W9-BPP-635

MARY LOGAN

REMINISCENCES OF THE CIVIL WAR AND RECONSTRUCTION

Edited with an Introduction by

GEORGE WORTHINGTON ADAMS

Carbondale and Edwardsville

SOUTHERN ILLINOIS UNIVERSITY PRESS

FEFFER & SIMONS, INC.

London and Amsterdam

Printed in the United States of America
Designed by Andor Braun
Standard Book Number 8093–0425–2
Library of Congress Catalog Card Number 73–93878

CONTENTS

LIST OF ILLUSTRATIONS

INTRODUCTION

George Worthington Adams

ON OCTOBER 16, 1859, John Brown and his little group of sons and other followers seized the U. S. Arsenal at Harper's Ferry, Virginia, in the hope of bringing about a great slave uprising in the South. This event and the amount of applause it elicited from some conspicuous Northerners shocked and alarmed the South and set in operation a series of events which were to culminate in the Civil War—the fiercest and greatest internal strife which has afflicted any Western country. The attitude of the people of the Ohio Valley was to be decisive in the military victory of the forces of the Union. For twelve years after the war, under the name of "Reconstruction," the sectional struggle was carried on "by other means."

Reconstruction brought about constitutional changes which legally abolished slavery, legally enfranchised the black Americans and supposedly guaranteed their civil rights. The North burgeoned economically, becoming a businessman's paradise controlled by the Republican party. After languishing for years, the Southern economy began to improve, with a small but important group of Southern businessmen playing important roles. With the disputed election of 1876 as their fulcrum, these Southerners extracted the "Compromise of 1877" from a faction of the Republican party that, in exchange for putting Rutherford B. Hayes in the White House, was willing to call Reconstruction a failure, to withdraw the Federal garrisons from the South and to leave the control of Southern affairs in white Southern hands. Modern Times and the "New South" had begun.

Mrs. John A. Logan, born Mary Cunningham, had a grandstand seat to watch the events of the period. She and her husband were essentially Southerners in what was technically a "Northern" state. As the country drifted toward the falls of sectional war the Logans were understandably distressed. Their regional racism and southernism pushed them in one direction, their loyalties and views of practicality in another. With secession a reality and the war begun, Logan painfully brought himself to a Union position and took his wife with him. More importantly, he was influential in persuading a majority of southern Illinoisans to follow him. Painfully and slowly, while fighting the war, he came to accept the necessity of abolishing slavery. When he became a Republican he did not take long to become a "radical" one and to give strong support to Reconstruction. He continued to support it after it had passed from the scene, gallantly "waving the bloody shirt" to the last, trying to win a changed northern public back to hard-line reconstructionism.

The adoring Mrs. Logan always managed to follow her husband in his changes, to endure the opposition and taunts of "Judas" that came from former friends and neighbors. This is the more remarkable as she was a woman with a mind of her own. But once convinced she was unchanging. After thirty-one years as Logan's wife she made his commemoration the principal mission of her thirty-eight years as a widow.

Mrs. Logan, although she became a professional writer, was not one of the leading women writers of her time. She was a supporter of women's rights, but not an outstanding one. With a good mind and a keen eye, she was an interested and interesting observer of the people and events of her time. In her *Reminiscences of a Soldier's Wife: An Autobiography* she occupies a unique position. She was the only wife of an outstanding soldier and outstanding politician of the era to write and publish an autobiography. Here the reader may learn what it was like to be the young and attractive wife of a man who was very much in the public eye. The very personal nature of her book makes it of less value to the historian than some other works. Her unbending loyalty leads her to see everyone and everything through jealous eyes: General Logan never did anything wrong; all who opposed him were suspect or misguided. Also, the fact that she wrote at the age of seventy-five has given her too much time for hindsight views and has sometimes blurred her memory. The editor has tried to provide necessary corrections as well as background information in the endnotes. But those who read this book will want to see things as the persistently feminine Mary Logan saw them. Objective history can be found in other books, such as those by Allan Nevins and by Bruce Catton.

A WORD as to the nature of this version of the *Reminiscences.* The book is too long to warrant reproduction in its entirety. Since it is most interesting during that portion of the author's life which took place while her husband was functioning as an important person in the era of Civil War and Reconstruction, it seemed desirable that the work be abridged in a way that would emphasize that era. The first three chapters of the *Reminiscences* are summed up in a "Prelude" (1838–59) and the greater part of the last four chapters in a "Postlude" (1877–1923). Each of these units is a synopsis of the more interesting portions of the original, peppered with enough direct quotation to allow the author's personality to come through.

The editorial work has been performed at various places over a number of years. The editor is grateful for the assistance of the library staffs at Morris Library, Southern Illinois University; the Library of Congress; Widener Library, Harvard University, and the Huntington Library, San Marino, California. He is indebted to Southern Illinois University for a sabbatical leave, a portion of which was spent on this work, and to the University's Office of Research and Projects which assisted with funds. He is grateful to Professor William Eidson of Ball State University for the opportunity of reading his manuscript biography of General Logan. This last indebtedness is greater than the number of citations would indicate because the editor later had the opportunity of reading all of the correspondence of John and Mary Logan in the Logan Family Papers at the Library of Congress, as well as numerous letters to or from General and Mrs. Logan in that collection.

Southern Illinois University
July 1969

REMINISCENCES
OF THE
CIVIL WAR

PRELUDE

1838–1859

MARY SIMMERSON CUNNINGHAM—called "Molly" until she was seventeen—was born August 15, 1838, at Petersburgh, Missouri. Her father, John M. Cunningham, was the son of a Tennessee farmer and slaveholder and had come to Petersburgh to manage a store. Her mother, Elizabeth Hicks La Fontaine, was the daughter of a French protestant landowner of the vicinity who was the proprietor of "many" slaves. His wedding present to the young Cunninghams was a slave family of man, wife, and two children.[1]

While Molly was still a small baby her Tennessean grandfather liberated his slaves, moved to Marion, Illinois, and appealed to his son to do likewise. Since the advice was accepted her childhood years were spent in Marion.

Southern Illinois was a frontier and was to remain in that condition throughout Mrs. Logan's girlhood. In her *Reminiscences* she praises the backbreaking labor of the pioneers in putting their land into cultivation. She also states that "southern Illinois at that time was not so advanced as the Far Western States of today," and adds that its people "were far behind in matters of education and progress. Free schools were unknown, much prejudice existing against the education of the masses, through the influence of the Southerners who were greatly in the majority among the settlers." They "opposed education on the ground that they could not 'keep the niggers down if they had larnin.'"

In that primitive time men and boys worked hard with ploughing while "the women and weaker or aged men followed in the furrows dropping the seed in by hand." Reaping was done "with cradle, scythe, or sickle"; threshing was accomplished by the stamp of horses' feet.

The inside tasks of the women seemed prodigious to Mrs. Logan as she looked back from old age. Cooking, baking, brewing; the manufacture of many yards of jeans, blankets, flannel, cotton cloth and carpeting. The making of clothes for the whole family, and the endless washing and cleaning. And all this along with the bearing and rearing of large families of children. "Household duties devolved absolutely upon the female members of the family," she recalled, "it being effeminate for any male member to perform any labor of a domestic nature. Many stalwart sons have stood idly by while their delicate mothers, wives, or sisters exposed themselves in inclement weather, milking the cows and performing the hardships which were considered women's work. On the other hand, the men did not hesitate to insist upon the same mothers, wives, and sisters trudging up and down the rows, dropping and covering the corn with a hoe, or following the reapers, turning and raking the grain as it fell before the sickle." As the oldest child of a large family Molly Cunningham had her hands full helping her mother and developing executive capacity as foreman in getting work out of the younger children. In her maturity she became a staunch supporter of woman's rights and woman suffrage.

But if life was hard, it was not without its rewarding moments. Mrs. Logan remembered that "old and young joined in the sports and pastimes in an abandon of enthusiasm." The jollifications were frequently the sequels of cooperating in something useful such as a house-raising or cooperative land clearing where the men worked, or a "quilting party" among the women. Young people looked forward to "corn-huskings" where the sexes paired off for the work. "They talked, they sang, and merrily chaffed each other as they rapidly husked the corn. Every time a red ear was found a scuffle ensued, as the finder claimed a kiss from his partner," who was duty-bound to try to resist—and who always surrendered. "After the work was over everything was set aside, and the merriest dances indulged in, lasting until the wee small hours."

Patriotism was to be a major facet of Molly's character as long as she lived. It was nursed in such major frontier holidays as Washington's Birthday, Independence Day, and Training Day. February 22 was a day of banquets and toasts when "thrilling stories were told of Washington and the Battles of the Revolutionary War," always followed by a grand ball. Training Day—usually in midsummer—was the annual gathering of the men of military age, with firearms in their hands, who enjoyed the admiration of the populance in an atmosphere of flags and red, white, and blue bunting. "They imagined that annual meetings were quite sufficient to cultivate the proper military spirit and keep aglow the fires of patriotism in the hearts of the people." Everyone of every age was present—it would have been unpatriotic to stay away—and the military exercises were suspended for an hour at noon so that the "soldiers" and their admiring families could all share in a splendid feast, which was the contribution of the women. Independence Day was much the same, but with the more patriotic oratory and even more martial music, usually by fife and drum.

The great nonmilitary holidays—Christmas, New Year's Day, and Thanksgiving—were likewise celebrated as community occasions. They did much to provide little Molly Cunningham with memories of a happy childhood—of kind hearts and friendly people.

Religion was held in high esteem. A dearth of preachers held the number of services down but made them memorable and prolonged social and religious events. The Methodists and Baptists who made up much of the population would hold only one set of services a month, but these would usually be spread over Friday and Saturday with a great culminating gathering on Sunday. After the harvest, the faithful would gather at a camp meeting site for two weeks of continuous services. The affluent would maintain simple log huts, into which they would proudly move for the duration of the "revival." Looking back with a sophisticated eye, Mrs. Logan commented that "Many people were converted and thereafter led better lives," but it seemed "incredible that intelligent people could have been impressed by the illiterate sermons and riotous services that often characterized the 'protracted campmeetings.'" As a girl her "sympathies were always deeply aroused for the poor women who were the hostesses on these occasions."[2]

Frequent demands for manual labor by the young cut school down to a few months a year. Fortunately, in the early 1850's the governor of Massachusetts at the request of the Western states made bevies of young teachers available. One of these, a "Miss C.," made a special impression upon Molly Cunningham. "She was a bright, pretty girl of twenty, of just the spirit to be thrown among good-hearted people; and, before the term was out, she had captured the affections of everyone and was regarded as a veritable Minerva, not only by her pupils but by everybody with whom she came in contact. She was the leader in all amusements and everything which tended to improve and cultivate the people." She was a great boon to a community a majority of whose citizens were then illiterate.

The outbreak of the Mexican War was marked by an upsurge of southern Illinois patriotism. John Cunningham volunteered for three years or the duration. Having been sheriff, and "probably the most popular man in Williamson County," he was elected captain of the local company "by acclamation," and marched off leaving a proud but grieving family to await his infrequent letters.[3]

Captain Cunningham was fated to be a member of the Santa Fe expedition which saw few Mexican soldiers but experienced many hardships in crossing "the Great American desert on foot," chased by Indians, and tortured by hunger and thirst. For daughter Molly the most momentous aspect of her father's war service was the strong friendship he established with young John Logan who was first lieutenant of the company from neighboring Jackson County. Jack "was full of fun, of a genial disposition, brave as a lion, and delighted in adventure." The affection of the older for the younger man became so great that the captain promised Molly's hand in marriage, a promise he kept to himself until Logan turned up at Shawneetown some seven years later to claim his "bride." Since the young people had never met, this was the surprize of Molly's life.[4]

Captain Cunningham had not been home long when he learned of the great gold discoveries in California and, being the adventurer he was, joined the Forty-Niners. Twelve year old Molly ran to the post office to meet every mail until finally, after months had passed, a letter arrived. Other letters came more frequently, but the disappointed father did not give up and return home until March of 1853.

Shortly after his return the captain moved his family to Shawneetown, Illinois, where he was to assume the duties of registrar of the United States Land Office. Wishing a superior education for their bright and energetic daughter, the Cunninghams decided to send Molly to Saint Vincent's Academy near Morganfield, Kentucky, "a branch of the celebrated Nazareth Convent, and one of the outstanding schools of the time."

If she learned anything from the formal curriculum at Saint Vincent's, Mrs. Logan leaves the fact unmentioned in her *Reminiscences*. But the two years there were a liberating and generally joyful experience for the fourteen year old "Campbellite-Baptist" girl from southern Illinois, who down until then had had no experience of Catholics or Catholicism and who had never been away from home before. Although she loved the nuns and respected the elderly priest she delighted in wholehearted participation in numerous pranks which she describes with relish.

This was also her introduction to the slave system, the convent having rented a number of families from neighboring owners. She and her friends became fond of these people. They liked "to take our finery and deck out the pickaninnies and mammies in harlequin colors, and enjoyed seeing them sally forth to attend parties."

Molly was deeply shocked by at least one aspect of slavery. The convent students were fond of "Uncle Henry," a farm hand, and "Aunt Agnes," the head cook, who were the parents of several children. When the owners of Aunt Agnes sold her to be sent to New Orleans pandemonium broke loose. "Uncle Henry rebelled; the sisters pleaded with the buyers to let them keep her, but they heeded nothing. They came with . . . a wagon, seized Aunt Agnes, tied, and bore her away. She fought them like a tigress and screamed as loud as she could. The children screamed and cried so that the girls discovered what was going on, and, before the sisters could stop them, they rushed out to rescue Aunt Agnes. Seeing them come pell-mell, the brutal men grabbed hold of her and tried to bandage her mouth. The sisters could not bear to hear her cries and they too joined in the pleas for the innocent creature who was being torn away from her husband and family. The men ordered the driver to whip up the horses, and they galloped away, Agnes' piteous cries reaching us above the clatter of the horses feet." This traumatic experience had a sequel. "From being one of the most docile, respectful negroes, Uncle Harry had become a veritable demon." Upon being disciplined by the overseer, he "went at the overseer with an axe, and came near decapitating him." Molly did not become an abolitionist, but this memory may have made it easier for her to accept her husband's decision many years later when he turned his back on the southern Illinois proslavery attitude and cast his lot with the "black Republicans."

Graduated from Saint Vincent's in May, 1855, Molly returned to Shawneetown where she helped her mother with the management of the younger children and her father in his work at the land office. In the meantime John Logan had been elected prosecuting attorney of the Third Judicial District, which included sixteen counties. He came to Shawneetown, where he was introduced to the unsuspecting Molly during her Christmas vacation of 1854 and began corresponding with her when she returned to school. When she had graduated and was at home again, he returned to Shawneetown and was so taken with her that he adopted a schedule which brought him back most week ends, no matter how much all-night riding that might involve. He was not without competition from boys of Mary's age [Logan always refused to call her Molly], but he persisted, and between the frequent visits and the letters he wrote he succeeded in winning her.[5] Almost sixty years later she wrote: "To this day I marvel that a young man of Logan's rare ability, ambition, and mature years—he being twenty-nine should hazard his career by marrying a girl of seventeen." They were married November 27, 1855, and went immediately to Benton, Illinois, which was to be their home until shortly before the Civil War when politics necessitated a move to Marion. If there is any doubt about Mrs. Logan's feelings toward her husband before marriage there can be none after it. From the start she was a paragon of a wife whose devotion expressed itself equally at home and in efforts to advance Logan's career.

Her first test was as a perpetual hostess. "As I discovered," she wrote, "we were supposed to extend boundless hospitality. Visitors and friends arrived unannounced, coming at any time that suited their convenience, without inquiring whether or not it was agreeable to us. They frequently brought children with them . . . You had to welcome them with a smiling face, notwithstanding the fact that your heart might sink within you. By eleven o'clock you had to go to your kitchen to begin preparations for the midday meal . . . Fortunately they were unconventional and followed you to the kitchen. You had to keep up a conversation with them, while you endeavored to think what it was possible to set before them. . . . Older housekeepers had well-filled larders, but brides like myself were not so thoughtful and often found themselves with an empty pantry. There were no markets, caterers, bakers, or greengrocers." As hostess "you had to play the part of entertainer while standing over a hot stove . . . You had to lay the table for adults and children, no matter how many, rushing meanwhile from the kitchen to the pantry lest something go awry. Many a hostess has collapsed as soon as her guests departed."

Mrs. Logan was so proud of the leading role her husband was playing in the community and the region, and of the devotion so many of the people had for him that she put up with the entertaining, and with even more. "Notwithstanding the fact that I was but little over seventeen years old," she remarked, "I soon discovered that I was expected to know everything; to be an efficient milliner, dressmaker, and to assist in the work of an undertaker in preparing the bodies of the dead for their coffins. I was sent for almost daily to perform some of these offices." But she was strong, accustomed to work and, liking the people, she managed to enjoy life thoroughly, especially the Agricultural Fairs and the horse racing that went on at them.

In the midst of these activities at Benton she discovered the joys and sorrows of motherhood. John Cunningham Logan was born there in 1856, and "Dolly" [Mary] in 1859. Baby John was to die there; Dolly was to outlive her mother.

If this enthusiastic wife had any defect it was the reverse of her virtues: she loathed being parted from her husband when he went on circuit as prosecuting attorney and when he had to be present in Springfield as a member of the legislature. The depth of this feeling is not indicated in the *Reminiscences,* but in her letters to him she was sometimes peevish and complaining on this score.[6] Anxious to be of service to him in his profession, and having watched him sit up late writing out indictments [this was before the day of printed forms for such papers] she conceived the idea of writing out multiple copies on which he could then fill in the appropriate blanks. As an old lady she remembered with "warm emotion the gratification I experienced when, after timidly submitting them to the prosecuting attorney, he pronounced them well done and declared they would be of valuable service to him."

Logan's reputation both as prosecutor and practicing lawyer was growing rapidly in the early years of his marriage, as was his standing in the legislature.[7] In his wife's opinion "he was probably the most conspicuous lawyer south of Springfield in 1860." With this regional prominence it is natural that when Stephen A. Douglas had to stump the state for Buchanan in 1856 he should seek Logan's support and should ask him to speak from the same platform on a number of occasions. Young Mrs. Logan was most pleased that she was invited to visit Chicago and to tour elsewhere in Illinois with the great leader of Illinois Democracy and her husband. She was greatly taken with Mrs. Douglas, who was a member of the electioneering group. As she put it: "Mr. Douglas had married the charming Adele Cutts, niece of Dolly Madison . . . one of the most queenly women of her day, quite as fascinating and captivating in her manner as her illustrious kinswoman." Shyness almost overcame Mrs. Logan at the thought of meeting this distinguished lady from the world of the great, people who "were little lower than the angels." Mrs. Douglas put her at her ease at once and the "timidity" vanished.

If the election of 1856 may be said to have fanned the fires of political enthusiasm in the breast of young Mrs. Logan, that of 1858 brought them to full blaze. In 1858 Douglas, who had become the only major leader of the Democrats outside the slave states, was fighting to hold his senate seat against the rising new party, the Republicans, whose senatorial candidate was the Springfield lawyer, Abraham Lincoln. What was even more exciting was that John A. Logan had decided to run for the southern Illinois congressional seat.

There was campaigning for and with Douglas, throughout the state, and campaigning for Logan closer to home.[8] To her great joy, Mrs. Logan was allowed to accompany her husband on a large part of this travel. Southern Illinois was heavily Democratic and had strong southern sympathies. As Mrs. Logan saw it, there were the mischief-making Republicans, intent on keeping slavery out of the territories, there were the ultra-"States Rights" Southerners, insisting that the territories be open to slavery, and there was the noble Douglas, the advocate of "Popular Sovereignty" who was trying to hold the country together by insisting that the people of each territory should democratically decide the status of slavery for themselves. Logan wanted Douglas reelected, Douglas wanted Logan in Congress, Douglas wanted peace, justice, and harmony, so Mary Logan could not be other than a warm Douglas partizan.

Having had fifty-five years to sort out her memories and writing as the widow of a prominent Republican politician, the aging Mrs. Logan was able to find kindly things to say about the Lincoln of 1858:

I always like to think of Mr. Lincoln as he was in the days when I saw him with the eyes of an opponent. His awkwardness has not been exaggerated, but it gave no effect of self-consciousness. There was something about his ungainliness and about his homely face which made any one who simply passed him in the street or saw him sitting on a platform remember him . . .

His very awkwardness was an asset in public life, in that it attracted attention to him, and it seemed to enhance the appeal of his personality when he spoke. Any one who was introduced to Lincoln without ever having heard of him before, though the talk was commonplace, would be inclined to want to know more about him.

Douglas won your personal support by the magnetism of his personality. Lincoln did not seem to have any magnetism, though of course he had the rarest and most precious kind. He seemed to brush away all irrelevant matters of discussion and to be earnestly and simply logical. In fact, he had the faculty of carrying conviction. At a time when the practice of oratory as an art was the rule he was without affectation. The ungainly form, the bony face, the strong sensitive mouth, the quiet, sad, and kindly eyes were taking you out of yourself into unselfish counsel.

Give Mr. Lincoln five minutes and Mr. Douglas five minutes before an audience who knew neither and Mr. Douglas would make the greater impression; but give them each an hour and the contrary would be true. This does not mean that Douglas was not sincere. No man could be more patriotic or sincere than Stephen A. Douglas was. He was as earnest in his belief in the rightness of his position as Lincoln was in the rightness of his; and when he found he had been in error no man of pride ever acted more courageously in admitting it.

Either because of or in spite of the series of confrontations known as the Lincoln-Douglas Debates, the voters of Illinois elected a Democratic legislature and thereby returned Douglas to his seat in the senate and sent Lincoln back to his law practice. John Logan won handily in his congressional race. Before he could take his seat in the House of Representatives the John Brown Raid occurred and there was a multiplicity of signs that the Union stood in grave danger. The curtain was about to go up on the period of "Civil War and Reconstruction." [9] It is time that Mrs. Logan be allowed to tell her own story.

CHAPTER 1

The Eve of Secession

As soon as the election returns were in and Mr. Logan was declared elected to represent the Ninth Congressional District in the Thirty-seventh Congress, he began to arrange his affairs to go on to Washington to be sworn in March 4, 1859. We went to Marion, Williamson County, to spend the Christmas holidays with my father and mother, and to visit Mother Logan who lived twenty-four miles west of Marion, at Murphysboro, Jackson County. On account of the discomfort of travelling in winter, we were afraid to take our little daughter, then but a few months old, on so long a journey in February. My husband therefore went on to Washington without baby and me. He arranged everything for our home, when we should come the following December.

I spent the summer arranging our household affairs that I might close our house, and in the far more difficult task of preparing a suitable wardrobe in which to make my début as the wife of a popular Congressman from the West. I spent many sleepless nights designing costumes, hats, and other necessities for a lady's wardrobe. We were too far from Saint Louis or Chicago for me to avail myself of city dressmakers and milliners; consequently, after getting together what I thought would be passable, I waited until I reached Washington to obtain what I should require further.[1]

A few days before Thanksgiving we bade good-by to the numerous friends and neighbors and started, via the Illinois Central and the Ohio and Mississippi Railroad, to Cincinnati; thence, via the Baltimore and Ohio Railroad, to the national capital.

Going to Washington in those days was a very different affair from that of the present. The crude railroading, the uncomfortable, barren, low-berthed sleeping-cars can never be forgotten. The road-beds were rough, and the rolling-stock worse. This, together with the zigzag track of the Baltimore and Ohio Railroad through the Alleghany Mountains, made travelling a question of physical endurance; getting over ground more rapidly than by the primitive stagecoach was at the cost of many an aching bone and dizzy head. The untidy condition of the best sleeping-cars was intolerable. I had never before crossed the Alleghany Mountains, and remember vividly the struggle between the desire to sit up and feast my eyes upon the grand scenery of the mountains and the Cheat River Valley, with that enchanting river appearing and disappearing from view as the train sped on through tunnels and around the craggy points of the range through which the river flows, and the tremendous effort it required to keep from yielding to the desperate car-sickness and fatigue incident to travelling under circumstances then inevitable. All trains were late, overcrowded, and uncomfortable. We had to change frequently. At Bellaire the cars were transported across the river on a boat; the mountains at some places were crossed by the switchback system. From the time one embarked till [he was] dropped at the old Baltimore and Ohio Depot in Washington one suffered incessantly either with fatigue, terror on account of the tortuous heights and crooked track, or suffocation from the tunnels and vile air of the cars. Eating-stations were few and far between, and the improvident, who had no luncheon provided, had to endure the pangs of hunger; and when children were of the number their cries added additional annoyance to passengers. We had, among others, as travelling companions, the

Hon. and Mrs. S. S. Cox. Mr. Cox was then a member of Congress from Ohio, and was full of life and good stories, which he told so well that he made everybody cheerful and enabled many to forget their discomfort. Others included the eloquent Dick Barrett of Saint Louis; Colonel Ross and J. C. Robinson, members of Congress from Illinois; Mr. and Mrs. Oscar Turner of Louisville, Kentucky; Mr. and Mrs. Stillwell of Indiana.

The Relay House was then the last stopping-place for meals before reaching Washington. Hungry and weary, we all responded with avidity to the supper-call, entering the typical Southern dining-room of the hotel, to be served with a delicious Southern supper of fried chicken, corn bread, baked sweet potatoes, fresh biscuit, butter, honey, tea, and coffee. As the door swung open between the kitchen and dining-room, while the waiters went in and out serving the supper, the old black cook with her bandanna turban could be seen busy with implements of her profession, dishing toothsome fruits of her cunning in the art of the cuisine, and could be heard at the same time delivering lectures to the audacious Sambos and Cuffys for the want of manners they displayed while filling the orders of the guests. Before realizing that twenty minutes had expired, the conductor's cry of "all aboard" made us drop the biscuit and honey and hurry to the train.

Reaching Washington in the early evening, we had scarcely descended from the cars before the rush of burly hackmen crying: "This way for Brown's Hotel!" "This way for the National!" "This way for——" this and that hotel and lodging-house, almost deafened and completely terrified me. Unsophisticated as I then was, I felt I was to be the victim of a mob; but under the guidance of Mr. Logan, to whom the whole proceeding was not a novelty, we were soon ensconced in Brown's Hotel omnibus and driven to that hotel, and to my dying day I shall remember the kindly greeting of Mr. and Mrs. Brown (parents of Mrs. Richard Wallach), the worthy proprietors. Their son-in-law, Mayor Wallach, was a friend of Mr. Logan, and through him they had been advised of our coming, and right royally did they receive us.

I felt that in Mrs. Brown I had a refuge in all the dilemmas that awaited the timid young wife of a Western Congressman. This city was then dominated by the aristocratic slaveholders of the South, who looked upon the North and West as "mudsills and drudges," quite unworthy of much consideration; and far too often a swaggering manner and a retinue of colored slaves gave a man a prestige over others of scholarly attainments, simple habits, and no attendants. The hotel was quite full of the most pronounced of the aristocratic type who were then threatening disunion. Among them were Wigfall of Texas; Keit of South Carolina; Mason and Harris of Virginia; Benjamin of Louisiana; Slidell and Barksdale of Mississippi; and a legion of others who were subsequently leaders in the Confederacy, and who have since paid the debt that all must pay sooner or later. Daily, during the dinner-hour, discussions were heated and often quite boisterous. Sometimes it seemed that a collision was imminent at the table, ladies frequently appearing with secession cockades, which gave encouragement to the advocates of secession. At first I used to listen to these discussions in mortal terror, and sometimes was almost persuaded that the boasted prowess of the Southern men was a reality. I often wondered upon what they fed that they should be so boastful; my heart, meanwhile, praying that, should the conflict ever come, Heaven might protect the Union and give to its defenders strength to save it from dismemberment.

Impatient to secure a presentable wardrobe, and disliking to take up my husband's time or that of Mrs. Brown, to accompany me on a shopping tour, one morning I started out alone. It was easy enough to wander down Pennsylvania Avenue to Perry's and John T. Mitchell's dry-goods stores, and to find all I dared purchase with my limited purse. Feeling that I had achieved wonders, I started to return to the hotel; but, after walking quite a distance and looking about carefully for landmarks and failing to find one, I went to the corner of Seventh and C Streets, the old carriage stand, got into one of the vehicles and told the driver to take me to Brown's Hotel. Turning around the corner he halted at the ladies' entrance half a block from where I had entered the carriage. He charged me a dollar which I paid without demurring, and hurried to my room. Subsequently, I discovered that I had gone down C Street in the rear of the hotel, forgetting, when I attempted to return, the oblique direction of the avenue. I waited many months before telling my experience to my husband, who enjoyed repeating the story at my expense for the amusement of his friends, and it was a long time before I heard the last of my first shopping expedition in Washington.

To visit the Capitol and public buildings and familiarize myself with the objects of interest which the city contained kept me busy for some time. Congress had adjourned for the holidays before we felt prepared to make our début, and begin the rounds of calls obligatory upon the wife of a new member, if she expects to hold any place in the social world at the capital. New Year's, 1860, I first witnessed the ceremonies of that day. Going to the White House, upon invitation of Mr. Buchanan, we watched with admiration the President, with all the dignity natural to him, and Miss Lane, with graciousness unsurpassed by any of her predecessors or successors, receive the official calls.[2] The Diplomatic Corps, Cabinet, Supreme Court, Congress, and the whole list of officials then, as now, paid their respects to the President on that day. The music of the Marine Band under the direction of Professor Scala, the gay uniforms and decorations of the foreigners, our army and navy, and the beautiful toilets of the ladies made an impression upon me that can never be effaced. My ideas of democratic simplicity fled precipitately, and I stood aghast fancying no imperial court could rival our republican government in ostentatious display. While Washington was not the city it is to-day in population and improvement, there were aristocratic and pretentious people who made the most of such occasions, and allowed no opportunity to pass without availing themselves of it to display their gorgeous resources.

Senator and Mrs. Douglas had invited me to come and assist them in receiving their friends. This was my first experience in participating as an assistant to a hostess on such an occasion. Senator and Mrs. Douglas lived on I Street in the house more recently occupied by the late Justice Bradley. Their home was one of the most ambitious in the city, with its lovely picture gallery, spacious drawing-rooms, fine library, and luxurious surroundings. Adjoining was the home of Senator Rice of Minnesota; that of Senator Breckenridge of Kentucky, adjoined Rice's. All day the callers came and went. Mrs. Douglas, one of the most diplomatic women of her time, received her guests with matchless grace and cordiality, presenting them to her assistants in such a way as to put them at ease and banish their shyness. Most elaborate refreshments, including egg-nog and wines of all kinds, were served in the dining-room; while Senator Douglas, with his wonderful charm of manner, entertained in the library those who lingered as long as politeness would permit. It was long before we slept that night: the excitement of the day, the glittering panorama of the reception, the novelty of meeting so many people, the enjoyment of hearing the bright sallies and conversation of the distinguished callers had enchanted me, but through it all forebodings of the impending "crisis" stirred my soul. The ambition of reckless spirits, who had for so long ruled the land, the arrogance of the slaveholders in their possessions, all tended to keep the political excitement at fever heat. Events occurring in the Capitol were reflected in society. The absorbing topics under discussion could not be dropped even in the drawing-room. Participants in the debates in the halls of Congress could not forget the subject when they met for social intercourse. The very sight of each other suggested continuation of their discussions. Illinois was then represented in the United States Senate by William A. Richardson and Stephen A. Douglas. Douglas's time was to expire on the 4th of March following. In the House of Representatives there were elected in November 1858: from the First Congressional District, [the] Hon. E. B. Washburne; [from the] Second, John F. Farnsworth; [the] Third, Owen Lovejoy; [the] Fourth, William Kellogg; [the] Fifth, I. N. Morris; [the] Sixth, John A. McClernand; [the] Seventh, James C. Robinson; [the] Eighth, P. B. Foulke; [the] Ninth, John A. Logan—forming a galaxy of as strong men as the State has ever had in Congress; and it was not surprising that such representatives were destined to be conspicuous in the thrilling events that took place in the decade following. While the legislature was Democratic, Mr. Lincoln having carried the State by the popular vote, the fear that Mr. Douglas would not be returned to the Senate was greatly augmented. When the legislature convened, there assembled at Springfield a great number of persons from all over the State who desired to influence its action. It was evident to the most stupid observer that Mr. Lincoln had made a national reputation during the campaign and especially in the joint discussions, and that in his questions put to Douglas on the subject of slavery in the Territories he had set many men to questioning whether or not the policy of Mr. Douglas was a safe one for the best interests of the country north of the Mason and Dixon line; whether it was not true that the country could no longer exist "half slave and half free," and whether or not, also, the slaveholders were determined to extend slavery or dissolve the Union. Every man in the legislature was watched with jealous eyes lest he might falter in his allegiance to his party, and thereby defeat party supremacy. The contest was long and bitter, until, finally, Douglas was re-elected to the Senate, but, as was predicted at the time, at the expense of his Presidential hopes and prospects, as beyond all doubt the fame acquired by Mr. Lincoln as the nominee of the Republican party for the Senate in the celebrated campaign of 1858 and the division of Democratic sentiment as to Douglas gave Lincoln the nomination for the Presidency in 1860.

But one issue was before the people, and that was the question of slavery and its extension in the Territories. The proslavery party would listen to nothing but an espousal of their cause absolutely; and the antislavery party would listen to no uncertain sound on that question—nothing but the prohibition of slavery in the Territories would satisfy their demands. Hence there was little chance for a compromise man to accomplish much. The two wings of the Democratic party were just as much at variance as were the Republican and Democratic parties, and when the conventions met the rupture came with full force, so that the result of the campaign of 1860 was not a surprise to Mr. Douglas and his adherents. But with his hopeful spirit, he thought something might still be done, and we remember well how, during the whole winter preceding the firing on Sumter, day after day he pleaded with leaders for a compromise, and with what anxiety he watched the gathering storm and longed to avert the "irrepressible conflict." I remember, too, how eagerly he joined the venerable John J. Crittenden in his "compromise" proposition, and how, night after night, the young men of his party met at his house and counselled with him as to what should be done, and how his great soul recoiled at the thought of a dismemberment of the Union! [3] I remember his likening himself to a shuttle, going from side to side, between the warp and the woof of party threads, trying to weave a harmonious fabric, but often entangled in the meshes of the political web. He was loyal to the core, and yet his affiliations had all been with the South. His first wife was a Southern lady, and his sons were then with their kindred in North Carolina. At times he felt most keenly his impotency to accomplish anything on the peace commission, even to postpone the evil hour. I remember once when it was discovered that the conspirators had been holding secret meetings in the room of the Senate military committee, of which Jefferson Davis was chairman, Douglas came to our rooms manifesting the greatest possible distress. They had been arranging for secession and even for the resistance of [*sic*] Mr. Lincoln's inauguration. As Douglas talked the matter over with Mr. Logan (then a member of the House) great tears stood in his earnest eyes, and he said: "It is no use. If you gave these men a blank sheet of paper and asked them to write down terms of compromise under which they would agree to remain in the Union, they would not write them." He added: "I, for one, can not be a party to the destruction of the Government, if every man in the Democratic party is with them." He said he would do all in his power to give Mr. Lincoln a hearty welcome to Washington and insure his inauguration; that he was elected by the people, and should be inaugurated at all hazards. As a senator from Illinois, he was most active on the committee of arrangements for the inaugural ceremonies, going with the Illinois delegation to pay their respects to Mr. Lincoln as soon as he arrived. He shared the deep solicitude felt by the friends of Mr. Lincoln lest some

General Logan, 1864

U. S. Signal Corps Photo
(Brady Collection in the National Archives)

Mary Logan at 75—when writing her *Reminiscences*

courtesy of the Illinois State Historical Library

madman or rampant secessionists might do him violence before his inauguration. I saw much of Mr. Douglas during those anxious days, and know that he suffered acutely all the time over the condition of affairs, and more over the approaching storm of rebellion than over his own disappointment and waning political power.

Matters had reached such a climax that the most indifferent realized that the nation's weal was paramount to any individual consideration. Men of affairs moved about with grave countenances, absorbed with the awful thought that a civil war was inevitable. We remember perfectly the arrival of Mr. Lincoln in Washington, and the relief it was to know that nothing had befallen him *en route*, and with what intense anxiety many watched every move of the most violent secessionists all Inauguration Day. With bated breath I stood on the balcony of the Metropolitan Hotel (then called Brown's) and watched the procession wending its way down Pennsylvania Avenue to the Capitol. I can remember exactly how Mr. Lincoln looked as he sat beside Senator John P. Hale of New Hampshire (father of Mrs. W. E. Chandler), so calm and so apparently unaware of the imminent danger that his dearest friends apprehended. I saw them returning after the ceremonies, and was deeply impressed by the change in spirit and manner of the multitudes that followed. *En route* for the inauguration ceremonies anxiety and apprehension were depicted on every face. Returning, they followed the carriage of the new President, shouting: "Long live the President!" But when nightfall was gathering over the city, again the timid began to quake lest some evil soul might improve his opportunity to commit some violent deed under the cover of darkness. For days hope and fear, security and doubt, succeeded each other in the public and private mind. Nominations for the Cabinet were sent in and were, of course, considered firebrands to [by] the South, whose representatives one by one departed from the city and began their work all over the South for the establishment of the Confederacy. Each day some prominent member or senator failed to answer the roll-call. Mr. Lincoln's assurances that he knew "no North, no South, no East, no West," made no impression, and were considered unreliable by the leaders of the secession movement. First one State and then another passed secession resolutions. Then came echoes of the fatal firing on Sumter and all the fearful consequences that followed.[4] Mr. Lincoln, with the deepest anxiety depicted on his face, was tireless in his efforts to restrain the madmen who were precipitating the nation into a civil war. He remained almost incessantly in his office or closeted with some leading spirit through whom he hoped to work a change and heal the breach. His most loyal adherents were untried men. He was ignorant of their abilities and doubted their discretion. The executive departments were completely demoralized. The Treasury and arsenals were empty. General Winfield Scott, the general of the army, was old and decrepit. The army was at its lowest ebb in numbers, and was scattered all over the vast extent of the country, with the most meagre and inefficient communications or means of transportation. The Indians were more numerous and savage than to-day. Our frail naval fleet, insignificant in the number of ships and efficiency of the officers and men, was for the most part on foreign seas, the rest in Southern waters. Fearing the Supreme Court to be in sympathy with secession, apparently a great republic was tottering to its fall. Was a President-elect ever so circumstanced? Upon him alone rested the responsibility of so directing affairs as to save the Union from dismemberment. Yet he was without absolute authority, and wholly dependent upon the legislative branch of the government and the loyalty of the people, albeit there were sounds of disloyalty everywhere, even north of the Mason and Dixon line.

Fortunately, the electric shock of the firing on Sumter startled the whole country, awakened the latent patriotism of the nation, and brought to Mr. Lincoln the much-needed assurance that there was in the hearts of the people an indomitable love of country that would sustain him in all respects and enable him to fulfil the mission for which, in the [*sic*] retrospect, he seems to have been especially called. I have often thought that persons who to-day criticise the manner in which things were done then—particularly the tardiness which characterized the organization and movements of the army and the preparations which were necessary to prosecute the war, seem not to remember the difference between the situation then and now or the wonderful progress that has been made for the transportation and mobilization of an army.

Notwithstanding the undercurrent of political excitement, social gayety at the capital was attempted, and, like all novices, I was entranced by the brilliancy of the receptions, balls, dinners, and other entertainments which my husband and myself attended. At times I felt timid and so unsophisticated that I feared my embarrassment would provoke many a smile from the experienced women who chaperoned me on occasions of great importance. No more courtly President has ever been in the White House than James Buchanan, whose innate refinement and dignified manners had been greatly enhanced by his experience at the court of Saint James. His charming niece, Miss Harriet Lane, who presided as mistress of the White House, was so queenly and gracious always that she has had no superior as the first lady of the land. I shall ever bless them for the cordial greeting extended to Mr. Logan and myself in the executive mansion.

Our first state dinner was an event of so much importance to me that the picture of the table will be in my mind evermore. It was an elegant affair, notwithstanding the fact that the decorations of that time were very unlike the richer displays of the present day. I remember at each end of the Van Buren mirror, with its filigree railing of gold bronze, that formerly adorned the centre of the table on all state occasions, there were two tall gilt baskets in which were arranged plaster-of-Paris fruits painted in very unnaturally bright colors. The variety included oranges, apples, peaches, grapes, etc., with artificial leaves here and there among the mimic fruits. I remember, too, the historic china, with the red band and coat of arms of the United States in the centre. The gold-plated spoons, solid-silver service, and cut glass, though familiar to me since from frequent dinings at the executive mansion, have never looked half so gorgeous.

Though delighted over the invitation, for days before the affair I was wholly engrossed by the momentous questions of what I should wear; what I should do when I got there; and how I should ever command ideas enough to carry me safely through a long state dinner and not become a bore to my escort —that was the rub. Who that unfortunate individual was to be it was impossible to find out. Was he to be a personage of agreeable manners, or arrogant, pedantic, and probably patronizing? Any of these latter characteristics would make me so unhappy that I should be unable to appear to any advantage. Then if he betrayed in the slightest degree that he was bored or really endured me because there was no escape I should have suffered intensely. I was proud of my husband, whose handsome face and brilliant conversation would charm all about him, but for myself I had many misgivings and visions of hours of agony.

However, the desire to see the pomp and display of a state dinner and to hear the conversation of the distinguished guests I expected to meet at such a ceremonious affair overcame every scruple. Stephen A. Douglas and his universally admired wife, Mr. and Mrs. John C. Breckenridge, Senator and Mrs. Jefferson Davis, Senator and Mrs. Yulee, Senator and Mrs. Mason of Virginia, Senator and Mrs. Gwyn [Gwin] of California, Judah P. Benjamin, Senator and Mrs. John J. Crittenden, Colonel Syms of Kentucky, the Cabinet, and many others to the number of forty sat down to that stately dinner. My escort was Stephen A. Douglas, and of course I was supremely happy, because I had known him from girlhood and had looked up to him as a great leader and most charming man in conversation. He was the personal and political friend of my father and my husband, and was anxious to treat me with every consideration for their sakes. Under his tactful and fascinating conversation I soon forgot my misgivings, and, through the inspiration of the resplendent surroundings, felt never so proud and happy, although now and then in the sallies of the leading spirits in the conversation that went round the table, ominous expressions were made that caused one to tremble and ask one's self: "Is it possible that there is one of this distinguished company who would raise a hand against the flag of the Union or break the bonds that hold the grand constellation of States together?" I little thought that one of the number would in a brief time be the leader and President of the Confederacy, directing deadly blows against a government that had bestowed on him many high honors.

Senator and Mrs. Gwyn [Gwin] of California, entertained very handsomely, their grand balls being among the finest given in Washington.[5] For years their hospitable home had been the attraction for the most distinguished at the capital. People were still talking of their famous masquerade ball, given the winter before, in which the President appeared in the court dress he had worn at Saint James's. Members of the Cabinet, both houses of Congress, the diplomatic corps, army, navy, and citizens entered into its spirit with enthusiasm, and, all in fancy costumes, represented royalty, dramatic characters, historic personages, great warriors, celebrated admirals, men and women of literary distinction, artists, and many others.

Among those who took part in the occasion was Mrs. William E. Chandler, then young Miss Hale, daughter of Senator Hale of New Hampshire, who appeared as Sunrise, and of whom Major John De Havilland, who described the affair in verse, wrote:

> I marvel not, O sun, that unto thee
> In adoration men should bow the knee.

Mrs. Stephen A. Douglas, subsequently Mrs. Williams, then one of the most brilliant and beautiful women at the capital, representing Aurora, inspired the poet to the following description:

> The bright Aurora in our senses gleams,
> Nor yields to that fair daughter of the morn,
> Whom Guido saw on car triumphant borne.

She was, indeed, "*la belle au bal.*" Mr. and Mrs. Coyle, Mrs. Madison Cutts, Mrs. Emery, wife of General Emery, and Brady the artist were there, though not in masquerade. Nothing of later days has excelled the stateliness of the occasion in all its appointments or the illustrious characters taking part.

Mayor and Mrs. Wallach gave many grand dinners and receptions and one ball so resplendent as to rival anything, save a fancy-dress affair. We recall the venerable John J. Crittenden and his charming wife, whose dignified bearing and genial face were ever pleasing to see. Lord Napier; the French minister; Hon. Anson Burlingame; Mr. and Mrs. C. C. Clay of Alabama; Mrs. Greenough, wife of the sculptor; Hon. Horatio King; Hon. Daniel E. Sickles, still surviving; Mr. Bouligny of Louisiana, and his fascinating wife, *née* Miss Parker; the Livingstons; Minister Bodisco and his charming wife; Cochrane of New York; Banks of Alabama; General Magruder; Mr. Clingman; Mr. and Mrs. Vance; Mr. Harris of Virginia; John C. Breckenridge; Senator Rice of Minnesota; Chief Justice Taney; Barkesdale, member of Congress from Mississippi, who was later killed in the Confederate Army during the Civil War; Stephen A. Douglas; Hon. William Kellogg of Illinois; Mr. and Mrs. Roger A. Pryor; Doctor Garnett; Senator Judah P. Benjamin; General and Mrs. McClernand; Miss Dunlap, sister of Mrs. McClernand, who married General McClernand after her sister's death in the early sixties; Mr. and Mrs. Foulke of Illinois; Senator Edward Baker, killed at Ball's Bluff in 1862; Colonel and Mrs. Robert E. Lee; and a host of others—were familiar faces at social entertainments.[6]

On all occasions wine flowed freely, egg-nog being on every table on New Year's Day. Terrapin was as common as the simple bouillon of to-day, the colored cook who presided in every kitchen knowing better how to prepare terrapin than our most skilful chef.

At evening entertainments the guests arrived early and remained until the "wee sma' hours." The Inauguration Ball, March 4, 1861, was a grand affair, but not participated in by many of the opposition or residents of Washington whose sympathies were with the South, many flattering themselves to the very last that there would be some resistance to Mr. Lincoln's inauguration. Fortunately, the theory of bowing to the will of the majority was then a cardinal principle in the decalogue of American politics. It is a melancholy revery for one to think upon those momentous days, and to take up, one by one, the names of men and women who figured in the social and political drama then being enacted. Death has claimed nearly all, as more than half a century has rolled away, not a few having met sudden deaths in the real tragedies in which they took part; while others of the brilliant coterie played important parts in the Civil War that burst upon the country with such violence in 1861 as to stop completely their dalliance with pastimes and pleasures at the national capital, and precipitate the whole nation into its realities. Instead of making merry and dancing to the music of "stringed instruments" in the ball and drawing rooms, they hastened to the field of carnage to the thrilling notes of martial music, changing the light steps of the dancers to the tramp of the warriors' march. Before Ash Wednesday had stopped the festivities, rumors of the coming conflict, the defiant threatenings of seizing Sumter, and the seceding of States from the Union effectually stopped all gayety, and made serious and thoughtful the most giddy devotee of society.

Almost every one was so restless that he must needs be on the go all the time. Even the theatres were packed every night. The actors and actresses of that time were very fine. Forrest, Sothern, Joe Jefferson, Booth the elder, Charlotte Cushman, and other celebrated men and women were on the boards, *Lord Dundreary* furnishing recreation and amusement for the weary, *Rip Van Winkle* bringing tears from the sympathetic, while Charlotte Cushman's *Queen Catherine* and *Meg Merrilies* awakened the wildest enthusiasm for her great power in the rendition of such roles. In February she came to Washington to play for five nights: the first night giving *Queen Catherine*, supported by J. B. Studley, a fine actor; the second night, *Meg Merrilies*. When she delivered the curse upon poor Bertram, her figure seemed to rise to the stature of a giantess before her trembling, cringing victim. On this occasion she was brought before the curtain again and again, the whole audience, from orchestra to the top gallery, rising to their feet and cheering wildly. In imagination I can to this day see her majestic figure as she appeared to acknowledge the encores.

She followed the next night (her benefit) with Mrs. Haller, in Kotzebue's play, *The Stranger*, and as MRS. SIMPSON in *Simpson & Company*, to a superb audience of appreciative admirers. *Lady Macbeth*, *Cardinal Wolsey*, and *Nancy Sykes* were also given at the earnest request of a large number of distinguished people, who signed a petition to her to gratify them by prolonging the engagement seven nights. Each night the house was as full as the managers dared to allow. One never tired of seeing her. She was the personification of power and grace, and so forceful that one was impressed by her peerless physical and mental strength, and yet she seemed as gentle as a child. Few women have left a deeper impress upon the age in which they lived.

On the reassembling of Congress after Mr. Lincoln's inauguration the excitement grew greater and greater, reaching a higher pitch when the sound of the firing upon Sumter was flashed across the country. The seizure of the forts in Charleston Harbor and the firing on the flag aroused the whole nation. The people were completely demoralized between the conflicting impulses of their generous natures toward kindred in the South and duty to their country. At first they could do nothing. The hammer lay idle by the anvil; the bellows unused; the fires were out in engines and furnaces; the wheels of machinery still. The plough stood in the furrow, and men wandered about asking for news, and stood in groups for hours talking; crowded around every new arrival in the little town, or gathered about the fortunate possessor of a newspaper, while he read aloud to the anxious listeners every line of news or comment upon the situation of affairs. Wives, mothers, and sweethearts went about their household duties with melancholy faces, and often with tears rolling down their cheeks, as their loving hearts ached with ominous forebodings of what was coming, and what might happen to their loved ones in the near future. Unaccustomed to the suspense and anxiety of war, and the absence of loved ones whom they knew would enlist if war should be declared, they were wretched beyond expression.

Having no alternative, Mr. Lincoln made the call for seventy-five thousand men, and money to protect life and property and uphold the authority of the Government. To our peaceful citizens this seemed an innumerable army, but the response from every loyal State, that their quota would be supplied as rapidly as possible, according to their respective facilities of enlisting and organizing troops, inspired the President with hope and confidence.

To a nation that had only known the annual "Militia Day" in those States which had militia organizations—numbering only a few in the whole country—and whose idea of the militia rose scarcely above the standard of a parade by five companies, the announcement, over the signature of the Chief Magistrate, that the Union was in danger and needed defence at the hands of all loyal citizens, aroused the patriotism of the people. The small, regular army, then scattered to the farthermost borders of this vast country, could not furnish a sufficient number of drill sergeants or commissioned officers to drill the hastily recruited volunteers.

The few veterans of the Mexican War then surviving north of the Mason and Dixon line had well-nigh forgotten the obsolete manual of arms, which they had learned during the brief war with Mexico; and yet long-neglected tactics were taken down from the dusty shelves and eagerly read. Rusty swords that had done occasional duty on Militia Day since '48 were hunted up and buckled on over citizen dress; old fifes that had not known the touch of human lips for many years were soon responding to the inspiring notes of martial airs; old drummers regained their cunning, and beat an accompaniment calling men to arms. The few industrial establishments that had been kept in operation by a small number of faithful men for the furtherance of private enterprises were immediately converted into busy hives for the manufacture of implements of war, volunteers stepping into line until every place was filled. Those not needed in the field joined the busy army of workers who were occupied with the preparations for clothing, feeding, arming, and supporting the soldiers at the front.

Returning to our home in southern Illinois, we found that the proximity of that section to the slaveholding States and the close ties by nature of a majority of the people to those of the South had caused the most intense excitement. Almost every household was divided in sentiment. The theory of States' rights had so impregnated the minds of the people that they were unable to divest themselves of the feeling that the people of the South really owed their first duty to their States, and not to the Government of the United States. In the heat of discussions of the political campaign they had concluded that the South had a grievance in the election of an antislavery man and the supremacy of the Republican party. At heart they were loyal to their country, and in sympathizing with their kindred of the South it never occurred to them that they were guilty of disloyalty, or that they were aiding and abetting treason. They had an idea that concessions might be made which would in no wise compromise the dignity and power of the Government, and through which the Southern States might be induced to remain in the Union.[7]

We had taken advantage of the interim between the adjournment and the reassembling of Congress under the President's call to go home, I to remain to do what I could to prepare the people for the step Mr. Logan had decided he must take at an early day or be guilty of treason to his country. He felt that he must be for or against the Government, and that his duty demanded that he should enter the army and take with him as many men of his constituency as he could. Therefore he did not want them to continue their excitement, lest they might rashly commit themselves to secession. Mr. Logan, however, returned to Washington to take part in the proceedings of Congress at the extra session to provide ways and means for supporting, arming, and equipping the troops.

Arriving at Marion, Williamson County, Illinois, where we then resided, we were not prepared for the state of public mind that greeted us. Constituents hitherto full of enthusiasm and cordial greeting met us with restraint, expressing eagerness to know what was going to be done; finding fault with this, that, and the other action that had and had not been taken; insisting especially that there had not been given to the South enough guarantees that their institutions would in no wise be interfered with. They were reluctant to believe that everything had been offered and refused. At the same time they blamed the South for the attack on Fort Sumter. Many of them had kindred in the South whom they dearly loved, and still they could not leave their homes in the North and sacrifice everything to go to their friends whom they knew must, sooner or later, lose their all in the cause of the rebellion in which they were embarking. It was touching to see them. They looked to Mr. Logan, then their representative in Congress, to tell them what to do, and they knew instinctively that his advice would be hard to follow. Either horn of the dilemma was painful for them to contemplate.

A few reckless spirits had already departed for the Southern Confederacy, and had thus brought suspicion and opprobrium upon the section of the State south of the Ohio and Mississippi Railroad.[8]

The authorities at the capital of the State and in the office of the United States marshal were watching the movements of every man. Their only hope of restraining the sympathizers was through Mr. Logan, whose influence had been very great. Appreciating the grave responsibility resting upon him, he had occasion for much vigilance and solicitude, lest he should fail in saving the people from getting into trouble through rash acts until their own good judgment and sense should bring them to see whither they were drifting, and the inevitable results of rebellion. Many were the hours he paced the floor revolving in his mind how he should hold them to their duty by enlisting them in the service of the Government, thus preventing their taking steps that would involve them in ruin. He dared not tell them that he should [*sic*] enter the army himself. They would have spurned him and accused him of treachery to his party and to them, and of selling himself to the administration. The time had not arrived for them, with their former political teachings and affiliations, to think of the rebellion as treason against the general Government, and as a confederation for the destruction of the Federal Union. So, without intimating what he should do, he talked to them as though they were children, arguing in the line of patriotism and duty to one's country, warned them of the fate of traitors, the horrors of civil war, and the consequences of aiding and abetting revolution. He then departed for Washington, promising them his faithful devotion to their best interests and the perpetuity of the Union, assuring them that party ties should not be strong enough to drag any man into treason against his country. He tried to prepare them for what was coming—the severing of party allegiance and enlistment in the army.

To remain at home and be surrounded by all these people, to answer all their questions, to satisfy their curiosity and fault-finding with what was being done in Washington, to interpret the meaning of every move North and South, to keep them as nearly as I could in the channel in which Mr. Logan had adroitly drawn them, was an appalling task. Beset by fears lest I might make a mistake, and the awful foreboding that harm might come to Mr. Logan through the hate of some adventurous spirit whose sympathies were with the South, and the knowledge, too, that my husband would soon join the army and embark in all the hazardous movements and dangerous enterprises of a soldier's life in a fratricidal war made me the most unhappy of women.

My eldest brother, then a young man of twenty, at school at Lebanon, Illinois, suddenly returned home, and before we could prevent him left us to join the Confederate army. He was only two years my junior; we had always been together in our childhood and partners in all the joys and sorrows of life. After my marriage he had been much with us, and loved Mr. Logan devotedly, but in a mad moment he had ruthlessly placed himself in the attitude of an enemy. He was a dashing, thoughtless spirit, and had yielded to an impulse to follow the fate of his college chums who lived South and had gone to their homes at the mandate of their families in different States which had seceded.[9] This brought to my already overburdened heart another overwhelming sorrow. To see the blanched faces and tearful eyes of my dear father and mother as they went about fretting over the impending conflict, with my husband (whom they idolized) and their eldest son in opposing armies, was almost more than I could endure. Time flew rapidly, and Mr. Logan wrote me by every mail (then triweekly) of the progress of events, directing me to prepare the few we could trust for his return and to apprise them of his purpose to raise a regiment immediately upon his arrival.

In the South the seeming restless tide of secession was sweeping everything before it; in the North the timid and doubtful were wavering under the impress always made by success. What would be the result? No one could fortell; all felt the feverish state of the public mind. The spring had come and gone, the summer's heat was on, half the crops had not been planted, and those that had been were not properly cultivated. Wherever one went naught but the din of discussion was heard; every person seemed suspicious of every one else; friction and impatience were rife. The battle of Manassas, or first Bull Run, with its unsatisfactory result had discouraged and disheartened the not over sanguine, and had made it harder than ever to convince the sympathizers that there was no foundation for the boasted prowess of the Southern soldiers, and that their claim that one Southern man was worth five Northern men was baseless.

Events of the most thrilling character occurred daily, and kept every one in a state of excitement and apprehension. The very thought of civil war carried with it a heart-sickening terror, and completely demoralized the people. Senator Douglas had died very suddenly in Washington, and Mr. Logan was left almost alone to face the excited, reckless people of southern Illinois.

Finally the day arrived upon which Mr. Logan was to reach home. J. H. White, later lieutenant-colonel of the 31st Infantry, which Mr. Logan raised; Mr. Swindell, sheriff of Williamson County; one or two others; and myself had canvassed the county on horseback. Going to the houses of the coolest-headed and most reliable men, we asked them to come to the town of Marion on that day that they might hear Mr. Logan, who was advertised to speak to the people in the public square; also asking them to be ready to protect him or to quell any disturbance should mob violence be attempted if he failed to impress them favorably.

It was one of those hot, dusty days in that semitropical climate when man and beast panted for breath. At an early hour the people began to arrive, and before noon—the hour at which Mr. Logan was due—a surging throng of human beings filled the public square, impatiently watching the road over which he was to drive into town.

Getting into a buggy early that morning, I drove out on the road leading to Carbondale, a station on the Illinois Central Railroad, to meet my husband, who was to come to Marion in a carriage that had been sent to bring him from the train. It was a distance of twenty miles from Marion to Carbondale. I kept driving but did not meet him. Fearing something was wrong, I continued my journey to Carbondale, to learn that the eastern train on the Ohio and Mississippi Railroad, and the Illinois Central Railroad upon which he was to come had missed connection at the crossing at Odin. There was no possible chance for him to get down until two o'clock the following morning; hence he could not speak until the following day. Appreciating the disappointment it would be to the people of Marion, knowing their inflammable natures, and that many men among them had probably been drinking and were desperate by that time, I knew it was no time to trust a messenger with the simple message that my husband had been detained, but would come the following day, at which time they should return to hear what he had to say. I also wished to consult with the trusted friends we had as to the temper of the people when such numbers were together. I therefore took a fresh horse and drove back to Marion. Many eyes were still peering down the long road, and the moment they spied me coming alone they could hardly wait for me to reach the centre of the square when they gathered around the buggy, stopped the horse, and eagerly cried out: "Where is Logan?" "What is the matter?" "What does this mean?" "We have got to know all about this business," and many such questions and threats.

Heartsick, frightened, weary with the forty-mile drive, and choking with anxiety and discouragement over the seeming madness of the men, I could only beg them to be quiet; to call Mr. Swindell, the sheriff, that I might explain to him, and that he should stand up in the buggy and tell them all. I saw that many were drunk and muttering vengeance on somebody, and that they did not know what they were doing, and I was almost in despair. Very soon Mr. Swindell, a tall, distinguished-looking man, with a fine face, blue eyes as gentle as any woman's, and at the same time full of moral courage and coolness, came to me and I briefly told him the facts: that it was purely an accident occasioned by a delay on the then badly managed road. He stood up on the seat of the buggy and addressed the surging multitude, appealing to their manhood, their sense of right and propriety. He besought them to go home and go to sleep; to quiet down, and to come back by two o'clock on the following day when Logan, their leader and best friend, would be there and would tell them everything. He told them that, as they valued their liberty, their homes, and their country, it behooved them to follow him wherever he should go; that he had more at stake than they had; that all that he or they held dear was in the balance against anarchy and rebellion; that they and their posterity would reap the consequences of their sowing; that they knew that his all was at stake with them, and that he, personally, was ready to join Logan with all he had in whatever move Logan said would bring peace to the distracted country, without which they could expect nothing for themselves or their children. Many were deeply affected and did as he suggested, departing for their homes; others manifested an ugly spirit and continued their wrangling and dissipation, making threats, and in many ways causing me great solicitude.

When the crowd had dispersed I drove to my father's home, and, after consulting with our friends, I decided to take another horse and drive back to Carbondale to meet my husband, so that I could have a chance to tell him everything—the exact position of every man in the town, and of many who were in the country; to be able to give him the benefit of what we had done; and suggest to him what we considered the safest line in which he could move. It was a bright moonlight night, and, as it was before the day of tramps, I was not afraid to go alone, although I should not arrive in Carbondale before midnight. In those days the produce was freighted across the country to the railroad in large wagons, forming sometimes quite a train of ten or a dozen together. The drivers camped at the side of the road, parking their teams, sleeping in their wagons, building fires to cook their food and make their coffee—the men sometimes sitting up late, playing cards and telling stories. If one was alone on the highway and had to pass one of these camps, they presented rather a weird appearance, and in times of such excitement it was quite enough to startle the nerves of a weak woman. Driving along the road with a dense forest on either side, and seeing that at the sound of the approaching vehicle some of the men walked out toward the road as if they intended to stop the horse, or at least to know who was passing at so late an hour; fearing that they might not recognize me, and greatly frightened, my heart fluttered like a leaf in a gale of wind. Fortunately they knew me and also my horse, and they called out: "Where are you going—has anything happened?" I halted long enough to tell them, and they expressed regret that I had undertaken so lonely a journey and that none of them could leave their teams, as they were then returning to Marion with valuable freight, or they would not let me continue alone. I bade them good night and hurried on, congratulating myself upon my good fortune. I reached Carbondale two hours before Mr. Logan arrived. It was two o'clock A.M. before his train halted at the Illinois Central depot.

We were both weary and half-sick from fatigue, anxiety, and loss of sleep. We went to the hotel, and, as quickly as he could get away from the many who had been waiting for him, we retired to our room to rest till seven in the morning, when we must go to Marion to meet the crowd that would be waiting impatiently for him. There was no sleep for either of us, so anxious were we both. Events of such grave character had happened since we parted early in April, that it seemed ages since we had been together. The unknown was before us. A more or less reckless people surrounded us, all of them unreasonable in their expectation of what Mr. Logan could do; some going so far as to aver that he could have secured the adoption of the Crittenden compromise if he had tried, forgetting that Crittenden, Douglas, Caleb Cushing, and the oldest and ablest men in the nation had been unable to get anything done in the way of compromise. His former closest friends were the worst secessionists. Our families were much divided, and we felt that we could trust only each other. He had resolved to enter the army for the war with no alternative but to leave me to do the best I could; and, at the same time, to try to sustain my father and mother (my eldest brother, as before stated, having joined the Confederate army) and those who might be left alone should their husbands, fathers, or brothers volunteer to go with him. Not knowing what fate awaited us, we drove over the familiar road with sad hearts, feeling it was our only opportunity to be alone, or to talk over the plans for the present or the future.

As we approached Marion the people began to gather about the buggy, cheering and shouting their welcome to General Logan; crowding so near to grasp his hand that it was almost impossible for the horse we were driving to move. He assured them he would speak to them at two o'clock. It was then almost noon, and he had to go home long enough to remove the dust of travel from his clothing and to get his dinner. The very crowd was enough to alarm one; they were so excited—seemingly on the verge of violent demonstration. When the hour arrived, he came to me and begged me on no account to go into the street. He felt that there might be trouble, and assured me he should be unnerved if he thought I was in the crowd, should mob violence seize the half-crazed people. I gave my promise, with a mental reservation not to keep it; as I determined to be near him whatever happened, thinking by a disguise in dress and keeping behind him (as he was to speak standing in a wagon in the public square) that I could watch the actions of one or two persons who had made threats of a personal assault upon him should he declare for war or attempt to raise a regiment. I felt sure I could at least scream should they move toward him with evil intent.

I waited until he was gone and soon followed, keeping out of his sight, but where I could see him and every movement made toward him. I trembled in every limb, my head swam, and I dared not speak to any one, though surrounded by acquaintances who once were friends. He mounted the wagon, and, after waving salutation to the throng who surrounded him, he began to speak in a voice so clear and with such volume that every person, even those farthest from him on the outside of the crowd, could hear him distinctly. In a few moments a deathlike stillness prevailed; the most turbulent spirit in the crowd was as quiet as the dead. You could hear only his sonorous voice as he with great deliberation pictured the situation of affairs, the inevitable consequences of rebellion against the Government should the theory of secession prevail; telling them at what cost of blood and treasure the republic had been established, and how certainly liberty would be forfeited and anarchy reign were the Union once dissolved. Step by step he led them on for nearly two hours, intensity and earnestness depicted in every lineament of his face, his bright black eyes gleaming with emotion, every gesture emphasizing the truthfulness of his remarks, and his earnestness carrying conviction. The effect upon his hearers was magical. They were swayed by his eloquence until they fairly re-echoed his utterances. Toward the close he said: "The time has come when a man must be for or against his country, not for or against his State. How long could one State stand up against another, or two or three States against others? The Union once dissolved, we should have innumerable confederacies and rebellions. I, for one, shall stand or fall for this Union, and shall this day enroll for the war. I want as many of you as will to come with me. If you say No, and see your best interests and the welfare of your homes and your children in another direction, may God protect you."

There was an old fifer, six feet four inches tall, and very large in proportion, in the crowd. He had been a fifer in the same regiment with Mr. Logan in the Mexican War. We had seen him previously, and he had promised to come and bring his fife, and at a signal from J. H. White was to go up to Mr. Logan, give him his hand as a volunteer, and then was to play a patriotic air on his fife, whereat Mr. White and a few others were to step in line and start the volunteering. Mr. Logan did not know that Sanders, the fifer, was to be there, or that he was to lead off in that way, and when he saw the herculean figure of his old comrade striding through the crowd, making for him, he lost control of his feelings and wept like a child. It is needless to add that through my own tears I witnessed the most affecting scene that had ever occurred in that or any other town. At the sound of Sanders's fife and the beating of an old drum of Gabriel Cox, who was a member of the drum corps of the same regiment in which Mr. Logan served in the Mexican War, and whom Mr. White and Captain Looney, who was elected captain of the company, and other friends had hunted up, Mr. Logan jumped down from the wagon, stepped into the line that was speedily filling up, one after another "falling in" (my friend the teamster who had frightened me so two nights before being among the very first) gave the command, "Forward, march!" and started around the square, followed by one hundred and ten men, as good and true as ever carried musket. All were enrolled for "three years, or during the war." There was scarcely a dry eye in the whole crowd. The ugly spirits who a few hours before were boasting and threatening all sorts of bloody deeds had hied themselves to safer quarters till the volunteers were out of town. The company enlisted on that day, the 19th of August 1861, afterward became Company A of the gallant 31st, which Colonel Logan recruited and commanded till after the battle of Fort Donelson, where he won his star.

Those were trying times when the knowledge that one's husband had enlisted for a war and a hundred others had joined him brought to the heart a feeling of relief and respite from fear lest he might be the victim of an assassin or a mob. That one should construe such a *dernier ressort* as a guarantee for the preservation of life and the protection of homes seems an anomaly, but such was the condition of things that from that hour we hoped for the best, and felt relieved from cruel suspense and agonizing forebodings.

Colonel Logan was so absorbed with the details of raising his regiment, and so sure that southern Illinois would be true to the Union that he seemed almost happy, keeping me busy driving back and forth between Carbondale, the telegraph station on the Illinois Central Railroad, and other points where he went to recruit the ten companies of which his regiment was composed. He would not trust any one else to send or receive the despatches he was constantly sending and receiving from the governor and adjutant-general of the State, who was at Springfield, the capital of the State, and the Secretary of War at Washington, D.C. Consequently and fortunately, I had but little time to think of the future and all that it might hold for me.[10]

CHAPTER 2

Espousing the Union Cause

THE VAST territory lying to the south, southwest, and southeast of Cairo, Illinois, prior to the Rebellion, depended upon the Mississippi River as almost the only channel through which could be conveyed to the markets the cotton, molasses, and sugar. Through the same source they passed the larger supplies of grain, flour, and other commodities. The Mississippi River and its principal tributaries bounded the shores of several States that had cast in their lot with secession. The lands of these States were owned by the few wealthy slaveholders who had colonies of slaves but very few neighbors beyond the kindred and families of the same estate.

"King Cotton," as they were wont to style their chief product, brought them a rich harvest of money when shipped to distant marts, but could not be consumed or utilized within their own State borders, destitute as they were of manufactories. Hence many thousand bales of cotton, hogsheads of tobacco, and barrels of molasses and sugar found their way to the North on the steamers plying between the Northern cities of Cincinnati, Louisville, Saint Louis, Cairo, and Memphis, Vicksburg, Natchez, and New Orleans of the lower South.

Coming up the Mississippi River, the steamers touched at

Cairo before going on to Saint Louis, or to Louisville and Cincinnati on the Ohio. Here they dropped that which was intended for the extreme north and east, whither it was taken by rail. It was a weird sight to see the black stevedores, clad only in turbans and trousers, rolling these bales and barrels on to the levee at Cairo by the light of pine torches planted on the shore, all the while chanting some plantation song, as they pulled and tugged at the heavy burdens, as if to lighten their loads by their own strange melodies. As soon as all was off and the steamer again "pulled out" and went puffing on her way, one could hear the boatmen still singing their plantation melodies as they lay on the piles of freight on the deck, resting from their labors.

Cairo was in those days little better than the doleful picture of it given in *Martin Chuzzlewit* under the fictitious name of "Eden." It was as unlike one's idea of the Eden of Paradise as possible. Often it was deluged by overflows, whose waters stagnated in every depression and were soon covered by a green scum, almost cutting it off from the highlands by that dismal swamp which extended nearly across the State a few miles north of Cairo. There seemed little hope that a city of any importance could ever be built in that locality. Ague and other diseases from miasmatic influences frightened away many who came to make their homes and fortunes there. Wooden structures, standing pools of stagnant water, bilious and listless white people, shiftless and wretched negroes, were about all there was of Cairo prior to 1861, save a few enterprising men who are found everywhere.[1]

Geographically so well situated, the "great captains" saw that from Cairo there could be moved armies that would sweep the Mississippi Valley to the Gulf, southwestward, and through Kentucky, Tennessee, and the Carolinas to the Atlantic Ocean. Driving before them the best fighting elements of the Southern Confederacy, when once on the soil of these States, they could gather subsistence from the country over which they passed. They foresaw that the cotton-fields must soon be given up, and corn and grain for their own armies and people would take the place of cotton. It was not for the "great captains" to consider the inconvenience, difficulties, and discomforts attending the mobilizing and organizing of these armies, but to conceive and issue orders, and leave it to the patriotic volunteer officers and soldiers to execute their plans. The small regular army was in the East and on the frontier.

Hence Cairo was designated as the place of rendezvous for the brigade which it was proposed should be recruited from southern Illinois. The Confederate troops occupied Columbus, Kentucky, and Belmont, Missouri, a point on the opposite side of the Mississippi River. Price's army was being recruited, terrorizing and controlling all of southwest Missouri. The city of Cairo, occupying the peninsula point of the State at the junction of the Ohio and Mississippi Rivers, was subject to overflows, the levees encircling the city being its only protection from inundation. The very streets were impassable at times. These facts made the occupation of Cairo by troops almost impracticable, but commanding, as it did, the Ohio and Mississippi Rivers, it was imperative that it should be fortified and manned by troops to defend the approach to the north up the Mississippi River. The fathomless mud was not the only unpleasant feature of Cairo at that time. The sudden concentration of thousands of men in the little city, with its half-dozen small hotels and overflowed surroundings, rendered existence as much a problem as that of the occupancy recently of the Canal Zone. Transportation was inadequate to the great number struggling to reach the point from which the great army was eventually to move. Habitations of houses or tents were not obtainable for all these civilians and soldiers congregating there. Quartermasters and commissaries were inefficient, and without any conception of the requirements of a great army and its followers. One single-track railroad with insufficient rolling-stock was to carry all the men, all the supplies, all the horses, all the ordnance and freight necessary for the immediate organization and equipment of the Army of the Mississippi.

The river steamers were of the most primitive character, and, though busy night and day, were unequal to the prodigious emergency. A majority of the men and supplies came from the North under difficulties indescribable. The Illinois Central Railroad was almost the only means of conveying everything to the base of operations.[2] The continuous trains going and coming kept the people along the line of the road in a state of feverish excitement, and impressed them with the stupendous nature of the preparations for the conflict.

The most extravagant imagination had never thought that the little city of wooden houses sitting behind the levees which line the shores of the Ohio and Mississippi Rivers at their junction, could ever be of so much importance in the nation's weal. One could hardly realize that it was the key to the valley of the Mississippi, or that the army rendezvoused and equipped within its small limits was destined to "hew its way to the gulf." The men of the West would not believe that the South would ever establish a blockade or fire upon the "flag of the free." Finally the shot was heard, and the wide-mouthed cannon mounted on the river-bank at Columbus, turned toward the north, announced the establishment of the barrier. Fired by indignation and patriotism, the people rallied to their country's call like the hosts of Roderick Dhu. Accustomed to pioneering and "roughing it," they were equal to the exigencies of the times.

The spirits that controlled in the South and Southwest were so daring and so reckless that they would have undertaken any venture, no matter how mad, had they not learned of the preparations to prevent them from coming up the river. The volunteers waited not for the regulation appointments, but, with earnestness that meant success, began at once to acquire the profession of the soldier. The old Belgian muskets, with which they were first armed, served every purpose for mastering the manual of arms; many officers, studying the manual of arms themselves, practised by drilling their commands for hours each day. Cheerfulness, and a willingness to learn to do whatever was to be done, were invariably evinced by the men notwithstanding the revolting feelings that sometimes came over them before they became accustomed to receiving and cooking their own rations, and doing the police duty necessary in camp. As fast therefore as the troops were recruited at different points, they were hurried to Cairo. There they were mustered in regiments ready for organization into brigades. The 18th, 27th, 30th, and 31st—and later the 25th Infantry Volunteers, known as the Lead Mine Regiment from Galena—Swartz's and Taylor's Batteries, and some cavalry were to compose the First Brigade.

Very few of the men or officers of these regiments knew anything whatever of the art of war, except a man here and there who had served in the Mexican War. For the most part they were young men just entering manhood, who had never been away from their homes for any length of time, many of them never having been out of the State. They knew nothing of the hardships that awaited them or the full meaning of enlistment in their country's service. When the time came for them to say good-by to mothers, sisters, wives, and sweethearts, it was most pathetic. I remember once watching the face of a sentinel as he paced his beat and looked with intense disgust at the unloading with iron shovels of the loaves of bread out of a wagon-bed in front of the tent where it was to be issued to the companies. This young man had left a home of comfort and plenty, where his fond and fastidious mother presided. Visions of her delicious cookery, snowy table linen, and transparent china made the loaves, thrown from the shovels to a not over-clean board table, anything but tempting. A few months afterward the forbidding loaves would have been hailed with delight in place of the "hardtack" that had not been softened or rendered more palatable by being carried in a haversack for days.

Doing guard and police duty with a lowering sky above them, and mud and water beneath their feet, made many a soldier sick at heart, and caused his courage to drop in the scale of heroism, when first learning the duties of a son of Mars. The discipline of walking to and fro with a gun on his shoulder in the wee small hours of a stormy night was a different thing from marching away on a gala-day to the tune of "Yankee Doodle," or with the drums and fifes beating and whistling "The Girl I Left Behind Me."

I witnessed the departure of many of the men of the old 31st from cottages and more pretentious homes. At the sound of the roll-call could be seen great, manly fellows, folding their loved ones in a last fond embrace, and then, with the tears streaming down their blanched cheeks, rushing out of the door, and down the street to step into line and answer "Here," while their telltale faces betrayed the emotions of their brave hearts. The tearful eyes, pale faces, quivering lips, and sobs of those they were leaving behind; quivering lips, and sobs of those they were leaving behind; the anguish of the non-combatants who were to guard the hearthstones, care for the dependents, and send cheer to the loved ones gone to the front, told the sad story of what it cost those who volunteered and those who stayed at home.

After marching out of the towns, they found farm wagons and all kinds of vehicles drawn up in a line beside the roads. Into these the "boys" climbed, to be taken to the railroad, because they were destined to have enough of marching on Southern soil. The troops were not allowed to walk when there was no necessity for their doing so. Arriving at the depot they were transferred to the cars, when the last good-bys must be said to those who had accompanied them thus far on their long journey. Reaching Cairo they were deposited on the levee, which, like a great sea-wall, then encircled the city.

Gathering together their little all, they were soon marching to camp to be assigned to tents and begin their duties as soldiers for three years, or during the war, unless sooner discharged by reason of disability. That first night in camp can never be forgotten by a soldier enlisted in time of war: the confusion of being assigned; getting accustomed to the meagre accommodations of tent life; the building of fires; hanging the camp kettle; making the coffee, drinking it out of tin cups; and cooking the rations, eating them from tin plates, without knives, forks, or spoons. To those who had left comfortable homes, presided over by loving mothers and wives, it was a trying initiation into the life they were to lead. The posting of the guard who, in reliefs, were to pace their beats through the weary hours of night, broken only by the dismal call of the hours: "—— o'clock, and all is well!" continuing through rain or shine of the morrow, and of each succeeding day and night was a great trial to men accustomed to following the Franklin maxim of "Early to bed and early to rise." Police and guard duty, drilling in the falling rain or broiling sun, kept them busy all the time. There was no going where they pleased or declining to obey disagreeable orders; they had to become accustomed to the confinement of staying within the lines; master the manual of arms; keep their clothes and accoutrements clean; appear at dress parade at five o'clock daily; cook their meals, report for drill and guard duty; and observe other details without questioning the reason why. To men who had known no discipline or superior authority, this was very hard and left little opportunity for aught save the homesickness that every soldier experienced.

In the 31st Regiment there were many men whom both Colonel Logan and I had known for years. They were splendid men, but absolutely ignorant of military discipline or the proper deference due superior officers. It took them some time to learn to address an officer by the title of his rank. They had always called Colonel Logan "John" and me "Mary" and often greeted us both affectionately by our names without realizing there was any impropriety in the familiarity. One day a soldier whom we shall call "Sol," a fine specimen of man—a robust, tall, active, cheerful, willing soldier—came to the colonel's tent looking much depressed. He gave awkwardly the military salute. Colonel Logan inquired what was the matter. He said: "John, I have got to go home, but I swear I will be back in three days." Colonel Logan replied: "What has happened?" "Sol" took out of his pocket a much-blurred and tear-stained letter and said: "Just read that, and you will not refuse to let me go." This was the letter from his wife:

MY DEAR SOL:

For God sake do come home. I am sick. There is nothing in the house to live on. I can't do a dam thing with the children. The cows got in, and ate up the garden, and everything has gone to the devil and you jist have to come.

Your loving wife,

AMANDA.

Across the span of fifty years memory brings to mind the amused expression on Colonel Logan's face, as he read this graphic letter. After getting control of himself, he said: "Now, Sol, you know I can not grant you a leave. You know that the reasons your wife gives for wanting you to come would look badly if I sent them up to headquarters. Besides, we are likely to be ordered to the front any day, and you would hate to have it said you were absent from the regiment." Sol replied: "Now, John, do you really think there is any chance for a fight?" Colonel Logan replied: "Yes." "Then no furlough for me," said Sol. The proximity of their homes, the frequent communications with friends, and many other features made the volunteer service at the beginning of the war almost ludicrous.

Day after day they came, till almost every spot of dry ground around the city was covered with the white tents of the boys in blue. The novelty of camp life soon vanished; attacks of illness, unavoidable with so many together in an inhospitable climate, and the discomforts that beset them, brought on an irresistible longing to return to home and friends. But furloughs were not to be thought of with all they had to learn and to do. No law, however, could prevent friends from coming to them, and ere they had been encamped two months, a new army made its appearance. Fathers, mothers, brothers, sisters, wives, and sweethearts came sweeping down in caravans of carriages, wagons, and every conceivable vehicle, and in every imaginable manner, pitching their tents and building their brush houses as near the regiment in which they were interested as the commanding officers would permit. Every moment off duty one could see company officers and men wending their way to the camps outside the lines, where devoted ones were waiting to greet them. Many delicacies and "treats" brought from home were enjoyed during the brief hours of a pass outside the lines.

To add to the discomfort of camp life in muddy Cairo, the measles broke out and spread rapidly. Five hundred of the 31st Regiment (Colonel Logan's) were ill with measles at one time. Medical purveyors were as little skilled as many of the officers in other branches of the service, and knew, if possible, less about providing for the sick. The exigencies of the war at that time had not driven them to a disregard of rights of property-holders in the interest of the army, and property-holders were not anxious to furnish supplies in exchange for the little slips of paper called vouchers, which they feared were of doubtful value. Surgeons and medical purveyors, and, indeed, all the regimental officers, were at a loss to know what to do. Beyond the power to seize and condemn a building for hospital purposes, they could do but little. The supplies in that department had been as heavily drawn upon as any other. Requisitions remained unfilled for days, weeks, and even months. The West was so far from the seat of war that they were the last to receive consideration. Houses large enough for hospital use were hard to get, and in many instances not to be found. There were scarcely enough tents for the troops and none for hospital purposes, and there was no provision for the care of the rapidly increasing number of sick.[3]

Deeply sympathetic, Colonel Logan of the 31st, could not bear to see the men lying on the damp ground in their tents, so he caused a small hotel, known as the City Hotel and owned by a Mr. Yocum, to be seized for hospital purposes. The proprietor vacated at once, but as there was no authority to take the hotel furniture for hospital use, there was nothing save the empty rooms and bare floors when the men were brought there. The purveyor's supplies had been exhausted in the establishment of the brigade hospital. The helpless regimental surgeons were in a quandary. Hundreds of the sick were lying rolled up in their blankets, and with nothing but their knapsacks under their heads. Two or three had died, and Colonel Logan was in great distress; something had to be done to render the condition of the men more comfortable.

Despairing of immediate relief through the purveyor's office, I assured Colonel Logan that I could get on the train and go to Carbondale and Marion, sixty miles north of Cairo, and, by appealing to the friends I knew, in thirty-six hours I could secure supplies enough to furnish the hospital with the best of everything, and stock the larder with all the delicacies necessary to the sick. He was so anxious for relief for his men that he decided to let me carry out my suggestion. I was to leave on the first train, which left Cairo at two A.M. The city was under martial law; the provost marshal was Major Kuykendall of Logan's regiment. At six o'clock P.M. he closed the provost office and returned to the regimental headquarters. Colonel Logan was to get me a pass and send it to me by Captain Edwin S. McCook, who was to take me to the two A.M. train. When we reached the depot and I asked the captain for the pass, he said: "By George, I forgot to get it!" The headquarters were at least two miles away, and there was no time to get a pass. The captain was greatly excited as to how to get me on the train without one. Seeing an old friend come into the depot, who was evidently going on the train, the captain went to him and told him of the dilemma. He said: "Oh, that is all right. I have one for myself and wife, and my wife was ill this morning and could not accompany me. I will take Mrs. Logan." They came over and told me of the scheme. I said: "Oh, no, good friends as we are, I could not think of travelling with you as Mrs. Wilson. I am sure I can get on the train without a pass, if you two men will stand on the depot platform and see me try to pass the train guard. If I fail, Captain McCook can take me back to my hotel, and I will wait until to-morrow." In those days I knew almost every one south of the Ohio and Mississippi Railroad. As soon as the train pulled in I went down to the car, and seeing young Donahue standing on the platform as guard, I said: "Donahue, I want to get into that car before the crowd; will you let me in?" He replied: "Yes, you bet I will, Mrs. Logan, but where are you going by yourself these times?" I told him that I was going to Carbondale, our home at that time, and passed into the car. As soon as I was seated, seeing the captain standing on the depot platform, I knocked on the window and nodded to him that I was all right. Mr. Wilson came into the car soon afterward, and we had a good laugh over the episode. McCook hurried back to camp to tell Colonel Logan the whole story. Later the colonel expressed to me his gratification at my discretion, and told me never to allow myself to be placed in a position that might be misconstrued and bring me many regrets.

Arriving at Carbondale, it required but little time to enlist many volunteers to collect the much-needed comforts. In less than thirty-six hours I had succeeded, by the help of loyal men and women whose friends were in the regiments stationed at Cairo, in collecting car-loads of home-made blankets, pillows, homespun bed linen, jellies, marmalades, wines, fruits, and everything necessary, and more, for the hospital of Colonel Logan's regiment. These blankets were made in bright colors, not unlike the famous "Roman stripes" and were so showy and comfortable, and attracted so much attention, that the hospital was known during its existence as "The Striped Hospital of the 31st Regiment." Pavilion and hospital tents were afterward invented and used, but in the early days of the war there was nothing of the kind in use in the West. It never occurred to the surgeons to decline anything tendered for the sick and disabled soldiers. The brigade and regimental surgeons were only too glad to accept the generosity of patriotic people, and avail themselves of everything that tended to reduce the mortality to a minimum. We were far enough away to disregard the dilatory action of "red tape" methods, which have been many times responsible for the increased death-rate among sick and wounded men. Regimental surgeons were held responsible for the sick of their respective regiments, and no other class of officers had more trying experiences on account of the inefficiency of the surgeon-general's department during the early part of the Civil War. Had the present system of brigade division and corps hospitals been then established, thousands would have died who were saved through the vigilance of regimental surgeons who knew, and had a personal interest in, every man in the regiment to which he belonged. Many monuments should now mark the spot where noble, self-sacrificing army surgeons sleep that "sleep which knows no waking" until they are called to their reward in a better world.

The generals and colonels swore they would never be able to discipline the troops. They longed to move to the front, or to have the power to order the civilian army to their homes. It was no use; there they stayed till the storms and blasts of approaching winter forced them to say a last good-by and retreat. In many cases, it was literally the last farewell, for the fate of war bore many of the officers and men to that unknown land from which there is no returning.

So time moved on. One day word came that a company stationed at "Big Muddy Bridge" had completed their three-months' service and declined to renew their enlistment. Governor Yates urged them to re-enlist, but to no avail. A special train was ordered, and General John A. McClernand, who was in command of the First Brigade, composed of the 22d, 27th, 30th, and 31st Regiments, was directed to go up there and to take Colonel John A. Logan and see if they could not persuade the men to remain in the service. One bright morning our party set out. Arriving at the bridge sixty miles above Cairo, on the Illinois Central Railroad, we got off the train and wandered about the camp of a few tents which the men had occupied while protecting the bridge from the torch of the Southern sympathizers who lived in the vicinity, and who had hoped, by burning it, to delay transportation of troops en route for Cairo, over the Illinois Central Railroad. Mounting a box, General McClernand spoke feelingly to the men, and urged them to "stand by the flag." Still no signs came from them as to what they should do. Colonel Logan followed McClernand with an appeal to "Come on, boys, fear not death, but dishonor." Every man shouted: "We will go," and before the hour had arrived for the train to take the party back to Cairo, one by one the men had re-enlisted and taken the oath to serve for three years, unless sooner discharged by reason of disability or peace.

For weeks regiment after regiment arrived at Cairo, and were assigned the most available spots where the tents could possibly be pitched. Every one felt that extensive movements must be contemplated to have occasioned such gigantic preparations. Officers and men were impatient at the routine duties of camp life, and longed for marching orders. At last they were gratified. Orders came that rations were to be cooked, ammunition to be issued, and everything to be made ready for a march —whither they knew not and cared but little, so they were on the move. When the hour for starting arrived they filed out of camp. Marching by companies, they were soon drawn up in a position on the levee, ready to take the transports. The boats

Mary Logan, 1869

courtesy of the Illinois State Historical Library

Mr. and Mrs. Logan with their daughter Mary ("Dolly") and son John A., Jr., about 1871

photo from GAF Historical Photo Collection

came steaming round the point, and rounding to the wharfs all were embarked, as the soldiers imagined, for eventful fields. However, before they had settled down or taken in the situation, the boats put into the Mississippi shore, and they were landed and formed in marching order to push forward across the country.

All was expectancy, as they supposed the enemy was not far distant. They found, however, that it was foraging and not fighting that was before them. Jeff Thompson had collected together large quantities of corn, hay, bacon, etc., for his command of freebooters, which was duly reported to headquarters, and General Grant determined to send over there and press the farmers into hauling to the river all they could bring away in boats, and to destroy the rest. It was amusing to hear the soldiers talking about the expedition. Their idea then of war was that all engagements between contending forces must occur upon a field, where each army would be drawn up in a line in strict accordance with military tactics.

They freely canvassed the question of ability to keep their "courage up," or to prevent their legs from carrying them in the opposite direction when commanded to charge bayonets. Hitherto the enemy had not materialized; but as soldiering in camp had proved more real than the holiday training-day of militia service, they began to fear the enchantment of distance between them and the enemy was so rapidly shortening that they must soon face the foe, or play the coward; and while impatience had characterized their conversation, they did not exactly relish the prospect of an engagement.

When, however, they found it was nothing more serious than attacking corn-cribs and haymows, their daring impatience returned, and expressions of disgust were heard from every direction. For many days they continued the monotonous duties of camp life, with continuous rain and mud to contend with, till November 6, when again orders came for cooked rations and everything to be put in readiness for a bona fide expedition in pursuit of the enemy. The troops were quietly informed that this time they would be initiated into the mysteries of real war. All was bustle and confusion till each regiment was in line on the levee in the order in which they were to embark. Hurrying on board the transports, they waved a good-by to the multitude of men, women, and children who had flocked to the levees for a last adieu to fathers, husbands, brothers, or sweethearts. As they sailed away the band played "We are Coming, Father Abraham," and other patriotic airs.

All the next day, the 7th of November, 1861, the sound of cannonading told sadly and painfully that the battle of Belmont was on. The streets and levees of Cairo were thronged with anxious people trembling for the morrow, knowing only that some loved one was in the fight. Silently we trod the levees, trying to look beyond the "river bend," hoping to catch a glimpse of the returning transports. They knew from the direction of the sound of the firing that the troops were on the Missouri side, and that the gaping guns stationed on the shore at Columbus would prevent the frail wooden crafts, or even the gunboats, from going below that point. They were sure the boats would return. Hour after hour rolled slowly away, and still no tidings save the continuous knell of the cannon's roar. Darkness cut off every hope of seeing anything save the lights on the vessels, should they appear. Nothing daunted, still we lingered and watched. Finally, toward the early dawn a light like a meteor was seen to dart round the bend, another and still another came, until at last the outline of the fleet could be seen. The nearer they approached, the more intense the agony of the anxious watchers on shore. Slowly rounding in, the vessels soon touched the wharf, and the weary and depleted regiments solemnly disembarked and marched to the tented quarters they had quitted thirty-six hours before.

Eagerly the anxious people, myself among them, gazed at every officer and man as he walked the gangway from the boat to the wharf, each looking for some friend. Exclamations of joy rang out as they were recognized among the safe and sound as they passed. Again, cries of distress were heard as first one and then another was missed from their places in the lines. Then came the first prisoners of war I ever saw, and they were so forlorn, so thinly clad, so pitiful-looking, as they stood shivering on the hurricane deck, that my heart went out to them in the deepest sympathy. After the prisoners were all off, the civilians who failed to see their friends in the lines were allowed to go on board the boats, to find them among the wounded, dying, or dead, as they lay stretched in the cabins and on the decks of the vessels.

With tear-dimmed eyes, blanched faces, and quivering lips the friends moved cautiously from one to another in search of some loved one among the unfortunate. All the pomp and circumstance of chivalry and military display had vanished; naught but the agony of pain and terror of death remained.

Tenderly covering the faces of the dead with anything we could get, and trying to soothe the suffering of the wounded, brave men and women worked unceasingly until ambulances and wagons came and took the unfortunate ones away to the hospitals which had been hastily prepared for the sick and disabled so suddenly assigned to them. Hotels and private houses had been seized, and the inefficient purveyors and quartermasters had put them in as good condition as the meagre and ill-assorted supplies would permit. For days and weeks physicians, surgeons, and volunteer nurses kept their constant vigil, trying to save as many as possible from the roll of the dead. After the battle of Belmont the wounded were brought to the "Striped Hospital," and the casualties of their first battle were evident in the wounded who were destined to submit to amputations of arms and legs, Illinois soldiers [thus] beginning their painful experiences in real war before they left Cairo. It was a sad sight to see strong men pleading with tears in their eyes for a foot or an arm that must be taken off. Many flinched not under fire on the field, but when told they must part with a member of their bodies by the surgeon's knife and saw, they wept like children, more than one refusing to lose a limb, preferring, as many expressed it, to lose their lives and be "buried all at once." Inexperienced surgeons were too hasty in making amputations, and needlessly sacrificed limbs which might have been saved.[4] The men were all so cheerful after the battle, and tried so hard to encourage each other, that it was a pleasure to minister to their wants as volunteer nurses.

Captain Looney of Company A of the 31st, Colonel Logan's regiment, was taken to our rooms in a private house, he having been severely wounded in the shoulder. After weeks of suffering he was sent to his home, where for many months he hovered between life and death; though he lived many years afterward, he was never again fit for duty, the service thereby losing one of the most gallant of men.

One day, in the brigade hospital, I saw a captain of an Iowa regiment who had been wounded through the left breast sitting up on his cot writing to his wife. He was as bright and happy as could be. Mother Bickerdike, a volunteer nurse who followed the Army of the West from Cairo to the grand review, came in with a bowl of broth for him, which he took and drank with relish, after which I assisted him in getting into a comfortable position to resume his writing on a pad. He suddenly turned very pale and we laid him on his pillow. He looked up with a smile on his face and breathed his last. We were horrified and ran for the surgeon, who came, but too late; all was over with the brave man. Upon examination the surgeon found the minié ball had lodged just above the lung, and in moving it had dropped in such a way as to produce instant death. Other pathetic scenes of those days can never be erased from my memory.

Fortunately the ludicrous and the melancholy go hand in hand or we should not be able to endure the sadness of life. It was very hard for many of the young men to brook the restraint and the monotony of camp life and a soldier's duty, so they used to invent all sorts of excuses to get down into the city of Cairo. One evening I was sitting in Colonel Logan's tent when a young soldier whom we had known before his enlistment came to the door and said that his sister was coming to Cairo on a night train, and as she was unaccustomed to travelling he wished to go down to the city to await her arrival and desired permission for himself and comrade to go. It was an unusual request and should have been made through his captain. Colonel Logan was suspicious that it was not quite a straight story, but he ordered a pass to be given them. He then sent his adjutant to the soldier's captain with a request that he send Colonel Logan a corporal and a soldier. These he ordered to follow the first two, see where they went, and what they did, and if found in any improper place to arrest and bring the soldiers back to the guard-house of the camp, and leave them there till ten o'clock on the following morning. It was discovered that they were not expecting friends on the train and that they were in for a "high old time," as the corporal reported. The corporal waited until they were both quite drunk, then he arrested them and brought them to the guard-house as ordered. The next morning, when they were marched to the colonel's tent, they were the worst-looking culprits that could be imagined, and when Colonel Logan, with a serious face, inquired if the sister had arrived, where she was, and such questions, the poor fellow looked as if he were under sentence of death. He acknowledged the fraud he had practised and said he was willing to suffer any punishment the colonel might inflict; that he had forfeited all respect by lying and had nothing to say in extenuation of his conduct. The colonel looked at him sternly, administered a lecture on lying and his detestation of liars, and then ordered that the offenders should dig up by the roots an enormous stump which was in the rear of his tent, where he could see them while they worked. They saluted and were marched off to obtain the tools to begin their work, which it took them some days to finish. They said they did not mind the work, but to be obliged to do it under the eye of the colonel whom they had deceived was a bitter trial, but a lesson that served them through the war and both were as gallant men as ever faced a cannon. They used often to laugh over this escapade after having won their shoulder-straps for gallantry on the field.

Before another expedition was to be undertaken a new commander was ordered to Cairo. The new commander flew from regiment to regiment. He had relieved General Oglesby and put him in command of Bird's Point on the opposite side of the river. He was no other than the hitherto unknown General U. S. Grant. It was announced that he would at once inspect every regiment in and around Cairo, to inform himself of their efficiency and the full strength of his forces. Hurriedly, company and regimental officers began preparing for his visit. Soldiers polished up their muskets and accoutrements, brushed their shoddy uniforms, and were speedily ready to be "ordered out." Expecting every moment that General Grant and staff would appear in full uniform and much military display, they waited impatiently. Imagine their surprise when informed that the unpretending, sturdy gentleman in citizen's dress who had just ridden by on a very ordinary clay-bank horse, attended by one officer and one or two of the officers on duty at general headquarters, was General Grant. Going directly to the colonel's headquarters, he introduced himself, and signified his desire to go through the quarters of the regiment and see the men of his command. Leaving their horses at each colonel's tent, and accompanied by that officer, they walked through the company aisles and personally inspected everything and every man in camp. By this businesslike procedure, void of all display and pageantry, General Grant won the confidence and admiration of officers and men. He afterward said that they were as fine a body of men as he had ever seen; that he would trust them anywhere to meet any equal number in any engagement.

Almost continual drilling and manœuvring filled up every hour for many days subsequent. The soldiers had little time for "larks" or homesickness. The malarious climate, however, began to tell upon the troops, and many became seriously sick.

CHAPTER 3

Armageddon—a Wife's Vigil

After the battle of Belmont, many more troops were ordered to rendezvous at Cairo, Illinois. General Grant was designated to organize an expedition up the Tennessee and Cumberland Rivers. During the months of December and January, in the worst weather ever experienced in that climate, the troops in great numbers were mobilized in and around inhospitable Cairo. Munitions of war and commissary stores were accumulated in great quantity. The troops, while ignorant of their destination, knew instinctively that some important movement was soon to be inaugurated. Brief as was their engagement at Belmont, they began to realize fully that Sherman's definition, "War is hell," was correct.

Finally the transports began to come into the port at Cairo. Orders were issued for the troops to be ready to embark on the 5th of February. From the moment of the receipt of this order the camps were all excitement with the preparations. Camp equipment were to be packed, and personal belongings reduced to the smallest possible compact parcel; business affairs had to be arranged by writing; letters, wills, and farewells had to be written, and everything prepared for a speedy departure to an unknown destination and fate.

The transports set sail in a pitiless storm of snow and sleet. Going as far as they could up the river, the troops were landed and proceeded to surround Fort Henry, which was to be attacked by our gunboats. The whole country adjacent was submerged by water; the land was heavily timbered, and it was almost impassable for the quartermaster and ordnance wagons, while it was with great difficulty that the artillery could be moved at all; but so dauntless were the troops of Grant's command that Fort Henry soon succumbed.

As soon as the fall of Fort Henry was assured, General Grant pushed forward with redoubled vigor, the assault by the gunboats having already begun upon Fort Donelson. The storms of the winter of 1861–62 were unprecedented, being especially wild during the month of February. Everything was covered with ice and snow; night and day a raw, cold wind blew such bitter blasts that men and animals could scarcely stand against its force. They had to move about or freeze to death. More than one of the brave men in the siege died from the exposure they experienced. Their clothing was frozen on them. Officers and men fared alike during the entire siege of Fort Donelson, and there was little respite for either. Colonel Logan was in the saddle almost continuously, taking only brief rests by lying down on the ground with his saddle under his head, and over him his saddle-blanket, which was frozen when he rose to mount his horse again. From this exposure he contracted rheumatism from which he never recovered, and which finally cost him his life. So near the fortifications were they that they did not dare to build fires by which to warm themselves or cook anything to eat.

Colonel Ransom with the 11th, and Colonel John A. Logan with the 31st Illinois Infantry, had gone into the siege side by side. Finding the ammunition short, these gallant men made an agreement to stand or fall together. They were to alternate in holding their places in the besieging line and thereby make the ammunition last as long as possible. They supported each other until the victory was won, but at a terrible cost to themselves and the gallant regiments they commanded, every man of whom was ready to follow either leader into the very jaws of death, as attested by the number who fell before the capitulation of Fort Donelson.

The *Telegraph* announced that Fort Donelson had fallen February 15, 1862, and also gave a list of the killed and wounded; in the list of killed appeared the names of Colonel John A. Logan, Lieutenant-Colonel John H. White, four captains of the 31st Regiment of Illinois, and a great number of the men, all of whom I knew personally. There were many Illinois troops in General Grant's command, and consequently the State lost heavily of her officers and soldiers in the expedition against Forts Henry and Donelson.

On receipt of the overwhelming news of my husband's death, I started at once for Cairo, Illinois, determined if it were possible to go to Fort Donelson at all hazards. Transportation was very limited, and hundreds of people flocked to Cairo, anxious to go up the Tennessee and Cumberland Rivers in pursuit of friends who had been killed or wounded. Orders were issued from the War Department to allow no one on board the few transports then at the command of the army. General Grant was to be reinforced at once so that he could continue the march to Pittsburg Landing and on to Corinth. On my arrival at Cairo I learned that Colonel Logan was not killed but was severely wounded, news which made me all the more anxious to join him. Going to army headquarters at Cairo, I applied for permission to go up the river. The colonel commanding assumed an imperious air, informing me with much emphasis that military necessity compelled him to refuse me a pass. My heart was almost broken; I could hardly stand on my feet while I addressed this high and mighty personage; hence I could only reply that I trusted, "if the exigencies of the service should ever send him to the front, and he should be so unfortunate as to suffer any of the fatalities of war, a military necessity would not prevent Mrs. Graham from going to him." He answered savagely: "Thank you, madam, there is no Mrs. Graham." And I retorted: "If there was one intended, I hope she died in her infancy." With fast-falling tears I left headquarters, fully intending to go to Fort Donelson if I had to go in a rowboat, or cross the river and drive overland. When I reached the hotel I found that Governor Yates of Illinois, and Governor Morton of Indiana, had both arrived, and were going to charter steamers to go and bring the wounded and the remains of those who had been killed home to their respective States. I hastened to call on them and was assured I could go with either of them. Dear old Colonel Dunlap of Jacksonville, Illinois, brigade quartermaster of McClernand's brigade was present, and as I passed out of the room he followed me into the hall and whispered to me the name of the steamer which was going first and which was then being loaded at the wharf. He said: "Slip down to the boat, tell them you are a member of my family, and that you are to wait for me until I come to the boat a few hours later. After you are on board, hide in one of the staterooms and you will not be disturbed, as, in the mean while, I will give such instructions as will protect you." I lost no time in getting to the boat and, to my delight, found Captain Arter in command. Colonel Logan had a few years before defended and cleared him of a charge of manslaughter. He was an old river captain and had gotten into trouble with a roustabout employed on his boat. He welcomed me most cordially, and understood without asking that I had no pass. He said: "Come on board, and you shall see Logan." He conducted me up a veritable winding stairs to a stateroom on the hurricane-deck, and I did not stir abroad until we were under way and the stars were shining. Captain Arter came and knocked on my door, calling out: "The coast is clear. Come down to supper."

As we sailed up the river it seemed like a shoreless sheet of water and ice, as the waters were so high they extended over acres of ground far outside the banks. Mammoth trees rose out of the water like islands in the sea, and but for long experience the pilot could not have kept in the channel. The long, gray moss which hung like mystic veils from all the trees invested everything with a weird appearance and made one feel he was penetrating into a mysterious land. We arrived at an early hour in the morning, and as we approached we saw the stars and stripes flying over the ramparts of Fort Donelson. As we neared the landing our boat almost touched the guards of the decks of the steamer *Uncle Sam* upon which were General Grant's headquarters. Recognizing me, a number of the officers who came out on the deck hailed me, telling me to come on board, General Grant having had both Colonel Ransom and Colonel Logan carried to his headquarters after the surrender. In a briefer time than it has taken to write this story, I was ascending the companion-way of the *Uncle Sam,* to find my husband lying on a cot with his left arm strapped to his body, it having been wounded near the point of the shoulder, the rifle-ball passing through the shoulder-joint. Another ball struck the pistol he carried in his belt, and nearly broke his ribs, from which he suffered almost as much as from the wound in the arm and shoulder. Colonel Ransom and Colonel Logan lay on cots side by side on the *Uncle Sam,* where General Grant had done the very best he could for them.

From the severe weather and exposure hundreds had come down with pneumonia and typhoid fever. Transportation was so limited that General Grant could not send the sick and wounded North as rapidly as he desired. He therefore took possession of the many vacant houses and tried to establish hospitals, to make the sufferers as comfortable as possible, with the thermometer below zero and the meagre supplies attainable. As soon as possible, therefore, I made my two patients, Colonels Ransom and Logan, much happier than they had been, as I had not been so improvident as to go to Colonel Logan empty-handed, but had hastily laid in clothing, delicacies, and many necessities for the relief of the sick and wounded. As I was the eldest of a family of thirteen, my education in caring for the sick and preparing the proper diet for invalids had not been neglected, and so I lost no time in finding the stewards and their kitchens. Only those who have had like experience can appreciate what a sponge-bath of alcohol and hot water, clean clothes, and nourishing food meant to those brave men after the long, weary hours of suffering and discomfort that they had endured from the hour they had fallen on the bloody field.

After ministering to their relief and when they were sleeping quietly, I went with some friends to look after those whom we knew who were either sick or wounded and had been carried to improvised hospitals. We also attended the burial service which was held over the brave men of the 11th and 31st Illinois Regiments that had fought so bravely. While life lasts I shall never forget the sight upon which I looked through tears on the battle-field. The long trenches had been dug by their weary comrades. The heroic dead had been brought and laid side by side in them. Their overcoats and blankets were wrapped about their lifeless forms. Tents were ripped so as to make tarpaulins with which to cover them over. Chaplains standing close to the centre, with uncovered heads, prayed fervently for peace to the souls of the gallant dead about to be laid to rest in mother earth, where they would sleep their last sleep till the trump of the resurrection should call them to glory in that land where wars can never come. After the bugler's long, sad note I turned away with unspeakable sadness from this, the first interment on a battle-field I had ever witnessed, appreciating more keenly than I had ever done before the melancholy significance of the words: "Buried on the field where they had fallen," and realizing that it was barely possible, after sanguinary engagements, to pay as much tribute to the dead as had been done in this one of the early battles in the West during the Civil War.

For many days I continued my constant vigil over Colonels Ransom and Logan, as serious complications in both cases set in, and it required the surgeon's best skill to save them.

Meanwhile General Grant was steadily pushing his preparations for the continuation of the expedition to Pittsburg Landing (know also as Shiloh) en route to Corinth, Mississippi, then the headquarters of Beauregard's army. Transportation was finally secured for Colonel Ransom to take him North to his friends. The surgeons succeeded in finding quarters to which Colonel Logan was removed, as the *Uncle Sam* had to proceed up the river with General Grant and his staff.

It would seem hopeless now to care for an invalid with the scant supplies, crude utensils, and appliances we could then command; but, thanks to untiring surgeons and devoted friends, who were constantly coming from the North with sanitary stores and most generous commissaries, our larder was kept quite full. Tin pans gradually gave way to real saucepans; broilers succeeded the long forked stick which had been used for broiling and everything; coffee and tea pots took the place of tin cans; and wooden johnny-cake boards were supplanted by iron skillets with iron lids. Donations of glass, queensware, cutlery, blankets, bed and table linen increased our stores, until at the end of three weeks we were living in affluence and were able to provide for many more who were wounded or ill in other parts of the building.

I look back upon that experience now with infinite satisfaction, as I was able to nurse my husband back to health and strength and he was spared to me and to his country for a quarter of a century longer.

The surgeons and physicians deciding that Colonel Logan was able to be moved, he was taken on board a transport, and by exercising great care we reached our home, which was then at Murphysboro, Jackson County, Illinois. We had scarcely recovered from the fatigue of the journey when the news of the approaching battle of Shiloh was received. Like an impatient steed, Colonel (now Brigadier-General) Logan sniffed the battle from afar, and though unable to put his arm in his coat-sleeve, he insisted upon rejoining his command in time, if possible, to participate in the expected battle.[1] The stars he had won at Donelson would necessitate his assuming graver duties, and he was most anxious to have his old regiment assigned to his brigade. Ignoring appeals to remain until his wound was healed, he set out for Shiloh, arriving there late in the afternoon of the last day of that memorable engagement, disgusted with the delays of transportation that had prevented him from participating in that mighty struggle, when fortune apparently wavered from the Union to the Confederate army, and then back to the army of the Union.

Scarcely halting long enough to gather up the sick and wounded and to bury the dead, General Grant moved forward, hoping to capture Beauregard and his army. General Logan was placed in command of the First Brigade, Third Division, Seventeenth Army Corps. He was proud of his command, and would have been happy but for the fateful effect of the attacks of scandal-mongers upon General Grant, charging him with intemperance and incapacity to command the dauntless army, which was subsequently a part of the invincible Army of the Tennessee. The authorities at Washington were so impressed by these reports, supposed to come from loyal, honest persons, that, wishing to protect the army which had scored the first victories for the Union, they placed General Halleck in command and designated General Grant as second in command, a designation never before or since made in the American army. General Grant felt the indignity deeply, but, true soldier that he was, he pushed his plans for the capture of Corinth with unremitting vigor, though handicapped at every turn by Halleck's dilatory, technical methods.[2]

Grant and Logan were on the most intimate terms, and, being aggressive soldiers, they became restive under Halleck's over-cautious tactics. General Logan's command was placed astride the Mobile and Ohio Railroad which ran into Corinth. In this brigade there were a number of men formerly in the employ of railroads and who understood sounds conveyed by the rails. General Logan learned from the telegraphy of these sounds that empty trains were being taken into Corinth and that they were loaded when they were run out. Convinced that the Confederates were evacuating Corinth, and that if they escaped it would mean another long and weary chase which would cost many lives and great hardship to the army, he went to Grant and begged him to let him feel the enemy and attack them if he proved that he was right about their movements.

Grant believed Logan and wanted to let him try, but Halleck condemned the whole suggestion and intimated that if Logan repeated his impertinence by such reports he would put him under arrest and relieve him of his command. General Grant in his memoirs says: "May 28th 1862, Gen. Logan informed me that the enemy had been evacuating for several days, and that, if allowed, he could go into Corinth with his brigade." Beauregard had begun to evacuate on the 25th of May, but General Halleck would have no suggestions from Grant or Logan, and waited his own time to find, when he issued his celebrated order of attack of May 30, no enemy on his front. Soon after Halleck was called to Washington and Grant, untrammelled by a martinet, began his campaign in pursuit of the wily enemy. Our gallant army continued the chase, stopping ever and anon to fight a battle and scale fortifications or rout the enemy.

After Corinth came the trying and tedious march through the enemy's country to Jackson, Lagrange, and Memphis, Tennessee.

In the fall and winter of 1862–63 General Logan's command was encamped at Memphis, Tennessee. The general had been almost constantly in the saddle from the time he reached Shiloh and joined his command in the movement against Corinth. The weather was inclement and the condition of the roads dreadful, the streets of the city being well-nigh impassable.

On hearing that General Logan had reached Memphis, I applied for transportation to join him, and succeeded in getting it—a most difficult thing to accomplish in those days, with the meagre facilities at the command of the army. General Logan and his staff were staying at the Gayoso House, as were also General McPherson and his staff. When I arrived I found that our friends Mr. and Mrs. Sanger and their daughter, Miss Harriet, now the widow of George M. Pullman, were guests of the hotel. Miss Harriet Sanger was one of the most beautiful and captivating girls in the West. General McPherson admired her extravagantly. She had also a devotee in the person of Colonel F. A. Starring, of the 72d Illinois Infantry Regiment. The 72d was from Chicago and its vicinity and had an unusually fine band. One night Colonel Starring arranged for his band to serenade Miss Sanger. He had called for Miss Sanger, who came down to the parlor to receive him, and while they were listening to the music they heard cheering. Colonel Starring stepped out on the balcony and found General McPherson on another balcony a few feet away acknowledging the serenade. One of his staff had supposed, of course, that the serenade was for General McPherson, and ordered refreshments in the hotel dining-room for the band men. This naturally inspired the band to play vociferously after the repast. Miss Sanger induced Colonel Starring not to say anything about the serenade having been intended for her, so that General McPherson might enjoy the compliment ignorant of the fact that the serenade had not been intended for him. It was too good a joke, however, to be kept a secret. Somebody told General McPherson, who was much chagrined over the affair. He tried to treat the occurrence jocularly, but was unable to conceal his annoyance.

General McPherson was, without exception, the most unassuming and agreeable man I ever knew. His soldierly qualities were of the highest order. True nobility characterized his conduct as a man and a gentleman. His orders were military in every sense of the word, but without a note of the martinet running through them. The attachment between him and General Logan was very strong, and found expression in General Logan's heroic action after McPherson fell, July 22, 1864.

A few days after the episode related above General Logan's headquarters were established on the grounds surrounding the magnificent Lanier place on the outskirts of the city. General Logan and I were given rooms in the stately mansion. As soon as possible thereafter General Logan began to get his division ready to be reviewed. General McPherson reviewed the whole command, doing us the honor to dine with us in the Lanier mansion after the review was over.

The troops had been paid a day or two before, and naturally many of them went on a grand spree, and it was with great difficulty that the officers could get their troops sufficiently straightened out for the review. Colonel John D. Stephenson commanded a Missouri regiment, one of the bravest, most brilliant, and best of men. His regiment was made up of men from the docks of Saint Louis, and they were a pretty hard tribe. They had been fighting among themselves, and almost all of them appeared in line for the review with black eyes and otherwise "bummed up." The morning of the review Colonel Stephenson started to go into the sutler's tent. There was a piece of timber standing near by which fell and struck the colonel on the side of the head causing great discoloration of his cheeks and under his eyes. General McPherson was full of fun, and, on returning to Colonel Stephenson's tent after reviewing his regiment, he said: "Colonel, I am surprised to see that you have a black-eyed regiment," a facetious remark which we all enjoyed.

The day of the review was the last time that General Logan was really able to leave his bed. After his long exposure and hard work I acted as amanuensis and messenger for him, taking his orders to the headquarters tent on the grounds of the Lanier place. One day he wanted from his adjutant-general a particular paper which he was to use, and I told him that I could go over and get it as well as not. I started over, and as I passed Colonel Stolbrand's tent I saw his clerk was tied to a tree which stood almost in front of it. Poor Crutchfield looked so unhappy, having just recovered from a debauch, that he touched my heart and I ran into the cook's tent, got a butcher knife and cut the ropes to free him. I told Crutchfield to go to his tent and hide himself as soon as possible. Colonel Stolbrand was on duty somewhere and did not know who had cut the ropes to free Crutchfield. Colonel Stolbrand was a fine specimen of a Swedish officer, with his ruddy complexion and sandy hair. He wore the red of the artillery, and altogether was rather a flaming specimen when he came rushing into General Logan's room in a towering rage, reporting to the general that somebody had freed Crutchfield whom he had tied to discipline and sober up, insisting that he could not find out that it was anybody in the army. If it was they had got to be punished, and if it was an outsider he must be driven from the camp immediately. I had said nothing to the general about what I had done, and enjoyed very much Stolbrand's indignation.

A few days before, Colonel Stolbrand had been telegraphed to meet his wife, who was trying to join him at some station above Memphis. The general was not inclined to let him go. Colonel Stolbrand happened to ask permission in my presence, and I said to the general: "Oh, let him go, he will be back all right." After my pleading the general did let him go, and Colonel Stolbrand was very grateful to me. He went, and, of course, got back all right.

The incident involving Crutchfield occurred a day or two after Colonel Stolbrand's return. I listened quietly to what he was saying to the general, and when he had finished I said: "Now, colonel, suppose it turns out that the person who cut that rope does not belong to the army, and nobody has any authority to drive them [*sic*] out of the camp, what would you do?" He said: "I would drive them away from the camp at the point of my sword." I said: "I believe there was a man who wanted to join his wife a few days ago, and his commanding officer would not consent to let him go. Somebody interfered and the man finally got permission." This remark gave the stolid Swede an idea that I might have done this, and so he said: "Ah, Mrs. Logan, my dear lady, I have great reverence for you, but you must not do that thing again or I shall be obliged to make charges against you." The general saw at once that I was the guilty party, and kept up the joke with Stolbrand by saying that if any such thing ever occurred again he would have the culprit driven beyond the lines by a drum corps, which put Colonel Stolbrand in a good humor. I was not willing to let it go at that, so I said to Colonel Stolbrand, "Colonel, Crutchfield has sworn to me that he will never touch another drop of liquor while he is in your command and you know that he is a very valuable clerk and I am sure you do not wish to part with him. Now promise me that you will inflict a very light punishment on him for this misdemeanor and that you will give him a chance to keep his oath of total abstinence in the future." I saw no more of poor Crutchfield for many years, but I was on a Mississippi River steamer going up the river one day, when somebody called me by name from the shore, and, standing on the deck, I responded. He then called: "Mrs. Logan, this is Crutchfield, and I am sober yet."

Colonel Stolbrand won his star for his gallant and soldierly conduct, and continued to remain on the general's staff to the close of the war. He was subsequently elected to Congress from a district in South Carolina, and died in the South a good many years ago.

The troops remained in Memphis many weeks, and I stayed with the general until they were ready to march. He was very ill for some time with a fever, and worried all the time as to what to do to keep the soldiers from deserting. Hearing that they were going to serenade him, he concluded that when he made his speech on the balcony he would have an order ready to issue appealing to them not to disgrace themselves by yielding to the influence of letters from home, which had created so much dissatisfaction among the troops. We had a great time preparing this address and this order, because the general was almost too weak to get them into the shape in which he wished to have them. It seemed as though almost the entire Seventeenth Corps assembled on the grounds of the Lanier place on the night that they tendered him the serenade. Colonel Stephenson was to make a little speech to the general, pledging the devotion and fidelity of the troops to him and their hope that he would soon be able to be on duty again. We stood on the balcony in front of the mansion during and after the serenade. Colonel Stephenson then made his address, to which General Logan replied, reading a copy of the order urging them to stand by their colors until they were planted on the ramparts of Vicksburg and New Orleans. He said he knew they could do it if they determined to, and that he would never order them to do anything in which he was not willing to take the lead. He fulfilled that promise to them literally, as he and his command were ever in the van until the fall of Vicksburg and the lifting of the blockade from the Mississippi.

The general had a very delightful staff: Colonel Townes, Colonel Hotaling, Colonel Yorke, Colonel Lloyd Wheaton, now retired major-general of the regular army and on whose escutcheon there is not a blot after his many years of service. Major Whitehead, Major J. H. Hoover, Major Holcomb, and others were also on the staff, and were untiring in the discharge of their duties and in trying to make everything agreeable. They treated me always with the most distinguished consideration. General Logan had some cousins in his old regiment which was encamped quite a distance from where we were staying. Major Hoover wanted me to go and see them very much. I was very anxious to do so, and General Logan desired me to go and look after them and to visit the headquarters of the regiments under his command. Major Hoover had a very fine saddle-horse which he wanted me to ride when we made these visits. There was staying in the Lanier house the wife of Colonel Sloane, of the 24th Illinois. She was one of those women who are always interfering with and crossing the members of her husband's regiment. She came very near at one time breaking up the regiment altogether, and was only prevented by her husband's sending her home. She found out that Colonel Hoover was taking me around to make these visits, and was determined to go too. She asked the general if he did not think she ought to accompany us, and the general, always full of fun and liking to play practical jokes, insisted that she should join us. He ordered Hoover to get her a horse and saddle somewhere. Hoover did not want to do it, as he disliked her excessively. "I'll give her a John Gilpin ride if she insists upon going." The mud and water was something terrible on the morning on which we set out on this expedition, Mrs. Sloane mounted on an unreliable horse. Hoover, knowing that I could ride like a Comanche in those days, had trained the horses to follow a whistle which he gave. Away we went until we were perfectly covered with mud and water. Mrs. Sloane could not ride very well, and it was not long before she was landed in a bank of mud on the side of the road, as her horse would keep up with the others and she could not stay on. Hoover said he knew she could not get hurt, but would be covered with mud and he would have his revenge. We had to stop and I had to take her horse and give her mine, which was a very gentle animal, and return home as we were not presentable afterward. The general suspected that Hoover had played this trick because he had not wanted Mrs. Sloane to go. Hoover said it was not his fault. She could not ride and he could not help it, but got the best horse he could for her. For a long time afterward the staff were regaled with Hoover's description of Mrs. Sloane's ride, hat off, hair hanging down, and clothing all awry.

Such diversions were all we had to break the monotony and anxiety ever hanging over the army. The day dawned all too soon when camp was broken, and the march was begun to Lake Providence. I returned to my home to spend the next few months in unspeakable anxiety, knowing that the army was destined to invest Vicksburg.

Crossing the Mississippi River, the Army of the West began its worst experiences during the war. It was proposed to invest Vicksburg, Mississippi, then supposed to be impregnable, by transferring the army by way of Lake Providence to a position below Vicksburg, recross the river, and besiege the city from above, below, and rear. The swamps and shallow lakes of that region were fearful for men to pass through. They tried to convert them into canals, hoping they might be able to navigate some kind of craft through them by which they could transfer the troops to Port Gibson, the point chosen to try to land below Vicksburg. After weeks of struggling with mud and water, with little success, General Logan, after conferring with General Grant, called for volunteers from his command to run the blockade on transports, protected by cotton-bales from the frowning guns that guarded the river. More men responded than they could use. Selecting from the number those whom they thought best fitted for the hazardous undertaking, they were ready in a brief time. They waited for the darkest of nights, which finally came, and then the wooden steamers with their walls of cotton cast their moorings. Not a light was visible on any of the boats, not a sound could be heard. Like the weird craft with silent crew on the River Styx, they floated on the placid river, past the mammoth guns of the forts on the river front, on to the port of their destination before the sleeping sentinel knew anything of the daring enterprise. Once below Vicksburg, the transports carried the troops with rapidity from the western to the eastern shore of the river. At Port Gibson the Confederates made their first resistance to the invading army of the Mississippi, but they were completely routed. The bayous, swamps, and impenetrable forests of that whole valley of the Mississippi made it terrible for an army to move after they had landed safely; but the tireless and undaunted troops of the West were equal to that herculean task. The battles of the Big Black, Champion Hills—one of the most brilliant of the whole war—Raymond, 22d of May 1863, and other engagements around the beleaguered city, proved the indomitable courage and military skill of the officers and men of the Western army. General Grant, acting upon what he supposed was reliable information from Major-General John A. McClernand, one of his corps commanders, that he had captured a section of the outer works, ordered an assault May 22, 1863. General Logan disagreed with General Grant about the wisdom of this assault doubting the truth of the information which had been given General Grant, but as General Logan never faltered or hesitated to execute his orders, the First Brigade, Third Division of the Seventeenth Army Corps, with General Logan leading, started up the rugged sides of the hills surrounding Vicksburg. Again and again they charged, losing many gallant men in each ineffectual assault. Finally General Grant found he had been misinformed and that the whole force inside the walls had been concentrated against the Seventeenth Army Corps. He hastily ordered them to retire, and as speedily relieved the officer who had so prematurely announced a victory which he had hoped to win but which had not been accomplished.

General Logan considered May 22 one of the most disastrous and fearful undertakings of any siege during his service. The almost perpendicular side of the bluffs surrounding the well-fortified city of Vicksburg, the immense advantage of the besieged over the besiegers, and the almost hopeless task of accomplishing anything made it a most unsatisfactory and ill-advised attack. For six or eight weeks the siege was continued, every day adding to the casualties of the besiegers and the discomfort and certain doom of the besieged.

General Logan felt quite sure of success through the mining and sapping of Fort Hill, which was one of the strongest points in the cordon of fortifications that encircled the natural stronghold of the Confederacy. After a thorough investigation of the proposition, General Grant allowed General Logan to undertake the scheme in which he had so much confidence. His command had led the van from Lake Providence. Officers and men were anxious to continue in the lead, and were impatient to begin the work, which was to result in the explosion of Fort Hill and the making of a breach in the walls through which they might be the first to enter the city. No finer piece of engineering was ever performed. The experience of the veteran volunteers made them expert miners and sappers, and with incredible rapidity they achieved the prodigious feat of undermining and exploding Fort Hill. General Logan's old regiment, the 31st Illinois, waited impatiently to rush into the crater for a hand-to-hand engagement with the brave men who had gallantly defended their breastworks. The conflict was of short duration, but many heroic men fell in this last sally of the Union army upon the breastworks surrounding Vicksburg. With General Logan leading the van, they marched into Vicksburg on the morning of the 4th of July, 1863. All parts of the besieging line had been unflinchingly sustained, and no braver troops ever encompassed a fortified city than the dauntless Union soldiers who besieged and captured Vicksburg. General Logan and his command had been in the front from the beginning of the expedition; they had furnished the blockade-runners, the assaulting party on May 22, and they made the break in the fortifications by blowing up Fort Hill; consequently, General Grant felt it their due to be the first to occupy the captured city.

With the fall of Vicksburg the Mississippi River was open to the Gulf of Mexico, and from that hour the fate of the Confederacy was sealed.

The booming of the cannon announced the glorious victory on Independence Day, and the deafening shouts of the triumphant Union army were the death-knells of secession. General Logan was appointed commander of the post at Vicksburg, and immediately began the adjustment of affairs between the conquered and conquerors, desiring in every way in his power, consistent with fidelity to his country, to ameliorate the condition of the unfortunate people who had lived inside the walls of the besieged city. Many had lived in caves during the siege, their homes being uninhabitable because they were within range of the guns of the Union army. They had been reduced to the last extremity, and had lived on food never before eaten by Americans. He listened to their woes, ordered relief for thousands, and was so magnanimous in his administration as to win their admiration and gratitude.

As I stood in the crater of Fort Hill, from which point I could see Grant's, Sherman's, and Logan's headquarters, and looked across the chasms made by nature between the ridges which were occupied by the contending armies at Vicksburg, I marvelled more than ever at the military genius of our great commanders, and the fearless intrepidity of the Union troops, who captured that seemingly impregnable city, justly called the Gibraltar of the Mississippi, fortified by nature and by the most skilful engineering of any age, and defended by the bravest of the brave.

It is a source of infinite gratification that the great State of Illinois has built a Temple of Fame in the National Cemetery at Vicksburg, in the crater of Fort Hill, at a cost of a quarter of a million dollars for the preservation of the names and fame of the officers and men of the seventy-five regiments who were engaged in that matchless siege and victory.

The siege had lasted without cessation from early in May until July 4, 1863. Officers and men were well-nigh exhausted by the intense heat, burning sun, hot rains, and the long strain of the constant vigilance and the heavy burdens they had borne. It was deemed advisable to furlough as many as possible both of officers and men. Hastening to their homes in the North and West, they found the welcome due returning soldiers who have been valiant in their country's services. Their presence among the people soon dissipated the sentimental sympathies with the South which had been aroused over the Emancipation Proclamation. The descriptions the returning officers and soldiers gave of the dangers through which they had passed, the hardships they had endured, the sufferings they had experienced, the sacrifices they had made and witnessed as they saw their comrades fall on many bloody fields, not knowing what might be their own fate ere the conflict ceased, caused a renewed spirit of patriotism to spread rapidly. When, therefore, at the expiration of the leave the officers and men had enjoyed, they returned to their respective commands, they knew there would be no more lukewarm support of the army in the field by the people at home.

General Logan was wanted to help win victories for the party in the local elections, which were in great doubt because of the effect of the issuance of the Emancipation Proclamation. As soon, therefore, as General Logan could get in shape the complex affairs existing after the bitter contest for possession of the Gibraltar of the Mississippi, he caused the appointment of General John Maltby of the 45th Illinois Infantry Regiment from Galena, Illinois, as commander of the post at Vicksburg. As the city was under martial law, General Maltby would have the assistance of a competent provost-marshal, and, being himself a brave and discreet man, General Logan felt that the people would soon be glad that they were once more under the protection of the Stars and Stripes. With his staff General Logan embarked upon the Mississippi River steamboat, and after a tedious journey reached home for a brief leave of absence. Southern Illinois having furnished a large quota of the troops which had been in every engagement from Forts Henry and Donelson to the surrender of Vicksburg, a great many of them had been furloughed and had arrived at their homes before General Logan. The whole population had been fired with the wildest patriotic enthusiasm by their graphic description of their experiences on the march, in camp, in hospital, and in battle from the time they left Cairo, February 1862, till Vicksburg fell, July 4, 1863; consequently, by the time General Logan landed at Cairo his heroism, magnanimity, kindness to his men, and his military genius had been so often told by his faithful followers that he found multitudes waiting to do him honor. The citizens had told the soldiers of the reign of terror which the Knights of the Golden Circle had exercised over the non-combatants who had been left at home. The soldiers insisted upon guarding General Logan wherever he went, following him in citizens' clothing, in much the same way as the President is guarded from assassination in these days. The welcome accorded General Logan was so spontaneous and flattering that he scouted the idea of any one doing him harm; all the same the soldiers continued their self-appointed guardianship, relieving each other from time to time as their leaves expired and they had to return to their respective commands.

The local elections grew more exciting as the campaign proceeded. General Logan spoke almost daily to vast assemblages. The themes he dwelt most upon were the Emancipation Proclamation and its necessity, and the guarantee of final triumph of the Government through victories the Union army, especially the Western army, had achieved.[3] At heart loyal to their country, they were easily won away from their temporary disaffection.

Colonel R. P. Townes, Major Hotaling, Major Lloyd Wheaton, Major Hoover, and other members of my husband's staff were with us in our home in Carbondale, Jackson County, Illinois, almost all the time during General Logan's leave of absence. Dinners, excursions, picnics, balls, parties of all kinds, to which were added political demonstrations, kept all of us busy. Carbondale had an unusual number of pretty girls and the very best society south of Springfield, the capital of the State. They were all very patriotic, and had devoted much time to the soldiers, their families, and the refugees. From nearly every family some one had gone into the army or navy; hence they could not do enough for the soldiers and officers to make their brief visit delightful, and were ever ready to join in anything proposed for their entertainment and diversion. A round of pleasure was inaugurated and kept up till the very last moment of the stay of General Logan and his staff. When the time came for their departure it was noticed that one or two of the young ladies wore engagement rings on the third finger of the left hand, and that the gallant officers said good-by to the girls they were leaving behind them with tears in their eyes and very sad faces. Their fiancées came often to me afterward to be comforted while waiting for the "cruel war" to be over.

The double stars of a major-general, which General Logan had won by his distinguished service and desperate daring in the Vicksburg campaign, would, I knew, require his transfer to the command of a corps, and knowing that an expedition against Chickamauga was being organized, General Logan was impatient for his orders. They came, all too soon for me, assigning him to the Fifteenth Army Corps, Army of the Tennessee, then under General J. B. McPherson. General Logan was delighted to serve under McPherson but sorry to leave the veterans of the Seventeenth Corps especially his old regiment, to whose valor he felt he owed his promotion. General Frank Blair was given the Seventeenth Corps, in which were almost all the regiments that had composed the brigade and division which General Logan had commanded after his promotion to a brigadier-generalship; but as the Fifteenth and Seventeenth were both to be in the Army of the Tennessee, he felt he should be near them. General Logan always regretted that he could not have reached Chickamauga in time to have a greater share in the battle among the clouds of Lookout Mountain. Another anxiety was his knowledge of the fact that an undercurrent of disloyalty still existed among the people on account of their Southern proclivities.[4]

The few days intervening between the receipt of his orders and his proceeding to Chattanooga to assume command of the Fifteenth Army Corps, General Logan spent in making speeches for the local candidates of the Republican party and in final appeals to the people to defend the Emancipation Proclamation which Mr. Lincoln had issued in the name of humanity and freedom for all men. Many times when he was speaking he would be interrupted by bullies who were foolish enough to imagine they could neutralize his influence over the masses by asking questions, uttering insults, and indulging in braggadocio. These disturbers of the peace were always worsted by General Logan's replies. On one occasion he threw the glass tumbler on the stand before him squarely into the face of a bully whose insults he would not brook. The coward had to retreat to a near-by drug-store and submit to a surgeon's skill to save his face from disfigurement. It silenced all others, and enabled General Logan to do valuable service for his party as well as his country before leaving home to return to duty in the field.

The continued disaffection of the troops on the question of the Emancipation Proclamation through the influence of sympathizers with the South, and the great number of desertions assumed a most serious aspect. In every community these deserters were hiding and adding to the feverish excitement of the public mind. The recreant soldiers found that by their act of desertion they were delighting the disloyal and rapidly undoing what they had done for the Union cause; also, that they themselves were in great trouble, as they were liable to suffer the consequences of the violation of the articles of war, so severe upon deserters.[5]

Something had to be done to secure their return to duty and at the same time avoid the expense of long trials and loss to the service of the men should they be condemned to penal servitude in the military prisons. Hence the ablest men in the country appealed to Mr. Lincoln to issue another proclamation pardoning all deserters who would return to duty on or before a given date.

As can readily be imagined, the regiments and companies were speedily reinforced by greater numbers who were glad to escape the consequences of their rash act in impulsively yielding to their sympathy with Southern institutions born of prejudice and association. Victories along the lines heightened the prospects everywhere till the proposition to enlist negroes as soldiers was mooted. Again the ever-present prejudice against the negro which existed in the West and Southwest was rife, and mutterings were heard in every direction, soldiers swearing they would not serve with "niggers."

Some officers exhibited a spirit of insubordination, and but for the fact that the army was constantly on the move it would have suffered another shock of disaffection from political influence. In southern Illinois the situation was especially critical. As the majority of loyal, able-bodied men, old and young were by this time in the army, the disgruntled sympathizers were left in full possession of every field—business, politics, and everything else. These malcontents grew more and more bitter, and, while powerless to do anything but annoy, they indulged in all sorts of persecutions of furloughed Union soldiers and the families of the soldiers who were at the front.

Mr. William Bandy, father of two or three Union soldiers, was taken out, tied to a tree, and whipped unmercifully for his radical sentiments. The home of an officer whose family lived in the country was entered and the household effects broken and destroyed. The animals of the Union people were butchered; the hamstrings of the horses were cut so that the poor brutes could not work the crops but had to be shot.

Family feuds were increasing, murder was perpetrated, and all the horrors of civil war and its consequences, added to the never-ending solicitude for the fate of friends in the field made life one continuous routine of anxiety and suspense, especially for those in the West whose fathers, sons, husbands, and friends were in the army.

Lookout Mountain and Atlanta, in the mountain fastness, were considered almost impregnable, and the thought that the troops in the expedition were so indomitable that they would all die in the attempt or capture these points gave occasion for constant anguish. The approach of winter and the thought of the mountainous country through which the expedition was to be made added another cause for deep concern. In addition, many of the families of the soldiers had to be provided for at home, and the refugee contrabands were becoming so numerous and such a burden to the people of the border States that it was a question of the gravest nature what to do with them. They were unfitted, physically, to take the places of the troops in industrial fields. They had already suffered much from exposure. Among the most pathetic scenes of the war was the sight of the poor, helpless creatures, black and white, who were dumped under the woodsheds on the line of the Illinois Central and Ohio and Mississippi Railroads with nothing but a few clothes and little bundles of bedding and articles of household belongings. Sick, destitute, homeless, friendless, and among strangers, in an inhospitable climate, their condition was unutterably sad.

In company with noble women who worked all the time for charity or the soldiers we visited these people to try to alleviate their sufferings, and were deeply affected to see them, in their absolutely helpless situation, sitting or lying on the ground with folded hands, perfect pictures of despair.

One white family of eight I remember were, without exception, the most cheerless and forlorn we had ever seen. The mother and six daughters were lying on the floor of an old freight depot with nothing but their scanty clothing to cover them, the old man sitting shivering with the cold. The bleak winds of November were whistling through the cracks, and they had not a morsel to eat. Our aid society had very little money but we hoped to relieve their extreme wants, and asked the poor mother what she desired most. Imagine our consternation when, with bated breath, she said, in true Southern vernacular: "A little terbacker, if you please." Some of the ladies declared we ought to let her die, but charity prevailed and she was given the much-desired weed. The doctors attended all these poor people faithfully, furnishing medicines for their prescriptions gratuitously. Food and raiment were given them, and after being braced up by the invigorating Northern climate they went to work and made useful citizens.

The poor blacks were, if possible, more pitiful on account of their timidity and extreme destitution; the climate was worse on them than on the whites, and they died as if suffering from a contagion. After a while they began to feel that they were safe from their persecutors and that they were free. Many an old man sang "Old Shady" with enthusiasm:

Good-by, hard work, and nebber any pay,
I'm going up North, where de white folks stay,
White wheat bread and a dollar a day.

Chorus

Away den, away, for I can't stay any longer,
Hurrah, boys, hurrah,
For I am going home.

The poor creatures providentially supplied the places of the men who were in the army. In my own case I blessed the day when they came to southern Illinois, because before that I had been, with the assistance of my companion and friend, Miss Mary E. Tuthill, obliged to play the part of man and maid of all work, feeding, currying, and caring for the animals in the barn-yard, harnessing and driving the horses, washing the buggies and carriages, and performing every species of manual labor necessary to be done, at the same time trying to help others more dependent and timid. Besides this we had to protect ourselves from annoying persecutions inflicted by the senseless sympathizers with the rebellion who were too cowardly to go South and cast their lot with the people for whom they professed so much sympathy.

One day as Miss Tuthill and I were driving we passed a colored man who sat under a tree beside the road wondering where he should go for a home, food, and clothing. Our "copperhead" rulers of the community had forbidden negroes to stop in that part of the country. I was unable to secure the services of a man servant, and was about as desperate as poor "Albert" as he sat there, an exile and a wanderer. I stopped the horse I was driving and asked the poor fellow what he was doing there and where he was going. He timidly replied: "I ain't doin' nuffin', Miss, and God knows I doesn't know whar to go. Bless de Lord, I would be glad to get sumfin' to do, an' be 'lowed to stay sumwhar."

I told him that I wished to hire a man to work for me, and if he would come with me I would build him a little house in my yard; that if he would work and obey me, taking care of my cattle, horses, and garden, I would pay him fifteen dollars a month and give him his board.

The poor creature bowed his head to the ground almost, and said: "Bless you, Missus, I would be glad to mind you and do anything in the world dat you telled me to, but I'se afeard dat the big white bosses around here won't 'low me to stay here nohow."

I told him I would undertake to protect him if he knew how to shoot. He should have a good gun and plenty of ammunition in his house to protect himself with if anybody should molest him at night; that I was not afraid of their coming on the place in the daytime; that for a while he would have to sleep in the barn till I could put up a little house for him. He said: "Well, Miss, I leaves it all in your hands and hope de Lord will take keer of us bofe."

I directed him how to go to my house to wait for me till I should come. When I reached home he sat on the wood-pile waiting for me, his face shining like the setting sun. He had taken a survey of the premises and was highly delighted, declaring to me he "nebber expected to reach de promised land so soon." I ordered him to carry a wash-tub out to the barn and to take a bath. I bought him a new suit of cottonade at a neighboring store, and when he presented himself at the back door soon afterward for food and orders he looked like a black prince. He was six feet tall and was a fine specimen of his race, his honest face beaming with happiness. He was more efficient in the arts of hostlery and horticulture than my friend Miss Mary Tuthill—afterward Mrs. R. N. Pearson, wife of General R. N. Pearson, of Chicago—and myself, and the poor dumb brutes and the garden soon presented an improved appearance.

Not long after it was noised about that "John Logan's wife has hired a nigger to work for her, and he is on the place to stay." They resolved that he should not do so, and that "if she did not send him away, they would go there, and send him off in a jiffy, and if she interfered to protect him, they would thrash her too."

A member of the secret organization known as the Knights of the Golden Circle, who kept up their warfare and made so much trouble for every Unionist, had been raised with me and while he was intensely disloyal to his country he was the soul of honor and loyalty to his friends. He knew I would try to protect the colored man when they should attack him, and he could not bear the thought of any harm coming to me. So he came to me, begging that I send the "darky" away, warning me there would be trouble if I persisted in keeping him, because they were "not going to let the country be filled up with niggers." I thought of the matter long and seriously. It seemed so outrageous that men in a free land would undertake, by mob violence, to decide who should and who should not live in the country that I was inclined to test the question and see whether or not these men, avowed enemies of the nation, should dictate to loyal people what they should or should not do. The colored man had in no wise interfered with any one. He was respectful to everybody, was sober, industrious, and was entitled to life, liberty, and the pursuit of happiness both by the Declaration of Independence and President Lincoln's proclamation.

So I told my friend James Durham that, while I appreciated beyond expression his friendship and warning, I must be frank enough to tell him I intended to keep the man and protect him to the best of my ability. It might be selfishness that prompted this decision because I did need Albert's services, and as he wanted to stay I should certainly keep him; that if Durham would trust me still further by telling me who was going to take part in the dastardly deed of maltreating an inoffensive creature who had never even seen them I would under no circumstances betray him, but that I would make them afraid to come on my premises or to harm the negro. After some hesitancy he told me the names of the men who proposed to do the work for the society. He went away feeling much distressed and quite sure that I would have a serious experience.

I waited patiently that day for one of the men, whom I knew must pass my house going into and out of the town. As soon as I spied him coming down the road on his way to town I walked out to my front gate and called to him, asking him if he would not come in a moment as I desired to see him on a matter of business. He was much embarrassed but came in. I at once told him that I had been informed by a member of the "Circle" all about their proposed attack upon the colored man in my employ; that I was sorry to hear he was one of the most active parties in the matter; that I had a vivid recollection of having accommodated him in many ways by loaning him my horses, farming-utensils, wagons, etc.; that I should be sorry to cause his arrest and imprisonment, but I had made up my mind to single him out as the one person whom I should hold responsible for the welfare of the colored man. I told him if the colored man was molested in any way I should cause his arrest, and I thought I could prove that he had made threats of violence, not only to the man, but to me personally if I tried to protect Albert; that Miss Tuthill, the colored man, and myself were splendid shots; that we practised daily the use of firearms; that we had a sort of arsenal for our protection; and that the slightest intrusion on the premises would be greeted with a volley from the house and from the darky's quarters near by. The frequent change of color in his face betrayed his guilt in the matter, but of course he protested innocence of any knowledge of anything of the kind and avowed his willingness to protect the "nigger" for me. I assured him it was all right as long as he was willing to be that kind of a hostage for Albert's safety; that I should only have to ask the governor for protection and the provost marshal would be ordered to arrest any one against whom I might make accusation; that all I wanted was for them to be law-abiding citizens and attend to their own affairs; that I had no desire to inform against them, but I intended to keep the colored man and defend him as long as he behaved and did the work I desired him to do. The miserable wretch was glad when the interview was over, and beat a hasty retreat after telling me not to worry—it would be all right.

My friend reported to me afterward that at the next meeting of the "Circle" the fellow told them it would never do to trouble that "nigger" at John Logan's house, because he had found out that Mrs. Logan had heard about what they had talked of doing; that all their names were now in the hands of officers; that if anything was to happen to the "nigger" he was certain they would all be arrested and soldiers would be stationed there to protect Logan's family; therefore, they had better let the "nigger" alone. They did, and we kept the man long after General Logan's return home after the war, till Albert desired to go South to hunt up his family. When we paid him off he had three or four hundred dollars as the result of his labors and a partnership which he and I had had in a little cotton crop we had raised together. As he drove away from the door on the town express, with a big trunk full of clothes, well dressed himself, and his money in his pocket, he felt as happy as if he had been a millionaire. I confess I too felt glad that I had saved at least one poor creature from being maltreated. We had taught him to read and write and trained him to be a good and useful citizen, of whom we have often heard good reports.

General Logan was delayed so long in reaching Chattanooga from Vicksburg that he did not arrive there till after the battle, greatly to his disappointment, as he desired to take part in what he felt was to be a brilliant victory.

After assuming command of the Fifteenth Corps, Army of the Tennessee, they were some time in moving to Huntsville, that being the objective point, but with his command stretched out about "seventy miles" he had a hard time getting them thoroughly organized and ready for the siege of Atlanta.

They were much exhausted and almost destitute of good shoes and clothing for the approaching winter, which proved to be a very cold one. The supplies were slow in reaching them because of the meagre transportation. For days the troops were moving slowly, for the most part subsisting on the country. General Logan's headquarters were for some time at Bridgeport, where they had a trying experience from the inclement weather and the hardships of soldiering in the enemy's country. Finally they reached Huntsville, Alabama, where they were more comfortable, and where all their preparations for the Atlanta campaign and siege were perfected.

I had come to look upon the horrors of war with something akin to terror. During the sieges of Forts Henry and Donelson, Shiloh, Nashville, Corinth, and all the battles from Memphis to Vicksburg, and during the capture of that stronghold, so many brave men had fallen and so many widows and orphans were all around us constantly appealing to our sympathies that we had no respite. That "Hope long deferred maketh the heart sick" was experienced daily. It took moral courage to face the facts of the situation, and I sometimes think a special Providence must have sustained both the people and the soldiers through these trying times. The women of the country, both North and South, bore no small part of the burden of the war, and I have vivid recollections of seeing them display moral courage of the highest order.

Trained nurses and undertakers were unknown in southern Illinois. These important offices were performed by the neighbors and friends with the loving-kindness and faithfulness that can not be purchased at any price. Though quite young, it was often my melancholy duty to bear a part in these sad services.

One dreary November evening, just as the sun was setting, two ladies and myself went with a poor old striken grandfather to bury his little grandchild, the daughter of a soldier who was away at the front and whose mother was lying ill. When we reached the cemetery there was no one near to assist him in lowering the little body into the grave. We took hold of the ropes, two standing opposite each other and one opposite the old man, and gently lowered the coffin. We then alternated in helping him to fill the grave and fashion the mound over the remains of the soldier's child. Returning with the aged grandfather, we found the poor mother rapidly sinking into the same sleep that had taken her little one out of all suffering. After a long vigil she too slept well when, changing from sexton to undertaker, we prepared her poor body for the casket and remained with the family till stronger arms could be found to lay her beside her child.

We never knew a woman to falter or to be found wanting no matter how trying a duty she had to perform in the field or at home, where sometimes she had to face trials greater than those on a battle-field. North and South, the women of this great nation demonstrated the heroism and devotion to their loved ones and to the ties that bound them to their homes and families.

CHAPTER 4

"'Politicking'' in Illinois
1864

APPRECIATING as I did the prodigious undertakings that were planned for Sherman's army, I spent many midnight hours in sleepless anxiety. During the day we had plenty to do to help care for the families of the refugees and soldiers, who were subject to all the ills to which human flesh is heir. Playing nurse, comforter, providing ways and means, and soliciting and dispensing relief kept my friends and myself very busy. Meanwhile we watched and waited impatiently for the meagre tidings that came irregularly from the advancing army.

All the winter of 1863 and the spring of 1864 Sherman was preparing for the campaign and siege of Atlanta. His old friend and associate, Johnston, was in command of the forces in and about Atlanta. Sherman had the most exalted opinion of Johnston's military abilities and courage; he was, therefore, very careful that every precaution should be observed.

The almost impregnable mountain barriers encircling the well-fortified city of Atlanta added much to the advantage of the enemy. With an army of less courage and experience, Sherman would have had reason for solicitude. Vicksburg, Lookout Mountain, and Chattanooga were ours. General Grant and the Army of the East had scored many victories; the enemy were dispirited and rapidly reaching the point of desperation; therefore, the Union troops had reason to expect intrepid resistance to their advance. This, however, in no wise deterred them, and they were only impatient for active operations, growing quite restive under the delays incident to the mobilization of such an army.

May 1, 1864, they started breaking up the headquarters at Huntsville, Alabama, from which date until the 1st of September they were constantly on the move, fighting their way over almost every foot of territory to the frowning breastworks surrounding Atlanta.

At Resaca they first drove the enemy from their works and pursued them in their retreat to Adairsville. General Logan desired to follow up this victory and capture the flower of Johnston's army, but was not permitted to do so. Subsequently it was proved that General Logan was correct in his military judgment, and that his proposition could have been successfully executed. From Adairsville the Union forces marched to Kingston and Dallas, where, in a severe engagement against Hardee's veteran corps, General Logan was shot through the arm about half-way between the elbow and the shoulder. They seemed determined to deprive him of his left arm, as he had been shot through that arm at the point of the shoulder at Fort Donelson. He paid little attention to the wound received at Dallas, feeling that there was no time to be off duty for a single hour. General Logan always claimed that Dallas, for the length of time and number of troops engaged, was one of the most hotly contested battles of the war. The attack of the Fifteenth Corps on Kenesaw Mountain, up its perpendicular sides, was one of the most daring and tragic in history. It was made in obedience to orders against the advice of General Logan, who considered the impossible feat little short of madness, an opinion in which General McPherson coincided, but both were subordinate to the general commanding the movements around Atlanta.

Yet the gallant leader of the Fifteenth Corps never hesitated to obey an order, even though it would lead to dire disaster. His brave followers tried to go wherever he led; so, at eight o'clock on the morning of June 27, 1864, they went bravely forward over two lines of works, driving the enemy still higher on the precipitous sides of the mountain, to be mowed down like grass by the enemy intrenched above. Huge stones, a torrent of iron hail, and canister were hurled down upon them like the avalanches of the Rocky Mountains. To proceed further or remain where they were was impossible. Besides the hundreds of dauntless men, such grand heroes as Generals Harker and McCook were killed. Finally, the advice of General Logan to flank the position was adopted, but not until the scaling experiment had cost many valuable lives. Johnston, seeing that his rear was threatened by the flank movement, fell back toward Atlanta from Kenesaw.

General Logan commanded the Fifteenth Corps, General Dodge the Sixteenth Corps, General Blair the Seventeenth Corps, of the Army of the Tennessee.[1] Between these officers and General McPherson there existed the most perfect harmony. General Logan and General McPherson were thoroughly impressed with the fact that in front of the Fifteenth Corps there was massed a large force of the enemy after the fighting that had taken place around Decatur. General Sherman believed the Confederates were evacuating Atlanta and were retreating toward East Point; therefore he ordered General McPherson to pursue them with the Army of the Tennessee and, if possible, cut off a portion of them.

McPherson felt this to be a terrible mistake, but he was too good a soldier to hesitate long over an order. So, early in the morning of the 22d of July, he rode over to General Logan's headquarters to confer with him, and at the same time order General Logan to put the troops in position to carry out General Sherman's orders, "while I will ride over to Sherman's headquarters, and try to convince him of his error," he said. General Logan has often, with tears in his eyes, related the thrilling circumstances and how he proceeded at once to obey McPherson, feeling that they were to be met by an opposing army greatly in excess of their commands.

Scarcely had the sound of the clatter of McPherson's horse's hoofs died away, as he galloped off in the direction of

General Sherman's headquarters, when an orderly came on a flying steed to General Logan to announce that McPherson had been killed by Claiborne's Cavalry, which was rapidly swinging around to the rear of the Union army.

Thus, in a twinkling, upon General Logan was thrust the awful responsibility of extricating the troops from the direful position in which they were placed—almost cut off, the enemy in the rear, the Union cavalry sent off to burn a bridge at Covington, and with the command as nearly as possible under the orders given by General Sherman to McPherson, and carried by him in person to General Logan, as mentioned above, in the early morning of July 22, 1864.

The order read as follows:

Three miles and a half east of Atlanta, Ga.,
MAJOR-GENERAL JOHN A. LOGAN,
Commanding Fifteenth Army Corps.

The enemy having evacuated their works in front of our lines, the supposition of Major-General Sherman is that they have given up Atlanta without entering the town. You will take a route to the left of that taken by the enemy, and try to cut off a portion of them, while they are pressed in the rear and on the right by Generals Schofield and Thomas.

Major-General Sherman desires and expects a vigorous pursuit.

Very respectfully your obedient servant,
JAMES B. MCPHERSON,
Major-General.

It was proved afterward to have been wholly impracticable.

With the sounds of the guns of the attacking enemy coming from every direction, General Logan as the ranking officer, and with only the orders which he received from McPherson a few minutes before he was killed, assumed command. General Logan rode with magic swiftness from one end of the line to the other, rallying the troops with the tragic cry of "McPherson and revenge!" and appealing to officers and men to do or die. Hand to hand was the order of the day—victory wavering from one side to the other from early morning until the day was far spent. The irresistible force and intrepid valor of the Union army, led by a dauntless leader, compelled the enemy to fall back. The day was ours and McPherson was revenged solely through General Logan's matchless genius, indomitable courage, and leadership of men—men who would have followed him to the jaws of death. He fought the battle without orders, winning a victory when the tide of battle was almost overwhelmingly against him.

I can not resist quoting, from General Logan's address on the occasion of the unveiling of McPherson's monument in McPherson Square in Washington in 1876, his graphic description of McPherson's death:

> The news of his death spread with lightning-speed along the lines, sending a pang of deepest sorrow to every heart as it reached the ear; but, especially terrible was the effect on the Army of the Tennessee. It seemed as though a burning, fiery dart had pierced each breast, tearing asunder the flood-gates of grief, but, at the same time, heaving to their very depths the fountains of revenge. The clenched hands seemed to sink into the weapons they held, and from the eyes gleamed forth flashes terrible as lightning. The cry "McPherson, McPherson!" and "McPherson and revenge!" rose above the din of battle and, as it rang along the lines, swelled in power until the roll of musketry and booming of cannon seemed drowned by its echoes.
>
> McPherson again seemed to lead his troops—and where McPherson leads victory is sure. Each officer and soldier from the succeeding commander to the lowest private beheld, as it were, the form of their bleeding chief leading them on to the battle. "McPherson!" and "Onward to victory!" were their only thoughts; bitter, terrible revenge their only aim.

There was no such thought that day as stopping short of victory or death. The firm, spontaneous resolve was to win the day or perish with their slain leader on the bloody field. Fearfully was his death avenged. His army, maddened by his death and utterly reckless of life, rushed with savage delight into the fiercest onslaughts, and fearlessly plunged into the very jaws of destruction. As wave after wave of Hood's daring troops dashed with terrible fury upon our lines, they were hurled back with a fearful shock, breaking their columns into fragments, as the granite headland breaks into foam the ocean billows that strike against it. Across the narrow line of works raged the fierce storm of battle, the hissing shot and shell raining death on every hand. Seven times Hood's, Hardee's, and Wheeler's commands charged and were as many times repulsed.[2] Once they broke the Union lines and captured De Grass's battery and he, with tears streaming down his brave cheeks, rode as fast as his horse could carry him to General Logan begging him to send a brigade of the invincible Fifteenth Army Corps to recover his beloved guns. Fired by the gallant De Grass's heroism, General Logan appealed to the men who had never failed him. Off they went, crying: "The guns! the guns! we will have them or die!" Logan led the way, the very incarnation of desperate daring, and in a brief time the battery was recaptured.

Over dead and dying, friends and foes, rushed the swaying host, the shouts of rebels confident of victory only drowned by the cry of "McPherson and revenge!" which went up from the Army of the Tennessee. Twelve thousand gallant men bit the dust ere the night closed in, and the defeated and baffled enemy, after failing in repeated and desperate assaults upon our lines, was compelled to give up the hopeless contest. Notwithstanding the fact that our troops had to fight front and rear, victory crowned our arms.

That night after the battle, General Logan received orders commanding him to report to General Sherman's headquarters, which he reached at the midnight hour, to be congratulated and praised without stint for the work he had done that day. Continuance of the command of the Army of the Tennessee was promised him again and again, as he in detail reported to General Sherman the events of the battle. No intimation was given of his unfitness for the command or of his lacks in the profession of a soldier. His military sense was considered of the highest order; if he was a soldier from civilian ranks, he had never been defeated in any engagement, which can not be said of all the professional soldiers of the Civil War. He felt, as he returned to his headquarters that night, that all was propitious, that he had done his duty well, and that merit would receive its just reward. He was anxious to fulfill every requirement of so responsible a position, so, when orders came that the army under his command should withdraw from their intrenchments and move seven miles to the right under the cover of darkness, that the enemy might not discover the movement, General Logan personally superintended the execution of the command. He ordered the wheels of the wagon-trains and artillery to be muffled with hay and straw, and was so explicit in his directions to the officers in command of the various corps and divisions that, in the stillness of the night they quietly gathered up all their belongings and all the paraphernalia of war, and were in their new position in the early morning, an unparalleled piece of strategy, and not excelled by any like movement by the greatest warriors of any age.

Imagine the feelings of a man, weary from midnight vigils, marching and personally superintending such gigantic movements as General Logan had directed for days preceding, and in a position to begin another big battle, to be confronted with an order to surrender the command to General O. O. Howard, not before conspicuously connected with the great Army of the Tennessee which Logan had led to victory after McPherson's death![3] The Army of the Tennessee had never known defeat under him and, to a man, they would have followed Logan through blood and carnage to the very abyss of death. A man of less noble mind and courage would have rebelled, and encouraged the just indignation expressed by the whole command; but he, with his great heart beating with patriotism and soldierly appreciation of the effect of his resentment, quietly returned to his old corps and led the van in the heroic deeds of the 28th of July, 1864, at Ezra Chapel, the most sanguinary battle of the whole campaign where the Fifteenth Army Corps captured many prisoners, arms, and battle-flags.

The victory was so complete that the enemy fled from the field, leaving their dead and wounded behind them. General Howard, General Logan's successor in command of the Army of the Tennessee, made special mention of the conduct of General Logan and his corps, attributing the success of the day as much to General Logan, personally, as to any one man. After frequent less important engagements the army reached Jonesboro, where the last great battle before the evacuation of Atlanta occurred.

General Logan did not reach Jonesboro until midnight of

August 30. Realizing that they were likely to be assaulted by the corps of Hardee and Lee at any moment, he ordered intrenchments to be made to protect his lines and his men from needless exposure. This was done without orders from either of his superior officers, but from the promptings of his own military genius and wisdom.

At three o'clock the expected assault was made but, protected by their trenches, the Union forces were able to repel the attacks of the enemy. The artillery were so well posted that they could rake the foe mercilessly. The day resulted in the fall of Atlanta, which had been doomed since the bloody battle of July 22.

General Sherman, in his report of the Atlanta campaign, heaped encomiums upon General Logan, and said no one could possibly have done better than he after the death of McPherson, but admitted that he had recommended General O. O. Howard to supersede General Logan.

It is needless to recapitulate, but General Logan's noble conduct in the most trying experience of his life is beyond exaggeration. I need not dwell upon his matchless achievements after he returned to the command of the Fifteenth Army Corps who, to a man, would have died for him. Logan never swerved one iota from his loyalty to his commanders, or in the least lessened his energies or his heroism till Atlanta had fallen. After the battle of Ezra Chapel, on August 28, 1864, which was won by the daring of the Fifteenth Army Corps with Logan at its head, General O. O. Howard issued an order congratulating the army, and mentioning General Logan in laudatory terms. General Logan was incapable of inciting or allowing a mutinous spirit to prevail, but he was not able to prevent the army from feeling resentment at the appointment of General O. O. Howard. Had not General Logan gone North at the solicitation of President Lincoln to take part in the Presidential campaign of 1864—after the fall of Atlanta—and had not the army started on its holiday march to the sea, the incident might not have ended as it did. Suffice it to say, that the authorities at Washington deemed it expedient to transfer Major-General O. O. Howard to the command of the Freedman's Bureau in Washington, and restore General Logan to the command of the Army of the Tennessee. Major-General Logan, therefore, rode at the head of that invincible army at the grand review. The Army of the Tennessee manifested their gratification at his return to the command in every possible way. General O. O. Howard was naturally chagrined, and a few years ago, in a public way, tried to explain that the restoration of Major-General Logan to the command of the Army of the Tennessee was brought about by political influence. It was at least strange that this explanation was not given while General Logan and General Sherman were living. Ever since the war closed and the patriotic societies were organized, on every occasion of their meetings or rather reunions, General Logan was hailed with enthusiasm as the great commander of the Army of the Tennessee.

It may not be inappropriate for me on this occasion to say that whatever of misunderstanding and estrangement there may have existed at one time between the two great commanders of the Army of the Tennessee, Sherman and Logan, it was wholly obliterated by General Logan's tribute to General Sherman at a notable banquet given by Colonel Corkhill to General Sherman on his retirement as general of the army, in which Logan said in replying to the toast "The Volunteer Soldier":

> There were no questions of numbers or time and, for General Sherman, I will say there was not a soldier who bore the American flag or followed it, not a soldier who carried a musket or drew a sabre, who did not respect him as his commander. There was not one, sir, but would have drawn his sword at any time to have preserved his life. There is not one to-day, no matter what may have been said, that would dim in the slightest degree the lustre of that bright name, achieved by ability, by integrity, and by true bravery as an officer. And in conclusion let me say this: While that army, when it was disbanded, was absorbed in the community like rain-drops in the sand, all citizens in the twinkling of an eye and back to their professions and their business, there is not one of these men, scattered as they are from ocean to ocean, who does not honor the name of the man who led them in triumph through the

enemy's land. Wherever he may go, wherever he may be, whatever may be his condition in life, there is not one who would not stretch out a helping hand to that brave commander who led them to glory. Speaking for that army, if I may be permitted to speak for it, I have to say: May the choicest blessings that God showers upon the head of man go with him along down through his life, is the prayer of every soldier who served under Sherman.

When General Logan finished, General Sherman arose, went around to General Logan, put his arm around Logan's neck, and shook his hand cordially, while the tears ran down his cheeks. His emotions were too great for words.

It was on a Saturday night and, notwithstanding the approach of the wee sma' hours before the tearful parting of the distinguished guests, General Sherman went home and wrote the following most manly and feeling letter to General Logan, explaining his reasons for certain actions touching General Logan and expressing his gratitude for General Logan's tribute to him.

WASHINGTON, D.C., *Sunday, February* 11, 1883.

GENERAL JOHN A. LOGAN,

U. S. Senate, Washington, D. C.

Dear General:

This is a rainy Sunday, a good day to clear up old scores, and I hope you will receive what I propose to write in the same friendly spirit in which I offer it.

I was very much touched by the kind and most complimentary terms in which you spoke of me personally at the recent Corkhill banquet, on the anniversary of my sixty-third birthday, and have since learned that you still feel a wish that I should somewhat qualify the language I used in my *Memoirs*, column 2, pages 85 and 86, giving the reasons why General O. O. Howard was recommended by me to succeed McPherson in the command of the Army of the Tennessee when, by the ordinary rules of the service, the choice should have fallen to you. I confess frankly that my ardent wish is to retire from the command of the army with the kind and respectful feelings of all men, especially of those who were with me in the days of the Civil War, which must give to me and to my family a chief claim on the gratitude of the people of the United States.

I confess that I have tortured and twisted the words used on the pages referred to, so as to contain my meaning better without offending you, but so far without success. I honestly believe that no man to-day holds in higher honor than myself the conduct and action of John A. Logan, from that hour when he realized that the South meant war. Prior to the war all men had doubts, but the moment Fort Sumter was fired on from batteries in Charleston, these doubts dissipated as a fog, and from the hour thenceforth your course was manly, patriotic, sublime. Throughout the war, I know of no single man's career more complete than yours.

Now, as to the specific matter of this letter. I left Vicksburg in the fall of 1863, by order of General Grant in person, with three divisions of my own corps (15th) and one of McPherson's (16th) to hasten to the assistance of the Army of the Cumberland (General Rosecrans commanding) which, according to the then belief, had been worsted at Chickamauga. Blair was with us, you were not. We marched through mud and water four hundred miles from Memphis, and you joined me on the march, with an order to succeed me in command of the Fifteenth Corps, a presidential appointment which Blair had exercised temporarily. Blair was at that time a member of Congress, and was afterward named to command the 17th Corps, and actually remained so long in Washington that we had got to Big Shanty before he overtook us. Again, after the battles of Missionary Ridge and Knoxville, when Howard served with me, I went back to Vicksburg and Meridian, leaving you in command of the Fifteenth Corps along the railroad from Stevenson to Decatur. I was gone three months and, when I got back, you complained to me bitterly against George H. Thomas, that he claimed for the Army of the Cumberland everything, and almost denied the Army of the Tennessee any use of the railroads. I sustained you, and put all army and corps commanders on an equal footing, making their orders and requisitions of equal force on the depot officers and railroad officials in Nashville. Thomas was extremely sensitive on that point and, as you well know, had much feeling against you personally, which he did not conceal. You also went to Illinois more than once to make speeches and were so absent after the capture of Atlanta, at the time we started for Savannah, and did not join us until we had reached Savannah.

Now, I have never questioned the right or propriety of you and Blair holding fast to your constituents by the usual methods; it was natural and right, but it did trouble me to have my corps commanders serving two distinct causes, one military and the other civil or political; and this did influence me when I was forced to make choice of an army commander to succeed McPherson. This is all I record in my *Memoirs.* It was so and I can not amend them. Never in speech, writing, or record, surely not in the *Memoirs,* do I recall applying to you and Blair, for I always speak of you together, the term of "political general." If there be such an expression, I can not find it now, nor can I recall its use. The only place wherein the word "politics" occurs is in the pages which I have referred to, and wherein I explain my own motive and reason for nominating Howard over you and Blair for the vacant post.

My reason may have been bad, nevertheless it was the reason which decided me then and, as a man of honor, I was bound to record it. At this time, 1883, Thomas being dead, I can not say more than is in the text, viz.: that he took strong ground against you, and I was naturally strongly influenced by his outspoken opinion. Still, I will not throw off on him, but will state to you frankly that I then believed that the advice I gave Mr. Lincoln was the best practicable. General Howard had been with me up to Knoxville, and had displayed a zeal and ability which then elicited my hearty approbation and, as I trusted in a measure to skilful manœuvres rather than to downright hard fighting, I recommended him. My *Memoirs* were designed to give the impressions of the hour and not to pass judgment on the qualities as exemplified in after life.

If you will point out to me a page or line where I can better portray your fighting qualities, your personal courage, and magnificent example in actual combat, I will be most happy to add to or correct the *Memoirs,* but when I attempt to explain my own motives or reasons, you surely will be the first man to see that outside influence will fail.

My course is run and for better or worse I can not amend it, but if ever in your future you want a witness to your intense zeal and patriotism, your heroic personal qualities, you may safely call on me as long as I live. I surely have watched with pride and interest your career in the United States Senate, and will be your advocate if you aim at higher honors. I assert with emphasis that I never styled you or Blair "political generals" and if I used the word "politics" in an offensive sense, it was to explain my own motives for action and not as descriptive.

Wishing you all honor and happiness on this earth, I am as always, your friend,

W. T. Sherman.[4]

This letter General Logan acknowledged promptly, responding cordially to the sentiments of regard expressed by his beloved commander.

UNITED STATES SENATE,
WASHINGTON, D. C.,
Sunday, Feb. 18, 1883.

GENERAL W. T. SHERMAN,
My dear Sir:

I have delayed acknowledging your letter of the 11th inst. up to this time for the reason that I have been so much engaged every moment of the time that I could not sooner do so; for your expression of kindly feelings toward me I tender my grateful acknowledgments.

I am inclined however, my dear general, to the opinion that, had you fully understood the situation in which I was placed at the times mentioned by you, that I returned North from the army for the purpose of taking part in the political contests then going on, that perhaps your criticisms on my (then) course would not have been made. I did not do it for the purpose of "keeping a hold on my people." I refused a nomination in my own State for a very high position for the reason that I would not have anything to do with parties while the war should last. In 1863, when I went home to canvass in Illinois and to help in Ohio, General Grant was fully advised and knows that although I had to make application for leave of absence, I did not do it of my own volition, but at the request of those high in authority. So, when I left on leave after the Atlanta campaign, to canvass for Mr. Lincoln, I did it at the special and private request of the then President. This I kept to myself, and have never made it public, nor do I propose to do so now, but feel that I may in confidence say this to you, that you may see what prompted my action in the premises. I have borne for this reason whatever I may have suffered by way of criticism, rather than turn criticism on the dead.

So far as General Thomas having feeling in the matter you mention, I presume he entertained the same feeling that seemed to be general, that no one without a military education was to be trusted to command an army; this, I think, was the feeling then, is now, and will ever be. I find no fault with it; this as a rule is probably correct, but the experience of the world has occasionally found exceptions to this rule. I certainly never gave General Thomas any occasion to have strong feelings against me. I did complain that I was not on an equality with him while I commanded between Decatur and Stevenson; that my passes on the roads were not recognized, and I have General Thomas's letter afterward, admitting the fact, and apologizing to me for the conduct of his officers in this matter. I at all times co-operated with him cordially and promptly during my stay at Huntsville and at all other times subsequent. Certainly I did for him afterward what few men would have done. When ordered to Nashville, with a view of superseding him at Louisville, when I found the situation of matters, I wrote and telegraphed to Grant that he, Thomas, was doing all he could and asked to be ordered back to my own command, which was done. This I say to show my kind feeling for him, and to say that if I ever did anything to cause him to complain of me I was not aware of it.

One thing, my dear general, that I feel conscious of, and that is that no man ever obeyed your orders more promptly, and but few ever did you more faithful service in carrying out your plans and military movements than myself.

I may have done yourself and myself an injustice by not disclosing to you the cause of my returning to the North at the time I did, but you have my reasons for it. I felt in honor that I could rest.

This letter is intended only for full explanation, and for yourself only. I do not feel aggrieved as you think, but will ever remain your friend,

Yours truly,
JOHN A. LOGAN.

The few brief years that intervened before General Logan preceded General Sherman to that land of eternal bliss they saw much of each other, forgetting in the happy circumstance of reunited friendship, the unfavorable winds that had temporarily estranged them. The Corkhill banquet was probably one of the most impressive dinners ever given in Washington, including the names of the most illustrious men of that time. Nearly every one of that distinguished company have [*sic*] joined the mighty throng in the great beyond.

The correspondence between Sherman and himself, General Logan regarded as confidential and therefore he would not discuss the matter or give it to the public. Amicable relations having been restored between himself and his revered commander, to whom he was sincerely attached, he was willing the matter should be dropped as it was impossible for General Logan, with his generous and big-hearted nature, to long bear malice or be indefinitely estranged from any one to whom he had once been attached.

Prior to the dinner above mentioned General Sherman had at various times and in many ways tried to explain why he was so inconsistent as to recommend General O. O. Howard to the authorities at Washington as successor to General McPherson in command of the Army of the Tennessee, after he had acknowledged that General Logan had rescued that army from defeat and won one of the most signal victories of the war. It was not until Sherman's retirement, as explained by the correspondence between General Sherman and General Logan and published after General Logan's death, that General Sherman gave to the public the true reason for the injustice done General Logan in returning him to his corps, and in taking General O. O. Howard from another army and giving him command of the Army of the Tennessee. It will be seen that one among others of Sherman's reasons for this action was that General Logan was a volunteer, and not a professional soldier graduated from West Point, notwithstanding the fact that Logan's record showed he had never made a mistake in handling an army, though the same is not claimed for General Sherman and other West Point graduates. [5]

In connection with this matter, there has come into my possession recently a copy of a most valuable record made at the time by that dauntless, efficient, and incomparable officer, Major-General Granville M. Dodge. General Dodge commanded the Sixteenth Army Corps of Sherman's army during the eventful Atlanta campaign. The intimacy which grew up between General Dodge and General Logan while they were engaged in the prodigious work which each performed in that campaign continued through life, and I deem this report so important that I can not resist the temptation to insert it here. It will be remembered that General Dodge's great services to his country did not end with the close of the war, for it was through his indomitable energy and great skill as a civil engineer that the Union Pacific Railroad was completed. He has been president of the Society of the Army of the Tennessee since the death of General Sherman. General Dodge's report reads as follows:

On July 27th General O. O. Howard was assigned to the command of the Army of the Tennessee, which was a great disappointment to that army. They felt that an army which had followed Grant, Sherman, McPherson, and Logan, who had taken it successfully through its last battle, after the death of McPherson, had material enough in it to command it. On the movement from the extreme left to the right, I pulled out first and as I was moving to the rear of General Thomas's army, I saw General Logan sitting on the porch of a log building. I went up to speak to him and found that General Sherman was inside. After speaking a few words to General Logan, I went in and had a talk with General Sherman, inquiring about the change of commanders and expressing my wish that General Logan had been assigned to the command. He answered me by saying it was all right; that he would tell me the reasons sometime. When I came out, General Logan was still sitting on the porch and, as the door was open, I have no doubt he heard what I had to say to General Sherman for there were tears in his eyes. I spoke to him very cordially and said to him that I was greatly disappointed at the change, but hoped it would end all right. He, like a good soldier, said it would but he said it was pretty hard on him. Nothing more then was said about it. Years after, I had correspondence in relation to this matter with General Sherman, when the friends of Logan and myself were endeavoring to bring them together. For a long time after the war General Logan never forgot Sherman's treatment of him and at times felt it keenly, but one day, on the floor of the U. S. Senate, General Logan made a speech in defense of Sherman and in praise of him, which finally brought them together and their old troubles were forgotten. Some time after the war, I forget the place but I think it was when we were together at one of the reunions of the Army of the Tennessee, General Sherman made a full explanation to me of the matter and at the time I made full notes of it in my diary, and I quote here what he said:

"Sherman said that in the winter of 1863, after the battle of Missionary Ridge on his trip to Meridian, he left Logan in command at Huntsville with the 15th Corps, and Dodge in command on [the] line of railroad from Nashville to Decatur with the 16th Corps, both in General Thomas's Department. On his return, he found Logan much dissatisfied with Thomas and complained of his treatment of him. He could not send an officer or soldier to Nashville until he got his orders or passes approved by Thomas's provost marshal or some local commander. Sherman, when he saw Thomas, told him he should not have treated Logan in that way; that he was a corps commander and was entitled to better treatment. Thomas complained of Logan in several matters and said he was hard to get along with and that he had had no trouble with Dodge. Sherman said he had tried to smooth the matter over, but he discovered an unfriendly feeling that continued through the Atlanta campaign.

"When McPherson fell on the 22nd of July, in front of Atlanta, Logan by seniority of rank assumed command by his direction and handled the army well. After the battle Thomas came to Sherman and they discussed the question of a commander for the Army of the Tennessee. Sherman told Thomas that Logan was entitled to the command, was competent for it and he desired to place him in it. Thomas answered with much feeling that he was sorry to hear him say so, for, if Logan was assigned to the command of the Army of the Tennessee, he should consider it his duty to resign his command. Sherman answered General Thomas: 'You certainly would not do that and leave me here in that condition.' Thomas hesitated and finally said: 'No, I don't know as I would go so far as that,' but protested that Logan should not be assigned to the command. Sherman said: 'I don't see how I can pass him by; I don't want to do anything that will seem to reflect on Logan.' Thomas answered: 'Well, let the President or Secretary of War select a commander.' Sherman said: 'No. I do not want them to send a commander here that is outside of this army.' Sherman said: 'In other words you don't feel that with Logan in command you and he could act cordially and harmoniously together?' Thomas said: 'Yes, that's it, and I think, to insure success, that there should be not only harmony but entire cordiality between the army commanders.' Sherman's answer was that he could not afford to put Logan in command under such circumstances.

"Finally they sat down and discussed the merits of the different generals and settled upon Howard. 'I have,' said Sherman, 'always been a friend to Logan in a great many different ways. He was a good soldier. He handled the army splendidly on the 22d and in his movement to the right. But you see I had a great responsibility and had to do the best I could under the circumstances. I consider Logan the representative volunteer general of the war.' "

While I never knew the exact facts in the matter, I know the Army of the Tennessee wanted Logan and was greatly disappointed when Sherman went outside of it for a commander. The officers and men felt that the little army that had had for its commanders Grant, Sherman, McPherson, and Logan had filled every post of responsibility to which it had been assigned, and that there was material left in it to command it; but I think no one in it knew of this complication and it is well they did not.

Sherman showed himself a master when he took the responsibility and made no explanation, and thus preserved the good feeling throughout the great command. I heard the news of the appointment of Howard in place of Logan as we were marching from the left to right. I did not know Howard personally.

While these events were occurring at the front, the political excitement was waxing hot all over the North, and the old feeling between the war and anti-war parties in the North was growing more and more intense. Many Democrats, General Logan among them, had gone into the army to save the Union. Many others failed to see that the Emancipation Proclamation was the legitimate sequence of secession; the disasters in the East were seized upon as an excuse for declaring the war a failure. McClellan, the first general of the army, was nominated for the Presidency by the Democratic party; many War Democrats flocked to his standard, and it was supposed that all of them would do so. It was thought that the disaffection thus created would result in the defeat of Mr. Lincoln, and thereby the transfer of the Government and all its interests to Democratic hands. For weeks all communication with the army engaged in the siege of Atlanta had been cut off. The conventions had been held, and the candidates were regularly in the field. The deepest solicitude was felt all over the country as to which of the parties and candidates would receive the moral support of the army.

Illinois, as the home of Mr. Lincoln, was watched with great anxiety. General Logan had refused all political preferment after he entered the army in 1861. This election of 1864 was the first Presidential election since the war began, and his old-time friends thought to win him to the support of McClellan. Mr. Lincoln realized that Illinois was so important to the Republican party that he was anxious to have General Logan's support. Hence, the moment that General Sherman decided that the army should not continue the pursuit of Hood's army until they had rested after their superhuman labors in the siege and capture of Atlanta, and it was evident that there would be no movement requiring General Logan's presence, Mr. Lincoln requested him to come home and take part in the civil campaign, which was fraught with quite as much importance as the military one just closed so gloriously.

After the army had entered Atlanta and all were to have a respite, General Logan came home. The plaudits of the people followed him everywhere, and I shall remember as long as I live the eagerness with which they surrounded him and plied him with questions as to his future political course. To all of them he said: "Wait till the arrival of the date when I am to speak to you." He had been advertised to speak in the grove near Carbondale, Illinois, our home at that time. The grove was a most beautiful place, a natural amphitheatre shaded by grand old oak-trees where outdoor public meetings were held. On this occasion, fully twenty thousand people assembled there, all breathless to hear what General Logan had to say. A large majority of the residents of that section were War Democrats, and inclined to the support of McClellan, a brother-in-law of mine among the number. My relative was so enthusiastic that he declared over and over again, while communication was cut off during the siege of Atlanta, that he knew General Logan as a War Democrat, would espouse McClellan's cause, greatly to the vexation of General Logan's friends who were devoted to Mr. Lincoln. One day, in the presence of a number of persons, he became so sanguine that he offered to bet a fine span of mules he owned against five hundred dollars that Logan would support McClellan. Seeing the annoyance and unhappiness his statement produced upon the friends, though not given to such practices, I said: "All right, Mr. Campbell, I will take your bet, since you are so confident." A half-dozen hands were instantly thrust into plethoric pockets, and the money was proffered to be put up to pay if I lost, and to be sure that I would have the mules if I won.

I heard nothing from General Logan for many weeks, and

knew as little as any of them as to his position on political questions, except from intuition and an appreciation of the situation and his well-known devotion to his country.

At last the day arrived on which General Logan was to speak. He was much worn and looked haggard and weary from his ceaseless labors in the Atlanta campaign which had lasted from May till September. He was so sunburnt that he looked like an Indian. The scenes through which he had passed had furrowed his brow, but the flashing light of his eyes was still there, and the return to home and his family made him happy. We soon told him all that had transpired during the thirteen months since we had last seen him; especially about the political situation, and the claims of both parties for his support and influence. When told that I had committed him to the extent of actually betting that he would not support McClellan and the platform upon which he was nominated, he was greatly amused and I soon saw I had his approval, ever a requisite to my happiness. The incident had been telegraphed everywhere, and much comment indulged in, so, when General Logan mounted the beautifully decorated stand from which he was to speak, he was greeted by wild cheers and yells from the vast crowd: "Now he will win the mules." He spoke for some time, telling them the duty of all loyal men, of the cost of blood and treasure at which the victories of the Union had been won, and closed with a glowing appeal for Mr. Lincoln's re-election, that the war might speedily be brought to an end.

Scarcely a dry eye was to be seen among the thousands upturned to him, their idolized leader in civil as well as military campaigns. At the conclusion they made a rush for my brother-in-law's barn, and soon returned with the mules hitched to a carriage in which they insisted upon taking General Logan and driving him around the town to our home. For weeks he travelled over the country in a carriage drawn by the mules, canvassing the State in the interest of the Republican nominees and did as much as any other one man for the re-election of Mr. Lincoln.

After the lapse of so many years, and through the veil of oblivion that has obscured the circumstances then existing, it is hardly possible to fittingly portray the importance of General Logan's presence in the campaign for the re-election of Mr. Lincoln. It was the first Presidential election after the issuance of the Emancipation Proclamation; our victories had been won by great sacrifice. The platform upon which General McClellan was nominated had declared the war a failure and was in favor of an armistice and renewal of fruitless peace negotiations, thereby betraying a want of sympathy with the policy of the Government on the part of the party nominating him. Had the Government changed hands at this critical juncture, no one could have answered for the consequences. Mr. Lincoln felt this most deeply. His own perpetuation in office occupied little of his thoughts, but the vigorous prosecution of the war and the preservation of the Union were of infinite importance; hence he was as anxious for the success of his party in the civil campaign as he was for the army in the field.

General McClellan's acceptance of the nomination inspired the Democracy with much courage. They thought the element known as "War Democrats" in and out of the army would rally round their leader. The most prominent journalists and party leaders were untiring in their efforts. General Logan was known as a War Democrat, and they expected he would support McClellan. They wrote him earnest letters and appealed to him, the moment Atlanta had fallen, in such communications as the following, which was from one of the ablest journalists ever in Illinois, and a devoted friend and mentor of Senator Stephen A. Douglas during his eventful life:

Office of the Chicago Post,
93 Washington Street,
Chicago, *August* 31, 1864.

Dear General:

I enclose you a copy of the platform adopted by the convention. I want you, as a Democrat, to write a letter indorsing your fellow soldier, patriot, and Democrat. You never failed yet to meet any demand that the Democratic party or your country ever made upon your talents or even your life. Will you refuse both when they jointly ask your voice in the election? In God's name, dear Logan, by all your hopes for your country and yourself, let not the Democracy ask your arm and be refused. You and I persistently refused to join any party, refused to accept the title of "War Democrats" as distinguished from the old Democratic party of our early love and, now that that party gives a rational and a national platform, will you refuse to give your voice in behalf of our own soldier, patriot, Democrat, and statesman—McClellan? Give us one of your characteristic letters indorsing platform, nominee, and all, and from the very hearts of the party will go up a shout of thanks to you.

Yours truly,
J. W. SHEAHAN.

Equally earnest letters were written from every quarter, not only to General Logan but to other officers of Democratic antecedents at the front, and to their friends at home, urging upon them the importance of winning the Presidential campaign with "Little Mac" as the leader.

Mr. Lincoln's anxiety to have General Logan enter the canvass being under discussion in a correspondence years later between General Sherman and General Logan, General Sherman wrote:

HEADQUARTERS, ARMY OF THE UNITED STATES,
WASHINGTON, D. C., *Feb.* 20th, 1883.

GENERAL JOHN A. LOGAN,
U. S. Senate.

DEAR GENERAL:

I beg to acknowledge receipt of your good letter of February 18th, and recall well the fact that about September 20th, 1864, I received at Atlanta a telegram from some one in authority, I think Mr. Lincoln himself, to the effect that your presence in Illinois was important to the National cause. You probably know that all my records were transferred to Lt. General Sheridan at the time he succeeded me in command of the Military Division of the Mississippi, and were burned up in the great Chicago fire. I only retained the blotters from which the official records were made up. In one of them I find my letter to Gen. Howard, commanding Army of the Tennessee, East Point:

"I consent that you give Gen. Logan a leave. I have not yet heard from Gen. Grant, but in case of necessity, we can in Gen. Logan's absence take care of the 15th Corps. There seems to be a special reason why he should go home at once."

This fully confirms what you write me, and looking back

from the distance of time, I doubt not you were able to give material help in the election of Mr. Lincoln, which was the greatest consideration of that day.

With great respect,

Your friend,

W. T. Sherman.

Colonel D. L. Phillips was bearer of Mr. Lincoln's note to General Logan, expressing his fears and desiring Logan's services, which Mr. Lincoln believed would be potential on account of General Logan's affiliation with the Democratic party before the war. I regret extremely that Lincoln's request to General Logan was mislaid by a historian years ago and could never be recovered. General Logan often spoke of it to me, and of the pleasure it gave him to think that Mr. Lincoln had such implicit faith in his power to influence the people to stand firmly at that vital period.

As soon as General Logan's speech after his arrival home from Atlanta was telegraphed over the country, he was deluged with telegrams from every part of the State, urging him to speak in the more prominent places, declaring it was necessary to counteract the efforts that were being made to induce voters of Democratic proclivities at the beginning of the war to support McClellan. Mr. Lincoln's friends realized the jeopardy that would follow a division of the vote of Illinois in the Electoral College, and therefore were determined that no such calamity should occur, if it was possible to prevent it by vigilance and desperate effort.

A list of appointments was made out by General Logan and the committee which would consume nearly all the time intervening between his arrival home and the election. The list was published and a party made up to accompany him, including ladies and gentlemen who were well known in the State.

We left Carbondale in carriages, General Logan's carriage being drawn by the mules I had won from my brother-in-law. In this carriage were Colonel Phillips, General Logan, and myself.

When we reached the first town on the list the enthusiastic crowd that greeted General Logan was innumerable. Many soldiers were home on furlough after the fall of Atlanta, and they were important factors in arousing the patriotism of the people. As we neared the towns we were met by throngs who, impatient to see General Logan, had gone out on the roads for miles to intercept him. The nearer we approached the wilder the cheers, until, before the people could be restrained, they had unhitched the mules and, attaching a long rope to the axle, in a twinkling they were drawing the carriage, while others were following the mules, screaming: "Here's your mules, won by Mrs. Logan on Lincoln's election!" Gay streamers of red, white, and blue ribbons bedecked the dumb brutes that seemingly understood they were attracting attention and were as docile as lambs, though we expected to see them resent with their heels the familiarity with which they were being handled. The towns were ablaze with bunting; the brass bands filled the air with patriotic music. We sometimes trembled lest the people, in their exuberant spirits and manifestations of cordiality and admiration, might permanently disable General Logan. He had to manage adroitly to seize their hands before they could get hold of his, so that he could drop theirs and save his from being crushed by their vigorous shaking. As it was, he had occasionally to put his hand in a sling. The people seemed unhappy if they could not get hold of him, and if his right hand was bound up they would slap him on the shoulders, embracing him in a way that would make him wince though he knew their hearts were full of loyalty for him. Sometimes old fathers and mothers, whose sons had gone into the service under General Logan and had fallen in battle or died of disease or wounds in hospitals in the South, would come up to him and with tears running down their cheeks, would grasp his hands or pat him on the head affectionately. They could rarely speak for their emotions. When they could speak they would say: "Logan, can you tell us anything more about our boy? Was he a good soldier? Was his face always turned to the foe? We shall see him no more, but we will stand by the flag and Mr. Lincoln because our boy gave his life for his country, and Mr. Lincoln is trying to save the Union and our country." General Logan's great heart was deeply moved by such encounters, and the tears which ran down his cheeks told of his sympathy in stronger language than he could find words in which to express it.

Perhaps the next to push their way to him would be a company of men and women gotten up in grotesque uniforms of red, white, and blue, who were presented by their pseudo-captains, who usually had some amusing design worn as an insignia of the rank they held. Once, I remember, they carried a splendid live eagle, who sat his perch with becoming dignity while he was presented to General Logan in an elaborate speech which had to be repeated to the end by the voluble orator chosen for the important duty. General Logan accepted the gift, and assured his friends that he would carry the bird through the campaign; that he should be allowed to scream for the Republican party and its worthy nominees; and that with the eagle and the mules he was sure his canvass would not be in vain.

For six weeks we travelled from place to place, being at last obliged to take the train, and send the mules home, as we went farther North and the distance increased.

The farther North we went the greater the crowds and the wilder the excitement, convincing General Logan long before the election that Illinois could safely be counted for Lincoln and Johnson. Pathos and comedy followed each other in such quick succession during that memorable trip that we were constantly vibrating between tears and laughter over the grave and comic scenes we witnessed. [6]

We tried to be cheerful and to think that the worst of the war was over, but when the hour came for General Logan to return to the army it was with many forebodings that we bade him good-by.

He was ordered to report to General Grant at City Point, Virginia, as before mentioned. I was advised of the order sending him to relieve Thomas. With intense anxiety I watched the very meagre despatches in the papers and hailed with delight the news of Thomas's victory and General Logan's return to Washington and New York, en route to Savannah to join the Fifteenth Army Corps, which had made the holiday march from

Atlanta to the sea under General Sherman. I believed then that by the time he could reach his command all the fighting would be over.

It was, however, a long and anxious winter. The troops were marching through swamps, over almost impassable roads, through Georgia and the Carolinas to Washington, stopping now and again to dislodge the Confederates from their final attempts at resistance to the Union troops, who were driving everything before them in their triumphant progress toward ending the bitter struggles for the preservation of the Union and for peace. We could get news from the army far less frequently than we desired. The refugees came in hordes from the South, seeking homes as near the border of the Southland as they could find. Colored and white dreaded the cold of the North and as a consequence the people of the border States were overwhelmed with the numbers of impecunious creatures who had to leave the South. It was some time before they could adapt themselves to the changed conditions and accept the inevitable. New laws were passed giving the negroes protection on Southern soil, so that they came in very well as a solution of the problem of what to do for laborers with all the able-bodied men at the front. Although both races were insufferably slow, they could do something. If you tactfully kept away from them when they were engaged in any kind of work they would get through eventually, and were a great improvement on having no one to do the indispensable manual labor.

CHAPTER 5

New Horizons at War's End

After the November election, with its glorious victories and the triumph all along the line dividing the Union and Confederate armies from the Potomac to the Gulf of Mexico, every one was much encouraged and began to hope for an early cessation of hostilities. The Thanksgiving of that year was observed with fervent thankfulness to Him who holds the destinies of nations in the hollow of His hand. People greeted each other with—"Well, what is the good news of to-day?" "Grant will be in Richmond soon." "Lincoln will be inaugurated as President of a reunited country the 4th of March."

The approach of the holidays was hailed with delight. The old-time Christmas festivities were looked forward to with anticipations of much pleasure. Homes that had been shrouded in gloom for four long years began their wonted preparations for celebrating the happy season. The church societies which had been absorbed in the work for the sanitary commission and soldiers' families began to talk of a Christmas tree for the old and young of the whole town.[1] In Carbondale, Illinois, where I lived, it would have been considered heartless and treasonable to have suggested such a thing during the holidays of '61, '62, '63; but every one was full of enthusiasm for the tree of

Christmas, 1864. For weeks before many men and women were busy making presents for everybody, especially the children in the town, including those who only went to Sunday-school during the holidays. Mittens, caps, comforts, socks, stockings, pinafores, handkerchiefs, collars, ribbons, sleds, toys, candies, cakes, fruit, nuts, and all kinds of gifts were prepared to gladden old and young.

Two large cedars were secured and brought into the Methodist church, it being the largest in town. Willing and skilful hands were found to decorate the whole church in living green, with branches of evergreens, artificial flowers, and flags profusely interspersed. The tree was festooned with yards of popcorn strung on a cord by passing a needle through the snow-white kernels. Oranges were hung on the boughs, while tiny flags and glass balls of every color of the rainbow were hung on almost every branch. The tinner kindly donated little tin saucers with wires so arranged through the centre that they would hold the little candles and at the same time fasten them to the limbs of the tree. These were for the illumination. In the afternoon of Christmas Eve the presents were all brought to the church done up in packages and labelled with the name of the person for whom they were intended. They had to be tied on the strong limbs near the body of the trees. When completed and the mounds at the base had been covered over with mats made of green woollen ravellings to imitate grass, they looked majestic—no grander ever graced a royal palace or brought greater joy to hearts of imperial households. The ceremonies began at seven-thirty. The programme consisted of music, songs, recitations, and addresses by guests. It was a union of all denominations in the town to celebrate the Holy Nativity. Brief speeches from the pastors of the different churches followed. After this Santa Claus appeared in a long fur coat and cap, his white beard reaching nearly to his waist. He was hailed by a chorus of childish voices and the clapping of many hands. When it was found that his generosity extended to every one present, and that on all were bestowed the very things they wanted, exclamations of delight filled the church. No such sight as the merry children running from one to the other, comparing and exhibiting their treasures, had been witnessed since the sound of booming cannon had broken the spell of sweet peace of the nation. A cloud of anxiety and suspense had always overshadowed every entertainment during the years of the war. After singing with a zest the Christmas carols, and an eloquent benediction, the joyous people wended their way to their homes with hearts full of happiness, feeling that Christmas-tide was bringing the glad tidings of peace on earth and good will toward men.

The political triumphs emphasized by the military victories seemed to bring hope and gladness to the people who fancied through it all they could see the dawn of peace. Everywhere there was less of the spirit of revolution and disloyalty; grumblers and evil prognosticators were fewer; anxiety and solicitude were no longer in every face. As soon as the election was over and Mr. Lincoln was declared elected, General Logan asked for orders to return to his command. Much dissatisfaction still existed throughout the Army of the Tennessee because General Logan had not been restored to the command of that army. General Grant, therefore, bade him come to Washington, where he arrived on the 23d of December, 1864, and stopped at Brown's—now the Metropolitan—Hotel, where he spent Christmas Day, the most agreeable one to him since 1860. He was satisfied that it was only a question of a brief time before the war would be over, and he was consequently very happy. His corps had made the jolly march through Georgia without even a skirmish since he left them to take part in the presidential campaign after the fall of Atlanta. His corps was then at Savannah and impatient to begin the march through the Carolinas en route to Richmond. He was equally impatient to lead them, but General Grant had other plans for him.

After the fall of Atlanta Grant was anxious that Sherman should start out upon his march to the sea, which he and Sherman had considered the most effective movement that could be made at that time to bring the war to a close. In order to make this expedition and avoid a catastrophe, Grant was most anxious that General Thomas, then in command of the troops about Nashville, should drive Hood out of Tennessee. The history of this General Grant gives in his *Memoirs*,[2] including copies of orders which he had issued to General Thomas urging him to attack Hood, but which Thomas had ignored because he took it upon himself to decide as to the wisdom of these orders, steadily delaying to make the attack until he had succeeded in getting his army in the position he desired it should be before carrying out his orders. In the light of the glorious victories won by Thomas, one forgets what might have been the consequence of his disobedience to orders if defeat instead of victory had characterized these sanguinary engagements.

This was the situation when General Logan reached Washington, December 3, 1864, en route to join the Fifteenth Corps at Savannah by water. He reported to General Grant at City Point, Virginia. He found General Grant much exasperated at General Thomas's delay. Grant says in his *Memoirs:* "Knowing General Logan to be a prompt, gallant and efficient officer, I gave him an order to proceed to Nashville and relieve Thomas." General Logan disliked extremely to obey General Grant's order implicitly, because he felt quite sure that Thomas would consider that he had taken advantage of an opportunity to displace him and thereby be revenged for General Thomas's personal injustice to General Logan in urging that General Howard supersede General Logan in the command of the Army of the Tennessee after General McPherson was killed. However, he reluctantly departed promptly for Louisville, Kentucky, from which place he was to communicate with Thomas and advise him of the orders he had received. General Logan, however, stopped at Cincinnati and sent one of his staff-officers on a confidential mission to General Thomas at Nashville, with a copy of the order he held to relieve him, instructing the officer to try to induce Thomas to make the attack which General Grant had ordered him over and over again to do, and to impress upon Thomas General Logan's disinclination to take advantage of the orders he held. General Logan felt that Thomas's further persistency in delay, notwithstanding the fearful weather and almost impassable roads which had been his excuse, might result most unfortunately for the Union army by allowing the enemy to amass such a large force. Therefore General Logan wished to use his influence to have Thomas obey

Grant's orders at once and thereby relieve him of the necessity of superseding General Thomas. General Thomas, being convinced that longer delay would cause him to forfeit his command and that he would be superseded by General Logan, made the attack December 15, 1864.

General Logan, receiving at Louisville the news of the battle of Nashville, at once sent to General Grant the following telegram:

LOUISVILLE, *Dec.* 17, 1864.

LIEUT. GEN'L. U. S. GRANT, City Point, Va.

Have just arrived, weather bad, is raining since yesterday morning. People here all jubilant over Gen'l. Thomas's success. Confidence seems to be restored.

I will remain here to hear from you. All things going right, it would seem best that I return soon to join my command with Sherman.

JOHN A. LOGAN, *Maj. Gen'l.*

Thus it will be seen that General Logan made the suggestion to return to his command after Thomas's victory, ignoring the opportunity which had been given him to be revenged upon one who had done him so much injustice. He was not moved by any other consideration than that of doing unto others as he would that they should do unto him, albeit he felt that Thomas's long delay was inexcusable, and that he could have won even a more glorious victory weeks before if he had not been of so "slow" or deliberate a temperament. General Logan often said that, had he been in Thomas's place, he would have made the attack much sooner than Thomas did, and believed that he would have had a victory as brilliant as that of Thomas's on the 15th of December.

I often heard General Grant and General Logan discuss Thomas and his heroism as a soldier, but they expressed regret that his temperament was so obstinate and that he shrank from responsibility. General Logan always insisted that he was not deterred from obeying orders to relieve Thomas on any other ground than that he would not be guilty of snatching laurels which he knew Thomas could win if he would only obey orders to attack Hood promptly. Of course, whether it was General

Logan's appeal to Thomas to save himself and fight the battle or because Thomas had finally succeeded in making the preparations which he had spent so much time perfecting, no one will ever know, as General Thomas was of a peculiar disposition and was so set in his opinion as to the wisdom of his conception of a situation that he would never give utterance to an appreciation of indulgence extended to him or of gratitude to those who had done him great service.

Again General Logan telegraphed General Grant requesting that he be allowed to return to the Fifteenth Army Corps, then near Savannah, Georgia. His request was granted, and he accordingly repaired to Washington, thence to New York, and by sea to Savannah, and was soon with his much-loved and devoted corps, with whom he was destined to continue in their march through the Carolinas to Washington.

From incessant rains the whole country was inundated, every stream swollen beyond the confines of its banks, roads were almost impassable, and the entire command destitute of shoes or warm clothes, but happy as lords and eager to continue the march toward Richmond. A less practical commander or less courageous men would have faltered before the almost impassable barriers of mud, ice, and water which surrounded them on every hand, but Sherman's "bummers" and General Logan's gallant men, among whom was the 31st Illinois, his old regiment, knew no discouragement. Captain A. M. Jenkins, a cousin, frequently gallantly commanded the squads which waded waist deep in mud and water to build the corduroys across the swamp. They could build pontoons, fell trees, and make corduroy roads, and march over them dragging ordnance after them and subsist on the country while they did it.

From Savannah they went to Beaufort, thence to Columbia, Fayetteville, Goldsboro, Raleigh, and on to Richmond—not as they marched from Atlanta to the sea, but driving an intrepid army who fell back fighting. Reaching the Salkehatchie River, they found the enemy had determined to make another stand and had again intrenched themselves, thinking the swollen streams would serve like the moat of olden-time fortifications. But the Fifteenth Army Corps knew nothing of the tardiness of ancient warfare, so, dashing through the sluggish stream, they assaulted the enemy with such fury that they were soon in possession of their intrenchments and, pushing along the railroad, arrived at North Edisto by the 12th of February where, in an engagement, General Logan captured many prisoners. When they reached Columbia, South Carolina, they found the retreating Confederates had set a lot of cotton bales and other stores on fire, from which a general conflagration ensued. I have often heard General Logan tell, with tears in his eyes, of the horrors of the night his troops entered that burning city and of the wreck that the desperate and intoxicated enemy left behind them. Barrels of whiskey and wine were here and there and everywhere; the desperate troops had been drinking their fill, and those arriving were not behind them in bacchanalian propensities. Life and property were of little consequence to either the Union or the Confederate. Total destruction seemed inevitable, and but for General Logan's perfect command over his men and his herculean efforts there would not have been left one stone upon another of the houses, or a single soul of the inhabitants to tell the tale of the awful holocaust. People were flying to and fro in the streets, wild with excitement and fear, while the flames were consuming everything before them. There were poor facilities for extinguishing fires under most favorable circumstances and, with no one of the city authorities at his post, and the triumphant general and his army just entering the city, it seems incredible, even now, that they saved anything; but through wise management and superhuman efforts many houses were wrested from the devouring flames and order restored.[3]

Lynch Creek, Lumber, Cape Fear, South, and Neuse Rivers, with the bottomless swamps between presented the most formidable and trying obstacles every mile of the march to Goldsboro. The weary men had scarcely finished building roads, bridges, and causeways, and succeeded in dragging the wagons and artillery over them, when they would strike another seemingly impassable lagoon or swamp. The swamps were thickly timbered, fortunately for the army, for the men could wade into the water and fell the trees to form corduroy roads and build bridges. When it is remembered that this was done with a stubborn enemy in front of them, ready to take every advantage, it must be acknowledged that this march has no parallel in difficulty. The country about Goldsboro was almost devastated, and subsistence was difficult; but the invincible army pushed on, feeling sure that they were nearing the end of hardship and warfare. At Bentonville the Fifteenth Army Corps met the enemy and again repulsed them, after which Johnston retreated, burning the bridges behind him. Halting at Goldsboro to recuperate, they heard that Petersburg had fallen and that Richmond was in the hands of General Grant, and the attempted Confederacy was no more. Going into camp at Raleigh, North Carolina, they waited for the whole army to come up, and with the conclusion of negotiations between Sherman and Johnston Richmond was ours, and now they had nothing to do but to push on to Washington and behold a united country.

While rejoicing over this happy thought, they were startled by the overwhelming news of the assassination of Mr. Lincoln, which so exasperated the soldiery that, with the fury of madmen, they swore vengeance on every inhabitant of the South and but for their devotion to General Logan they would have destroyed the city of Raleigh, North Carolina, and every soul within its precincts. Hearing of the wild grief and intense indignation of the men, General Logan mounted his well-known horse, Black Jack, and flew from one command to another, calling on the men to be worthy of their own heroic deeds and innocent of the blood of guiltless people, to remember that he who had been sacrificed would not that they should thus avenge his death, but let the laws they had upheld take charge of the guilty. Weeping like children, these brave men went to their quarters. A perfect pall hung over the whole army, which the good news of so soon being mustered out of the service was not able to dispel. Thinking men could not divine where the conspiracy was to end or to what extent the military would be obliged to act. They were ready for anything, and would not have hesitated to seize any suspected persons; but seeing the magnanimity of Mr. Lincoln so ruthlessly betrayed, and such madness and desperation indulged in by the reckless spirits who sympathized with the rebellion, they feared the worst. In Washington no such gloom had ever been known. Such a tragedy as the assassination of the President and the attempted assassination of the cabinet officers, following the triumph of the Government, made the most indifferent feel that they were standing over a volcano that was likely to burst forth in fury at the most unexpected moment; that the lives of the executives were insecure, and that after all the sacrifices of human life and the nation's treasury, there was no peace or security of life; that the republic was a failure, and that, like Mexico and South America, we were destined to experience continuous revolutions. Nothing but the inherent wisdom that had guided us through the whirlpool of rebellion saved us from anarchy. Our people never dreamed that the methods which had characterized monarchies would ever be attempted in our republic, and it required time for them to rally from such a shock. But, as before, the deliberate judgment of cool heads soon regained the mastery, and order was maintained. In the country the people were overwhelmed with grief, and with folded hands presented sad pictures of despair, the strongest not ashamed of their tears. They even suspected Mr. Johnson, who was born on Southern soil. Their faith was only firm in the army and its great commanders. General Grant could have made himself dictator had his ambition prompted him to such daring. His timely support of Johnson and his assurance that the will of the President should be obeyed by the army did much toward quieting the excitement. In the mean time the army was gradually nearing the capital for the grand review and disbandment.

Every day after the assassination of President Lincoln the news which came to the army was of a succession of disasters to the Confederacy and its faithful adherents, till the last armed foe had to surrender. Even those remote from the armies were eager to hear of the final capitulation. Feeling that peace was near at hand, they were impatient for the return of loved ones who had now been away for more than four years. The crops and business had been neglected, because at the beginning of the war the people did little else but go to the station and to the telegraph office to hear everything possible. Finally Lee's surrender was telegraphed all over the country, and the Army of the Tennessee was ordered to Alexandria, Virginia. All the country around Washington was occupied by troops. The Army of the Potomac, having finished its work in Virginia, on the James, at Gettysburg, and all along the Chesapeake had retraced its steps, and was again encamped around the capital it had hastened to defend in 1861. The armies from the Southwest who had been from Cairo to New Orleans, on the coast from New York to Saint Augustine, from Vicksburg to Lookout Mountain, from Atlanta to the sea were all ordered to report to headquarters in Washington. The men of the Army of the Tennessee, ragged and worn by their long marches and desperate fighting, but with a glorious record for heroism and endurance were delighted that they were to have an opportunity to see the Capitol, the White House, where Mr. Lincoln had lived, and the theatre where he had been so cruelly murdered.

Reaching Alexandria May 12, 1865, they were encamped in and around that degenerate city, where brave young Ellsworth, the first martyr of the war, lost his life in hauling down a Confederate flag that had been hoisted over the Jackson Hotel, almost under the shadow of the dome of the Capitol. General Howard was ordered to take charge of the Freedmen's Bureau and General Logan was reinstated, as he should have been before, in command of the Army of the Tennessee. He was received by the soldiers with cheer after cheer, and was made happy by the feeling that justice, though tardy, had at last been awarded him.

When the negotiations of peace had all been signed, and were unchangeable, the President and cabinet and some wise counsellors said: "Now the war is over we shall never again see such an armed force in this country. We must have a grand review in Washington and allow the survivors of the gigantic rebellion to march up Pennsylvania Avenue with the commander of each army and his staff at its head." When Napoleon returned from Italy, the whole army of France and its allies passed in review down the Champs Elysées and were marshalled on the Champ de Mars; the trophies of arms, flags, and captured cannon that were arranged artistically on that broad plain inspired the whole of France with implicit faith in Napoleon. The spectacle of the victorious legions marching to the music of the Marseillaise on that great occasion so impressed the people that it was possible for the great conqueror to lead them, as he did, to the very jaws of death.

Our republic had been saved by our invincible army, and in order to confirm the faith of the nation in them, it was a wise suggestion to have the review; hence it was arranged for the 23d and 24th of May. No fairer days ever dawned. To the bright sunshine were added the magnificent accessories of military and spectacular scenery. General Logan once described the day as follows: "It looked as if the great Republic was on dress parade; the house-tops, the windows, the doors and balconies and all available space around, below and above was [*sic*] packed with men, women, and children. They were well clothed; the Nation had put on its best. Tens of thousands of bouquets made settings for the picture and were subsequently thrown to the officers and troops as they passed in review. Cannons boomed, engines whistled, flags fluttered in the breeze, innumerable brass bands and drum-corps filled the air with patriotic music. Every conceivable demonstration manifesting the enthusiastic welcome of a grateful people to their heroic defenders characterized the day."

For many hours of each day before, every soldier, to the most untidy and reckless in the ranks, was busy polishing his arms and accoutrements, repairing well-worn uniforms and soleless shoes. Artillery guns and caissons had not been so polished before, mountings and housings were never so bright, while bayonets were polished till they glittered like Damascus blades.

General Sherman, accompanied by his formidable staff, to which he added Major-General O. O. Howard and other general officers, preceded the almost endless columns from the Capitol west on Pennsylvania Avenue. First came the Army of the Potomac, trim and neat, marching like regulars on parade; then the Army of the Tennessee, composed of the Fifteenth, Sixteenth, Seventeenth, Twentieth, and Fourteenth Corps, with well-worn uniforms and almost shoeless feet, followed their dauntless and idolized leader, General John A. Logan, who sat his steed like a statue.[4] On horseback he was majestic, as erect and graceful as an Indian, his long black hair and mustache, flashing eyes, olive complexion, and broadbrimmed army hat giving him the air of a cavalier. On that day he was the recipient of such ringing cheers that he was very happy. Bouquets and wreaths of flowers were showered on him. The enthusiastic men in the street, rushing up to his horse, put the wreaths over the proud animal's head down on to the creature's neck until it was covered. When division after division was hailed with such deafening shouts, General Logan's heart beat high with pride and gratification. He cared little that they were called "Sherman's bummers," or that scarcely a uniform of officers or men in the whole army would have passed a regulation inspection. In the glory of that day Logan's men forgot the fathomless mud of Cairo, the sleet, mud, and water around Forts Henry and Donelson, the heat and long siege of Vicksburg, the rugged mountains of Kenesaw, the siege of Atlanta, the swamps and corduroys of Georgia and the Carolinas, the burning suns, and pitiless storms of winter, the marches, the battles, the suffering, and carnage of the long four years intervening between April 1861 and May 1865. General Logan forgot that he had been relieved unjustly of the command of the Army of the Tennessee after his great victory at Atlanta and speedy avenging of the death of McPherson, July 22, 1864. All were going home soon and only thought and dreamed of bliss, like Campbell's soldier. Even in the dead of the night "sweet visions" they saw, "and thrice ere the morning" they dreamed them again.

From morning till night, for two days, these victorious cohorts were marching through Pennsylvania Avenue, past the President, and back to their quarters. Banners were flying; battered flags were borne by proud color-bearers; the bands played the familiar airs that had inspired many a faltering heart in battle, while the glittering bayonets of the infantry and bright plumes of the cavalry and artillery presented a picture never to be effaced, and aroused the patriotism of every

American heart. Decimated ranks and riderless horses told the story of what the final triumph had cost, and was the one cloud over the matchless pageant that can never be repeated on American soil.

Immediately following the review were orders for the mustering out of the service of the Union army those whose heroic work had been so gloriously accomplished. General Logan and the Army of the Tennessee were ordered to Louisville, Kentucky, where they were to be honorably disbanded, the men to be allowed to go whithersoever they listed. It was most pathetic to see them anxious for a leave of absence to visit their loved ones, but loath to leave the army and their idolized commander; many of them pledged themselves to return speedily upon a call from him for service anywhere in the world. Time nor distance can ever break the bonds cemented by the experience of soldiers who have marched, suffered, and bivouacked together. Before disbanding, General Logan issued the following order, which very feebly expressed his feelings toward them and their gallant service:

HEADQUARTERS ARMY OF THE TENNESSEE,
LOUISVILLE, KY., *July* 13, 1865.

OFFICERS AND SOLDIERS OF THE ARMY OF THE TENNESSEE:

The profound gratification I feel in being authorized to release you from the onerous obligations of the camp, and return you, laden with laurels, to homes where warm hearts wait to welcome you, is somewhat embittered by the painful reflection that I am sundering the ties that trials have made true, time made tender, sufferings made sacred, perils made proud, heroism made honorable, and fame made forever fearless of the future. It is no common occasion that demands the disbandment of a military organization before the resistless power of which mountains bristling with bayonets have bowed, cities have surrendered, and millions of brave men have been conquered. Although I have been but a short period your commander, we are not strangers; affections have sprung up between us during the long years of doubt, gloom, and carnage which we have passed through together, nurtured by common perils, sufferings, and sacrifices, and riveted by the memories of gallant comrades whose bones repose beneath the sod of an hundred battle-fields, which neither time nor distance will weaken or efface. The many marches that you have made, the dangers you have despised, the haughtiness you have humbled, the duties you have discharged, the glory you have gained, the destiny you have discovered for the country for whose cause you have conquered, all recur at this moment in all the vividness that marked the scenes through which we have just passed. From the pens of the ablest historians of the land daily are drifting out upon the current of time, page upon page, volume upon volume of your heroic deeds which, floating down to future generations, will inspire the student of history with admiration, the patriotic American with veneration for his ancestors, and the lover of republican liberty with gratitude to those who, in a fresh baptism of blood, reconsecrated the powers and energies of the Republic to the cause of constitutional freedom.

Long may it be the happy fortune of each and every one of you to live in the full fruition of the boundless blessings you have secured to the human race. Only he whose heart has been thrilled with admiration for your impetuous and unyielding valor in the thickest of the fight, can appreciate with what pride I recount the brilliant achievements which immortalize you, and enrich the pages of our national history. Passing by the earlier but not less signal triumphs of the war in which most of you participated and inscribed upon your banners such victories as Donelson and Shiloh, I recur [refer] to your campaigns, sieges, and victories that challenge the admiration of the world and elicit the unwilling applause of all Europe. Turning your backs upon the blood-bathed heights of Vicksburg, you launched into a region swarming with enemies, fighting your way and marching, without adequate supplies, to answer the cry for succor that came to you from the noble but beleaguered Army of Chattanooga. Your steel next flashed among the mountains of Tennessee, and your weary limbs found rest before the embattled heights of Missionary Ridge, and there with dauntless courage you breasted again the enemy's destructive fire, and shared with your comrades of the Army of the Cumberland the glories of a victory than which no soldier can boast a prouder. In that unexampled campaign of vigilant and vigorous warfare from Chattanooga to Atlanta you freshened your laurels at Resaca, grappling with the enemy behind his works, hurling him back dismayed and broken. Pursuing him from thence, marking your path by the graves of fallen comrades, you again triumphed over superior numbers at Dallas, fighting your way from there to Kenesaw Mountain and under the murderous artillery that frowned from its rugged heights; with a tenacity and constancy that finds few parallels you labored, fought, and suffered through the boiling rays of a southern midsummer sun, until at last you planted your colors upon its topmost heights. Again, on the 22d of July 1864, rendered memorable through all time for the terrible struggle you so heroically maintained under discouraging disasters and that saddest of all reflections, the loss of that exemplary soldier and popular leader, the lamented McPherson, your matchless courage turned defeat into a glorious victory. Ezra Chapel and Jonesboro added new lustre to a radiant record, the latter unbarring to you the proud Gate City of the South. The daring of a desperate foe in thrusting his legion northward exposed the country in your front and, though rivers, swamps, and enemies opposed, you boldly surmounted every obstacle, beat down all opposition, and marched onward to the sea. Without any act to dim the brightness of your historic page, the world rang plaudits where your labors and struggles culminated at Savannah, and the old "Starry Banner" waved once more over the wall of one of our proudest cities of the seaboard. Scarce a breathing spell had passed when your colors faded from the coast, and your columns plunged into the swamps of the Carolinas. The suffering you endured, the labors you performed, and the successes you achieved in those morasses, deemed impassable, form a creditable episode in the history of the war. Pocataligo, Salkehatchie, Edisto, Branchville, Orangeburgh, Columbia, Bentonville, Charleston, and Raleigh are names that will ever be suggestive of the resistless sweep of your columns through the territory that cradled and nurtured, and from whence was sent forth on its mission of crime, misery, and blood, the disturbing and disorganizing spirits of secession and rebellion.

The work for which you pledged your brave hearts and brawny arms to the Government of your fathers you have nobly performed. You are seen in the past, gathering through the gloom that enveloped the land, rallying as the guardian of man's proudest heritage, forgetting the threat unwoven in the loom, quitting the anvil, abandoning the workshops, to vindicate the supremacy of the laws and the authority of the Constitution. Four years have you struggled in the bloodiest and most destructive war that ever drenched the earth with human gore; step by step you have borne our standard, until to-day, over every fortress and arsenal that rebellion wrenched from us, and over city, town, and hamlet, from the lakes to the gulf, and from ocean to ocean, proudly floats the "Starry Emblem" of our national unity and strength. Your rewards, my comrades, are the welcoming plaudits of a grateful people, the consciousness that, in saving the Republic, you have won for your country renewed respect and power at home and abroad; that, in the exampled era of growth and prosperity that dawns with peace, there attaches mightier wealth of pride and glory than ever before to that loved boast, "I am an American citizen." In relinquishing the implements of war for those of peace, let your conduct, which was that of warriors in time of war, be that of peaceful citizens in time of peace. Let not the lustre of that brighter name you have won as soldiers be dimmed by any improper acts as citizens, but as time rolls on let your record grow brighter and brighter still.

John A. Logan, *Major-General.*

When the last good-bys had to be said, heroes of many battles wept like children, feeling that they would probably meet no more in this world. Alas! if the muster-roll of the Army of the Tennessee of 1865 were called to-day, tears would dim the eyes of the few survivors who would answer "Here!"

Like patriots they took their several ways and in a few brief weeks the thousands who had followed the life of soldiers laid aside the accoutrements of war and took up the implements of peace, dissolving into citizens as rapidly as they had become soldiers.

At home, from the day of Lee's surrender there was continual rejoicing until the shock of Mr. Lincoln's assassination changed it to mourning. Then there was vibration between the emotions of joy over peace and grief over the sacrifice of his great life. Finally, the news came that the regiments raised in the vicinity of Carbondale, Illinois, would arrive within a few days of each other. Then all was activity and bustle to make suitable preparations for welcoming them home again. No building in the town was half large enough to hold the people or spacious enough for tables upon which to spread the bounteous repast they determined to lay before the returning soldiers; so the lovely grove heretofore mentioned was selected. Every twig or branch that had fallen, every dead leaf and unsightly bit of rubbish was cleaned away and the grass swept, leaving a lovely green sward beneath the spreading boughs of the majestic oaks. A grand stand was erected on one side, from which welcoming speeches were to be made by the hosts. The most prominent of the returning heroes were expected to tell some of their experiences and give expression to their joy that peace had at last brought them home. Canopies of red, white, and blue were thrown over the speakers and the band-stands, and the columns that supported them were wound with garlands, the whole being beautiful and effective. On the other side there were long tables spread with spotless linen, china, silver, glass, a profusion of flowers, and everything that a prolific country and an abundant harvest could produce. After the music and speeches every soldier was seated at these tables for such a feast as he had not known for many a weary day. Every man and woman in the town, no matter how proud their position, was ready to wait upon them, each one turning into as skilful a waiter as ever served at Delmonico's. With smiles for those who were there and tears for those who were not, they made their return as pleasant as possible, repeating the same welcome for the various commands as they arrived.

When it is remembered that everything that was cooked, the decorations and all the work done was accomplished by loving hands, it can be imagined that there was little necessity for gymnasiums, Swedish movements, or other exercises of which we hear in these modern days. The benevolent had plenty to do to look after the widows, orphans, and unfortunates and ere long affairs had assumed their wonted routine, each drifting into the channels he had followed before volunteering.

General Logan reached home on the 28th of July 1865, accompanied by two members of his staff. He brought his horses, camp equipage, and two colored men and a boy about sixteen years old, who were with him when they struck the tents in Louisville for the last time. He did not have the heart to turn these freedmen adrift without employment, with no home and away from the haunts of their childhood, so he brought them home, providing for them until he could secure them something to do and a chance to be self-supporting. "Boston," the boy, was as black as ebony. He had been the valet, jockey, and petted servant of a sporting-master who was killed in battle. He was a daring, mischievous, wiry little scamp, with many monkey instincts and antics and required constant watching. He was a born gambler and would slip out and gamble with the dissolute men about the town. He pretended to have been converted and joined the colored Baptist church, and together with a number of colored men and women was to be immersed in a large pond in a field near the town. Boston wanted us to attend; it was a cold, lowering Sunday afternoon in March. We drove out and sat in the carriage near the shore on the opposite side of the pond from where they had tents erected, one for the women and one for the men. One minister went to the tent-door and escorted the candidates for baptism down to the steps which had been placed at the edge of the water, while another minister led them one by one quite a distance toward the centre of the pond. When the water was waist-deep, the minister crossed their hands, took hold of the belt around their waist with one hand while with the other he caught them by the back of the neck and dipped them into the water. All their heads were tied up with white handkerchiefs, and as they rose out of the water they were so frightened it was with difficulty that they could walk to the steps. One thin little colored girl preceded our Boston. She was frightfully nervous and screeched as loud as she could the moment she was led into the water, and as the minister took hold of her she jerked away from him and went plunging through the water across the pond. Boston bolted after her and in a twinkling the impressive ceremony changed into the most ludicrous performance one could have imagined. Boston grabbed her around the waist, lifted her up in his arms, and bore her triumphantly to the women's tent, then darted to the men's tent, tore the white handkerchief from his head, the belt from around his waist, dressed himself, and fled precipitately from the place, the girl following on behind. The wild singing and shouting of the clergy and the members of the church was not sufficient to drown the laughter and jeering of the curious crowd.

That night, when Boston reported for his duties, General Logan began to scold him for his unseemly behavior. He replied: "General, I saw they was gwine to drown that girl, and I is her sweetheart and I was not gwine to let 'em. You wouldn't yourself stand still and see 'em drown the Missus. I was done clean 'gusted with that old parson, so I just lit out."

After a hopeless struggle with him for months, he ran away and the last we heard of him he was engaged as a jockey in Saint Louis. The men remained with us for some months, but returned to their Southern homes and were both conspicuous in the conflicts between the colored and white races in the early days of the reconstruction.

On the 30th of July 1865, occurred the grand welcoming of the returning volunteers at Carbondale, Jackson County, Illinois. For weeks our home was a hostelry for the accommodation of constantly arriving visitors who were not satisfied until they had greeted General Logan in person. Carbondale was a small town without markets, catering establishments, comfortable hotels or competent servants, and under such circumstances, it was not an easy matter to entertain unexpected guests who came by the score. In my happiness over the declaration of peace and General Logan's safe return I murmured not, and with the assistance of friends who insisted upon aiding me as a labor of love, we so managed that it was around well-laid, bountifully supplied tables, that we listened to stories of the trying and amusing experiences of the four years of the Civil War.

Another source of rejoicing in our home added much to our happiness: our son, John A. Logan, Jr., was born July 24, 1865 and was from the very hour of his birth so bright and handsome as to attract the attention of every one, and to us evermore a blessing beyond compare.

Early in September, having been notified by the departments in Washington that his accounts were all audited and that there was nothing against him on the records, General Logan tendered his resignation, as he was unwilling to continue on the pay-rolls without rendering active service. He had been importuned to remain in the service, having been offered a brigadier-general's commission in the regular army, a proffered honor which he highly appreciated; but knowing so well his restive disposition, he feared he would be unhappy in time of peace to be confined to the regulations in his coming and going, and declined the generous offer.[5] About that time there was an apprehension that we might have trouble in Mexico. Every one looked with suspicion upon the appearance of Maximilian in the city of Mexico. General Logan was requested to hold himself in readiness to go there as United States minister, should it be necessary to send him, and but for the discomfiture and the melancholy taking off of that ill-fated and deluded sovereign, Maximilian, General Logan would probably have entered the diplomatic service. He had no taste for it, however, when there was little probability of eventful times. Soon after he was requested to accept the mission to Japan, but having no desire to become isolated from his own country, he also declined that position, expecting to again return to the profession of the law.[6]

During the winter he was called to Washington to attend to some business affairs of his own and of some friends. He went thither, therefore, and while waiting for the settlement of these matters with the government he became much interested in the reconstruction and readjustment of national questions then under discussion. At the State convention held in May 1866, he was nominated by acclamation for Congressman-at-large, the State being entitled to an additional member who was chosen at large until the legislature assembled to redistrict the State. He could not well refuse to accept, notwithstanding the fact that he had not intended to again enter politics. His majority was overwhelming. March 4, 1867, he again took his seat as a member of Congress, after an absence of six years, having resigned his seat to enter the army in August, 1861.[7] Bringing to the position so much renown, he was immediately assigned to the most important committees of the House, and made chairman of the military committee which had before it the difficult task of providing for the reduction of the army to a peace basis. With his impetuous disposition and intense nature, it was impossible for General Logan to be an indifferent or passive member; hence he plunged into all the vexing details of the most knotty questions, working day and night that he might understand them thoroughly and be able to do that which would result in the greatest good to the greatest number. Every day, during the discussion of the problems of reconstruction, he was confronted by questions which he felt were vital to the perpetuity of the government. He appreciated the fact that if mistakes were made by the party in power, they would recoil in the future or spring up like Banquo's ghost to torment posterity.

We took up our residence in the old Willard Hotel, which had been the leading hotel of Washington during the war. It was of fearful and wonderful construction, the Fourteenth Street side having been built on to some buildings fronting on Pennsylvania Avenue. The floors of the Fourteenth Street addition of each story were three or four feet higher than those of the Pennsylvania Avenue buildings; the ceilings were low, the halls dismal, and the dining-room cheerless. From long occupancy and unsanitary sewerage it was anything but an agreeable abode. The house was, however, full of guests. Among them were General Francis E. Spinner, United States treasurer, whose autograph on the greenbacks was so famous all over the world, and his interesting family; Senator Simon Cameron of Pennsylvania, who was Mr. Lincoln's Secretary of War, and his wife and daughter; Senator Harris and his family; the eccentric bachelor, Senator Salisbury, and others.[8]

A number of members of Congress and their families were also in the house. Mr. and Mrs. James G. Blaine with their four children had a suite near ours. When Mrs. Blaine and I were out making calls, Emmons, Alice, and little J. G. Blaine, Jr., and Dollie and baby John A. Logan, Jr., had fine times impersonating different distinguished men and women of whom they had heard their elders talk. Frequently we returned home to find confusion reigning supreme in our rooms, the children having amused themselves by dressing up in their parents' clothes, playing grown-up people. Impromptu parties were organized, and the other children in the house invited to partake of the banquets they served through the indulgence of Hughes, the head waiter, who was so devoted to General Logan and Mr. Blaine that their children could have whatever they wanted. Emmons presided over their affairs with much suavity of manner inherited from his knightly father.

There were frequent exciting discussions at the dinner-table. The members and senators and prominent people assembling at that hour could not resist the temptation to continue their controversies.

Mr. Blaine's election as speaker, his appointment of the chairman and members of important committees, were matters of as much importance as they are to-day, and probably greater because of the momentous questions that had to be settled after the close of the Civil War.[9]

With all of his diplomacy and fascinating manners, Mr. Blaine did not escape bitter criticism on the announcement of the chairmanships. Personal disappointments were many and not concealed by aspirants for these important positions. It would have saved speakers of the past much vexation of soul if the present method of shifting the responsibility of selecting the committees and chairmen to a committee of the House, as is done in these progressive times, had then been in vogue.

After the departure of General Logan for the rendezvous of the troops at Cairo, Illinois, in 1861, we had decided that I had better reside in Carbondale, Jackson County, Illinois, on the Illinois Central Railroad, where I could be in communication by telegraph with the then Colonel Logan of the 31st Illinois or join him, if necessary, by rail.[10] We had formerly lived twenty-two miles east of the railroad and, in consequence, suffered great inconvenience on account of the overland travel necessary to reach a railroad. The uncertainty of the movement of the troops would have kept me anxious for my husband's welfare, and besides this the families of the members of his regiment depended upon me for information in regard to their soldier husbands, sons, and fathers.

The present generation is perfectly ignorant of the lack of facilities for communication and rapid transportation to and from the army in 1861 and 1862. We received the mail, part of the time, once a day. The newspapers were triweekly, and they contained very meagre reports of the direful things that were going on between the Union and Confederate armies. The telegraphic reports were censored so closely by the authorities that they did not dare to give out anything like full accounts of battle engagements and casualties of the war. Consequently, we did little else except to wait impatiently for news. Our daughter, now Mrs. Mary Logan Tucker, was in her second year and was my constant companion. I was afraid to leave her with any one and therefore took her with me wherever I went, whether on an errand of mercy to the unfortunate families of the soldiers at the front, or to attend to the business affairs which my husband had left in my care when he dropped everything and went into the army. The citizens of that part of the country were so divided in their sympathies between the North and the South that it caused many unpleasant situations and embarrassing meetings. Those whose friends were in the army of the Union were naturally sensitive and could not bear to hear their husbands, fathers, and sons accused of being Lincoln hirelings, negro-lovers, and many other opprobrious names which were applied to them, while those in sympathy with the South were just as resentful over being called rebels, traitors, and numerous other names. Mr. Lincoln was held directly responsible for all the calamities of the war, the secessionists and their friends insisting that he caused the conflict of armies by his demand for the abolition of slavery. After three long years I knew nothing but that we were solicitous for the unfortunate by whom we were surrounded.

When peace was declared there was universal rejoicing and excitement. We knew then that the soldiers and sailors would soon be returning to their homes and their friends, as they would be disbanded as soon as possible after the surrender of Lee's army. General Logan was in command of the Army of the Tennessee which, after the grand review, was mustered out of the service at Louisville, Kentucky. The families of the returning volunteers were overjoyed at the thought of having their loved ones with them again.

There was a class, however, who pretended to be very much troubled for fear the troops would prove a disturbing element as soon as they had recovered from the excitement of meeting those they had left behind them. Some went so far as to say they feared that they would form marauding parties who would be a terror in the vicinity where they resided, and would go about and take possession of whatever they wanted without regard to law, order, or the rights of others. This was an unfounded fear, because there never could have been a more orderly return to peaceful pursuits. To a man, the soldiers and sailors seemed to realize that they had been engaged in a war for the preservation of the Union, and when that had been accomplished they had nothing to do but to return to their homes and resume their various vocations which they had laid down when they volunteered. They soon became law-abiding, industrious citizens of the Union they had saved. There was no such thing as violation of the law, visits of vengeance, or any species of unlawful, riotous conduct on the part of any of these men. In thirty days from the time they were discharged, many of them had begun their work for the support of themselves and their families. Legions of them engaged in all kinds of industrial, commercial, professional, and other pursuits necessary for the preservation of life and liberty.[11] In a most exciting political campaign there were few personal conflicts or settlements of old scores on account of unjust and outrageous acts perpetrated during the warfare between the North and the South. Veterans met veterans and extended the right hand of fellowship to each other. There were reunions, reconciliations, and happy meetings between the bitterest of foes.

Naturally they differed much in political affiliations, some being most ardent Republicans while others returned to the Democratic party, to which they had belonged before they entered the service. Before going into the army General Logan had acted with the Democratic party, and left it when he had to choose between his party and his country. On account of the change of principles of that party during the war, he felt he had no desire to again become an advocate of the principles of Democracy, but would continue his adherence to the Republican party, whose platform advocated the principles for which he and thousands of others had stood during over four years of blood and strife.[12]

He did not intend to enter politics again, desiring to resume the practice of law, but this was not to be. In the very first campaign after his return home from Louisville, Kentucky, where he mustered out the entire Army of the Tennessee, our home was crowded with men from all over the country, insisting that he accept from the Republican party nominations for political positions. There were hordes and hordes of ex-Union soldiers from almost every State north of the Mason and Dixon line, who were untiring in their efforts to secure the adherence of the most distinguished men of the army. The assassination of Mr. Lincoln had left such a deep spirit of resentment that Republicans were busy in securing the support and advocacy of the ablest men who had been in the army, to fit elective official positions.

We kept open house and entertained legions of people, which was no small thing to do at that day and time, with the inconveniences of poor markets and independent employees upon whom we were obliged to depend. It would be an incredible story were I to describe graphically the chase for chickens, fresh meats, fish, and edibles considered fit to be placed before these numerous guests. It was the old, old story of choicest fruits, vegetables, poultry, and other good things being shipped to the higher-priced markets, and the cities and residences in the rural districts having a great scramble to get anything worth being put upon the table. As I look back upon it now, I think we performed miracles in the line of satisfying hungry men and women who joined in the petitions to General Logan to accept the various nominations for official positions. Illinois had been represented since the census of 1860 by a Congressman-at-large, as they had not redistricted the State. Hon. S. W. Molton, a most estimable man, was a candidate for re-election as a member of Congress in 1866, but, the soldiers being in the majority in the Republican party, they demanded that General Logan should succeed Mr. Molton in Congress because they anticipated serious trouble over the various questions that should follow the close of the war and the assassination of Mr. Lincoln. General Logan talked to me very seriously on the subject and I felt intensely interested in what he might do, as he had sent his resignation to Washington as soon as he got his affairs properly adjusted, but had not yet embarked in the legal profession, which it was his intention and ambition to do. Mr. Molton was a loyal friend of General Logan's and insisted that he would withdraw in favor of the general if the general would consent to allow his name to be used. Without waiting for his answer, the State convention convened and General Logan was nominated by acclamation on receipt of his reply. But for the fact that they insisted it was necessary for the success of the Republican party for him to make the race, he would not have done so. As soon as the convention was over and he had signified his acceptance, then [there?] began an indescribable scramble for him to make promises to almost every county in the State to speak in the interest of the State ticket.

The months of June and July we had spent in our headquarters in Saint Paul, Minnesota. Our party consisted of Eliza Logan Wood, the great tragedian, Katie Logan who was subsequently our adopted daughter, General Logan, myself, our daughter Dollie, and baby son, John A. Logan, Jr. We made Saint Paul our headquarters and went to all the important lakes in Minnesota, having a very delightful time fishing. The general had had no such respite from constant care and anxiety since he entered the army in 1861. He entered into all our plans for recreation and rest with the enthusiasm of a boy. When we visited the lakes we had our boats and went out in the morning, returning in the afternoon with boats laden with beautiful fish, all of us having participated in the catch. It can be said to have been one of the most delightful summers of our lives.

Upon the announcement of the general's nomination for Congress, we returned to Chicago and the general immediately entered upon the campaign. I remained at Joliet, Illinois, to visit cousins of General Logan, Mr. and Mrs. Henry Fish, Mrs. Fish being a daughter of Joel Manning, many years auditor of the Illinois Canal and one of the most splendid men of his time. In the midst of enjoying their hospitality I received a telegram telling me of the death of my mother at Marion, Illinois. A young man by the name of Henry Hopper of that town, having gone to a Democratic convention at Cairo, Illinois, was exposed to and attacked by cholera. He arrived home at noon and was dead at night. His wife followed him a few hours later; her mother, with whom they lived, was seized and having no one to aid her she sent for my mother, who went to her and remained until after her death, after which she secured some one to take charge of the body. Returning home, she was not at all alarmed about herself, as she was fearless of danger or disease and only very glad that she had been able to perform the last offices of nurse and physician for the poor woman. Before the dawn of another morning, August 24, 1866, she herself was a corpse. My father, in great grief and bewilderment, had directed that telegrams be sent to the Republican headquarters at the old Tremont House in Chicago. They arrived after we had left the city, and were laid on a table in the committee-room where they stayed until some one came in who felt that they should be opened. Finding the contents so sad, they tried to find General Logan, who immediately thereafter telegraphed me the overwhelming news. It was, up to that time, the greatest sorrow of my life, as my mother and I had been companions from my childhood. I appreciated her great mentality and remarkable executive ability. I knew that my father in his wonted dependence upon her was perfectly undone, so I lost no time in joining him, and to my dying day shall I remember his anguish and the desolation of our beloved old home. There were five children of the thirteen brothers and sisters at home, and my dear father to whom I had to give my immediate attention. Consequently, the remainder of the year was a very busy one for me, as I felt my first duty was to my husband and, of course, there were many occasions when he needed me to accompany him. I made it a point to look after him carefully, for after he made long speeches in the open air he was always completely exhausted. I was ever glad to be with him to give him my personal attention and to receive his friends and guests while he took a few hours' rest.

Travelling and canvassing in those days were a very different proposition from the present day. There were not so many railroads in any State as there are to-day, and various points had to be reached by driving overland, and not always upon the best of roads. This necessitated the spending of much time in covering the distance from point to point, and as these campaigns are always conducted in the heat of summer and the inclemency of fall rains, great fatigue and exposure were inevitable. The result of the campaign was most flattering to General Logan, as he received practically the largest number of votes that had ever been cast up to that date for any candidate.

Early in December General Logan went to Washington to attend to some matters before the departments and to settle the accounts of a number of officers under his command who had not been able to get a complete settlement with the Government when the troops were mustered out of the field. My father's family and my own two children requiring my attention, we decided that I had better remain at our home in Carbondale, Illinois, until the general should take his seat in Congress, March 4, 1867.

The people were so relieved by the close of the war and the prospects of great prosperity that, although I was in mourning myself, I found it far less depressing than it had been the preceding winter when the end of the war was so uncertain. It was interesting to see the activity of the men who had been in the service, who were so anxious to take up some sort of peaceful pursuit which promised success for them. The elections having resulted in such stupendous majorities for the Republican party, no one doubted that in a few brief months all the vexatious problems arising from the war would be settled, and that this country would enter upon an era of progress and prosperity.

REMINISCENCES
OF
RECONSTRUCTION

CHAPTER 6

Life Among the Reconstructionists

A WONDERFUL movement was started early in 1866 to carry out the organization of the Grand Army of the Republic, the history of which is as follows:

To an Illinoisan belongs the credit of conceiving the grandest organization ever thought out by man for the perpetuation of "Fraternity, Charity, and Loyalty." Reverend William J. Rutledge, while chaplain of the 14th Illinois Infantry, was the tent-mate of Major B. F. Stephenson, the surgeon of the regiment, to whom he was devotedly attached. In the weary hours of their marching and bivouac, Chaplain Rutledge had many conferences with Major Stephenson. Among the topics which they discussed was the future of the million and more of men who would soon lay down their arms and be scattered all over the Union, the chaplain insisting that they would naturally desire some form of association by which they could perpetuate their experiences as soldiers of the Union, and at the same time cultivate such a spirit of loyalty that a rebellion would be impossible in this country in the future.[1]

Major Stephenson was deeply impressed by this suggestion, and appreciated the fact that an organization that would include all honorably discharged soldiers and sailors and the gallant officers who commanded them, whose fundamental principles were fraternity, loyalty, and charity, would be far-reaching in its benefits, the important point being to formulate a ritual that would serve the high and noble purposes they had in mind for such an organization. After a long correspondence Chaplain Rutledge went to Springfield to consult with Major Stephenson and to read the rough draught that Major Stephenson had prepared. In March 1866, a conference was held in that city. To this conference, under bonds of secrecy, they invited Colonel J. M. Snyder, Doctor James Hamilton, Major Robert M. Woods, Major Robert Allen, Colonel Martin Flood, Colonel Daniel Grass, Colonel Edward Prince, Captain John S. Phelps, Captain John A. Lightfoot, Colonel B. F. Smith, Major A. A. North, Captain Henry F. Howe, and Lieutenant B. F. Hawkes (since colonel).

Captain John S. Phelps was so enthusiastic over the proposition that he worked untiringly with Major Stephenson in perfecting the ritual, charter, and by-laws for the order. It is possible that the name was suggested by an organization that bore the name of "The Grand Army of Progress" which was then in existence. The printing of the ritual was guarded so sacredly that the committee took it to Decatur, Illinois, so that they might put it into the hands of reliable friends whom [*sic*] they knew would join them, and who would not allow the matter to get out until they were ready to urge the formation of posts. Seeing the magnificent future of the order, the friends in Decatur determined to apply to Major Stephenson for a charter, and through him to organize the first post in that city. The 6th of April 1866, Major Stephenson, by virtue of his authority as departmental commander of Illinois, having been so elected at the first meeting in Springfield, went to Decatur and, assisted by Captain Phelps, organized the first post of the Grand Army of the Republic, the charter members being Captain M. F. Kana, Major G. R. Steele, Captain George H. Cunning, General Isaac C. Pugh, Major John H. Hale, Captain J. T. Bishop, Captain Christian Riebsame, Doctor J. W. Routh, Doctor B. F. Sibley, Isaac N. Coltrin, Sergeant J. M. Prior, and Lieutenant Aquilla Toland, all of whom had been in the service of their country and were keenly alive to the importance of the order as is shown by the Declaration of Principles expressed in the constitution of the Grand Army of the Republic, in the following heroic language:

Declaration of Principles

Article I. Section I. The soldiers of the Volunteer Army of the United States during the Rebellion of 1861–65, actuated by the impulses and convictions of patriotism and of eternal right, and combined in the strong bands of fellowship and unity by the toils, the dangers, and the victories of a long and vigorously waged war, feel themselves called upon to declare in definite form of words and in determined co-operative action those principles and rules which should guide the earnest patriot, the enlightened freedman, and the Christian citizen in his course of action, and to agree upon those plans and laws which should govern them in a united and systematic working method with which, in some measure, shall be effected the preservation of the grand results of the war, the fruits of their labor and toil, so as to benefit the deserving and worthy.

Section 2. The results which are designed to be accomplished by this organization are as follows:

1st. The preservation of those kind and fraternal feelings which have bound together, with the strong chords of love and affection, the comrades in arms of many battles, sieges, and marches.

2d. To make these ties available in works and ties of kindness, of favor, and material aid to those in need of assistance.

3d. To make provision where it is not already done for the support, care, and education of soldiers' orphans, and for the maintenance of the widows of deceased soldiers.

4th. For the protection and assistance of disabled soldiers, whether disabled by wounds, sickness, old age, or misfortune.

5th. For the establishment and defence of the late soldiery of the United States, morally, socially, and politically, with a view to inculcate a proper appreciation of their services to the country, and to a recognition of such services and claims by the American people.

At a subsequent national encampment, an additional section to Article I was added:

Section 6. The maintenance of true allegiance to the United States of America based upon paramount respect for and fidelity to the national Constitution and laws manifested by the discountenancing of whatever may tend to weaken loyalty, incite to insurrection, treason, or rebellion, or in any manner impair the efficiency and permanency of our free institutions, together with a defence of universal liberty, equal right, and justice to all men.

Following the organization of the posts at Decatur and Springfield, a call was made for a grand convention at Springfield for the launching of the Grand Army of the Republic. It was held July 12, 1866, and was largely attended by ex-Union officers and soldiers. This convention gave its unqualified indorsement to the plans formulated by Major Stephenson and his co-workers. They provided for the first national encampment, which was held at Indianapolis, November 20, 1866. General S. A. Hurlbut was elected commander-in-chief. The senior and junior vice-commanders, subordinate officers, and a council of administration were elected, and the order formally launched in its great work.

For some reason the national encampment was not called in 1867, but met in Philadelphia January 15, 1868, when General John A. Logan was elected commander-in-chief. As was his wont, he threw his whole soul into the work and, after a conference with the officers then elected and the council of administration, proceeded to encourage the extending of the order and increasing its good works. He established national headquarters in Washington, and drew around him an able staff.

General Logan was thrice elected commander-in-chief, and no service of his whole life was more satisfactory than that given in behalf of his comrades at arms. The destinies of the Grand Army have been presided over by the truest and the best. From its very inception the Grand Army of the Republic was destined to a great and noble work and to supply a place in the desires of patriotic men that no other had been able to do. The provision eschewing politics and religion and providing for the banding together under the most sacred secret obligations to work together for the defence of their country, for the alleviation of each other's woes, for the uplifting and betterment of each other and those dependent upon them, touched a responsive chord in the heart of every soldier, who knew by experience that every man who signed such an obligation would be true to it. The plan for the organization of posts in every hamlet, town, and city, and to unite them in departments in every State, and once a year to meet in a grand national encampment, would insure the perpetuity of their comradeship. The post would supply the place of the soldier's regiment; the convention of the department of the State his corps; and the national encampment that of the army to which he belonged. At the camp-fires of these meetings he could live over again scenes which were burned into his memory by the heat of battle. He would have a resource in every dilemma that might overtake him through life, and friends to succor him in sickness and misfortune and who would follow him to the grave when he was finally mustered out. The ritual appealed so strongly to the men that to-day, nearly fifty years after the war, the Grand Army of the Republic is many thousands strong. It has borne upon its rolls more than 300,000 ex-Union soldiers.[2] It has expended thousands of dollars in charity for its members and their families. To the Grand Army of the Republic more than to any other order do the unfortunate look for aid. If a comrade is sick, he sends to his post for sympathy and help. If he seeks employment, he can rely upon his comrades to vouch for him. He knows that when the end comes he will be laid to rest by the members of his post, and that a stone will mark his last resting-place, and that it will never be reared in a potter's field. He knows that each recurring 30th of May flowers will be strewn above the low green mounds where sleep the loyal dead.

It is a curious fact that the genius who was the author of so magnificent an organization should have been in his last days one of the very unfortunates for whom he was so solicitous in his days of prosperity. Overtaken by misfortune and an ill-starred fate, Major Stephenson, after years of discouragement, died and was buried at Rock Creek, Menard County, Illinois, August 30, 1871, though scarcely at the zenith of his manhood. August 29, 1882, Estill Post 71, Grand Army of the Republic, Department of Illinois, removed Major Stephenson's remains to Petersburgh, Illinois, and reinterred them among the soldiers of Rose Hill Cemetery with impressive ceremonies, thus rescuing him from the oblivion of an unmarked grave. A few years ago the national organization of the Grand Army of the Republic erected a monument to his memory in Washington.

In their stupendous work of succoring the suffering, comforting the living, caring for the dying and the dead, the Grand Army of the Republic has far exceeded the work of any other organization of the same age the world has ever known. In the cultivation of a spirit of patriotism it has accomplished more than has been done by any other methods ever adopted. The rush to enlist for the Spanish-American War and for service in the Philippines attests the patriotism of all American citizens from whatever section or nationality they may have sprung. This influence in retrospect doubtless inspired the organization of the Sons and Daughters of the American Revolution and other kindred societies. It is probably not too much to say that had there been a Grand Army of the Republic at the close of the War of the Revolution, there never would have been any War of the Rebellion. Fraternal ties in the interest of patriotism would have prevented the growth of sectionalism.

Realizing that a time would come when the last ex-Union soldier would lie down to peaceful slumber, a wise provision has been made for the perpetuation of the spirit and principles of the Grand Army of the Republic by the formation of the Society of Sons of Veterans, who are pledged:

> To keep green the memories of our fathers, and their services for the maintenance of the Union. To aid the members of the Grand Army of the Republic in caring for their helpless and disabled veterans. To extend aid and protection to the widows and orphans. To perpetuate the memory in history of their heroic deeds and the proper observance of Memorial Day. To inculcate patriotism and love of country, not only among our membership, but among all the people of the land, and to spread and sustain the doctrines of equal rights, universal liberty, and justice to all.

Thus we see another result of the inculcation of the principles of patriotic devotion to the land of our nativity or adoption, and can rest secure for the eternal preservation of a government that guarantees to its people the protection of life, liberty, and the pursuit of happiness. In executing their deeds of local charity the Grand Army of the Republic found they must call to their assistance the good and loyal women. There were innumerable cases where only a woman could minister to the unfortunate; hence almost every post has auxiliaries in the persons of noble women who do as much as the members of the posts for the helpless and indigent. In 1883, at the national encampment of the Grand Army, held at Denver, Colorado, such glorious women as Florence Barker of Massachusetts, Kate B. Sherwood of Ohio, Annie Wittenmyer of Pennsylvania, Mrs. L. A. Turner of Massachusetts, Clara Barton, and a score of others organized the Woman's Relief Corps as auxiliary to the Grand Army of the Republic. Since the time of the organization of this corps, the parent society has had to look well to its honors, as these noble women have raised and distributed their hundreds of thousands of dollars; built homes for the indigent widows, mothers, and daughters of ex-soldiers, and in all respects have performed heroic benevolent service. They have borne upon their rolls the names of gifted and famous women, and perhaps have had the largest membership of any benevolent society ever organized.

Their management of the enormous sums of money coming into the treasuries of the national and local corps has commanded the highest encomiums from the ablest financiers of the country, assuring the continuation of this great society of patriotic women, who in turn will be succeeded by the Daughters of Veterans, their worthy auxiliary.

Soon after Vice-President Johnson had assumed the reins of government murmurings were heard from every quarter of his disaffection toward the reconstruction plans of the party in power. It was feared by many that, upon the principle that "blood is thicker than water," Mr. Johnson would allow his Southern blood to influence him to such an extent that he would surrender everything that had been won to the parties late in rebellion, and for whom, notwithstanding their persecution of himself and family during the war, he had suddenly conceived the most intense infatuation.[3]

I have vivid recollections of the stirring events which occurred during the session of Congress which convened December 1867, at which time there were grave apprehensions over reconstruction. The political rivalries of the summer had intensified the partisan feeling. States lately in rebellion, seeing their advantage in the sympathy of the administration, were clamorous for rehabilitation in all their forfeited rights. The domination of the ignorant colored people, and their unfitness for a proper use of hitherto unknown privileges; their pliancy, in many instances, in the hands of unscrupulous men; the resentment and ugly spirit of the native Southerners toward all who came among them to make their homes in the Southern States; the absence of slaves to do their bidding, and the galling necessity that they must work like the hated "Northern mudsills," made the situation deplorable. It was a serious problem how these seemingly irreconcilable elements were to be harmonized and made to dwell in peace together, until Congress should pass a general law under which the seceded States could again take part in the Government.

Disagreement waxed hotter and hotter between the Republican party and President Johnson over the policy adopted by Mr. Johnson, and a serious conflict ensued. Congress, then Republican by a large majority, preferred articles of impeachment against Johnson and spent much time in an unsuccessful effort to convict him. During these long, eventful months Mr. Johnson, in a spirit of resentment as much as of clemency toward the criminals, pardoned a great many who had been convicted of various treasonable offences, reaching a climax during the last few days of his administration by the pardoning of Spangler and Arnold, conspirators in the assassination of Mr. Lincoln, who were then confined on the Dry Tortugas. The remains of Henry Wirz, the keeper of Andersonville prison, were surrendered to his friend Louis Schade who caused them to be interred at Mount Olivet Cemetery, in the District of Columbia, the 3d of March 1869. They were exhumed from the ground floor of Warehouse No. 2 of the arsenal.

About the same date the family of John Wilkes Booth secured an order from President Johnson for the surrender of Booth's body through his brother Edwin Booth, another famous tragedian of this illustrious family of actors. John T. Ford, owner of Ford's Theatre, who had suffered much on account of his supposed complicity in the assassination of Mr. Lincoln, but had succeeded in vindicating himself without any break in his friendship with the Booths, aided materially in bringing about the interview between Edwin Booth and President Johnson which resulted in the President making the order that the remains should be given to Edwin Booth's representatives. Mr. Booth was then playing an engagement in Baltimore and, while he had never visited Washington, nor could be induced to play at any of the theatres at the capital after his brother's mad act, came quickly to carry out his desire of recovering his brother's body and to inter it in the burial lot of the Booth family, in Greenmount Cemetery, Baltimore, Maryland. On what was to him a melancholy day he waited in the front room of the undertaking establishment of Harvey & Marr, then on F Street in the city of Washington, while a Baltimore undertaker, who had performed the service of undertaker for the Booths many times previously, Mr. Jacob H. Weaver and R. F. Harvey went to the arsenal, armed with the President's order for the body. The officer in charge promptly obeyed, causing a detail of soldiers to assist in exhuming and transporting the body to the wagon provided by Mr. Harvey, to whose establishment it was taken, where it was identified by Edwin Booth, and subsequently taken to Baltimore and buried privately beside his kindred. So carefully was the transfer made and so discreet was every one who had to be intrusted with the matter, that even the alert newspaper reporters failed to get a hint of the disinterment and removal of the body of the assassin until some time afterward. That these are the facts there is no doubt, though there is no record of the matter unless Mr. Weaver or his descendants have one, but up to this time none has ever been made public. Mr. Harvey died some years ago, but unfortunately the records of his business could never be found by his son, his successor. Public feeling at that time was so strong against every one connected with the conspiracy and the assassination that Mr. Johnson was execrated for these acts. Had it been known at the time, there might have been violent opposition to the execution of his orders for the surrendering of Booth's body. Fortunately time has softened the bitterness and cooled the passions of the people, and to-day there would be no opposition to the surrendering of the lifeless body of so great a criminal as John Wilkes Booth to those dear to him by the ties of nature after he had paid the penalty of his crime. There is probably not a single survivor of that appalling conspiracy or any one living who participated in the capture, trial, conviction, and punishment of the conspirators, or the restoration of their bodies to their relatives and friends.

Mr. Johnson conceived the idea that Mr. Stanton, Secretary of War under Lincoln, was inimical to the consummation of his designs, and decided that he would remove Stanton from his position. The party resented this step indignantly and insisted on Mr. Stanton remaining. The President as vigorously demanded that he should vacate his office until the matter became so serious that the President threatened forcible ejectment. At the request of his party Mr. Stanton remained continuously in the War Department, having a bed placed in his private office and his meals served there also lest, during his absence after office hours, the President should install General Lorenzo Thomas as Secretary of War, as he threatened to do.[4] General Grant, then General of the Army, was consulted as to calling out the troops, but happily, he advised against such a step. At that time General Logan was commander-in-chief of the Grand Army of the Republic and, realizing the delicacy of the situation, he called the members of the organization together secretly, there being many ex-Union officers and soldiers employed in the departments in Washington at that time. He formed battalions and placed them under the command of efficient officers. Sentinels in citizens' dress were on duty every hour of the day and night, especially in the vicinity of the White House and the old War Department building. Countersigns were given and signals agreed upon for an emergency, should it be necessary to protect Mr. Stanton. General Logan occupied a cot beside Secretary Stanton in the War Department, so that he could summon the Grand Army at a moment's notice.

During the imbroglio between Mr. Johnson and Congress, the greatest excitement since the assassination of President Lincoln prevailed. Every day startling announcements were made of the President's overt acts and of the resentment of Congress. The climax was reached when Brevet Brigadier-General Lorenzo Thomas was arrested on the charge of attempted usurpation of authority that did not belong to him as adjutant-general of the War Department. He was released on a bond of five thousand dollars, signed by a Mr. George R. Hall and Elias A. Eliason. President Johnson irritated Congress further by sending in the name of General Lorenzo Thomas for Lieutenant-General. He was not confirmed.

The warfare continued until articles of impeachment of President Johnson were prepared and presented in the House of Representatives. General Logan being chosen one of the managers on the part of the House, he was wholly engrossed with the case for many weeks, scarcely leaving our rooms except to attend the sessions of the House and, although they were unsuccessful, General Logan demonstrated his great ability as lawyer and statesman and has left on record an unanswerable argument for the prosecution. I was deeply interested in everything transpiring and spent many hours of the day and night hunting up authorities, marking paragraphs in law-reports and the newspapers which had any bearing on impeachment cases. This work, in addition to the care of my two children, receiving calls, returning visits, accepting and declining invitations kept me busy. I was, however, very happy as I enjoyed the interesting people who came as visitors and those who were temporary or permanent residents of the capital.

During the winter and spring the political excitement that invariably precedes a presidential campaign grew to a white heat, the Republican party almost unanimously desiring General Grant as the nominee for the presidency. The assembling of the national convention, the presenting of General Grant's name by General Logan, and Grant's unanimous nomination by the convention, with Schuyler Colfax as Vice-President, were brief affairs. With the overwhelming majority of the Republican party north of the Mason and Dixon line at that time, it would be superfluous to add that they were both elected at the November election of 1868.

Socially the winter of 1867 and 1868 was as brilliant as possible under the circumstances. Mr. Johnson's family were much out of health and though his charming daughters, Mrs. Stover and Mrs. Patterson, did all in their power, they were unable to dispel the gloom that ever overhangs a discordant administration. With the executive out of harmony with his party, it made it doubly hard for the cabinet to keep up social good feeling, notwithstanding the fact that Secretaries Seward, McCulloch, Browning, Randall, Welles, and General Grant as General of the Army, gave the regulation receptions and dinners. They were magnificent affairs, and under serene political skies would have been happy events. Many of the private entertainments were on a grand scale.

Senator and Mrs. Pomeroy of Kansas gave delightful parties, dinners, and receptions, as did also General and Mrs. Butler.[5] One magnificent party given by General and Mrs. Butler in their home on the corner of I and Fifteenth Streets on the occasion of the début of their daughter, Miss Blanche, has scarcely been rivalled by the superb affairs of later years. The house was decorated profusely with the rarest flowers of the season. The soulless, scentless camellias were then the fad. Thousands of these flowers, whose petals will not bear the slightest touch, were arranged in every conceivable shape, while ferns and palms made the whole house a bower. Everybody of any distinction was there and was loath to leave when the wee sma' hours announced the near approach of the dawn of another day.

Mr. Sumner gave many of his superb dinners where delicate viands lost their flavor in comparison with the "feast of reason and flow of soul" all enjoyed who sat at his board.[6] It is a melancholy thought that the march of time necessitates the removal of these historic houses. The dumb walls have not rehearsed for preservation the many occasions when, around Mr. Sumner's table, the most distinguished and cultured men and women of this and other lands have discussed the absorbing questions of the day. Under a recent arrangement by capitalists to erect a magnificent hotel on the grounds where once stood the Arlington, a conglomerate combination of the historic houses once the homes of Sumner, Reverdy Johnson, and [the] Hon. James A. Harlan, who was Mr. Lincoln's Secretary of the Interior and later senator from Iowa, these houses have been torn down and very soon these edifices and their illustrious occupants will be known no more.

Mr. Hooper of Massachusetts, who lived in a house on the corner of H and Fifteenth Streets, which has been supplanted by the Hotel Shoreham, also gave many delightful dinners, his inseparable friend, Mr. Sumner usually being one of the guests. I remember once, at a dinner given by General and Mrs. Butler, to have had the honor of Mr. Sumner's escort to the table, and shall ever recall it as one of the most delightful dinners of my life though I have long since forgotten all about what we had to eat. So charming was Mr. Sumner in conversation that the three hours we sat at the table in those days slipped by all too quickly.

February 1, 1868, Dickens came to Washington to give readings from his own inimitable writings. There was not a suitable auditorium in the city at that time and Mr. Dolby, agent for Dickens, could only secure old Carroll Hall which was formerly on F Street, between Ninth and Tenth Streets. Mr. Quimby of Detroit, Michigan, a devoted friend of General Logan, invited the general and myself to accompany him for the series. They were a rare treat. Notwithstanding Mr. Dickens's monotonous style of reading, the innate drollery of the man, manifested in his intonations and gestures, made his readings very interesting. Beginning February 6 with *Doctor Marigold* and the trial scene from *Pickwick*, he also read extracts from *Nicholas Nickleby*, *Old Curiosity Shop*, *Martin Chuzzlewit*, *Dombey and Son* and *The Christmas Carol*, using precisely the same intonations for every character, whether pathetic or comic.

During his stay he was entertained by Charles Sumner and many other distinguished people, enjoying particularly walking about the city at night with Captain Kelly, Charles Sumner, and Mr. Stanton. He was the guest of Sir Edward Thornton, the English minister, who had succeeded Sir Frederick Bruce on the death of that illustrious diplomat. Dickens carried away, as a result of his readings in America, thirteen thousand dollars, then considered a fabulous sum. At the time of his first visit, 1847, he had given much offence to the people of this country by his criticisms of America and Americans, and by his drastic description in *Martin Chuzzlewit* of Cairo, Illinois, and the swamps of that section, which, he declared, caused even the frogs to shake with the ague.

It is a curious coincidence that his son should have come to the United States so lately to deliver lectures, and that he should have been invited to Cairo, Illinois, in order to counteract, even at this late date, the impression which *Martin Chuzzlewit* had created of Cairo. He was royally entertained in that city and subsequently addressed a letter to the mayor that did him great credit. Unfortunately, the brilliant son of a brilliant father died in New York at the close of his tour.

It is not too much to say that the prima donnas, actresses, and actors of that time were greater artistes than those of to-day. The operas were finer, and the plays which came under the head of legitimate drama were of a higher order than those presented in these latter days. Washington was favored by the engagements of Adelina Patti, Brignoli, Ritter, Cellini, Boetti, and Herr Hermanus. Ole Bull gave two concerts during the winter. Parepa Rosa, cantatrice, gave two grand concerts in Metezrott Hall during January. Mrs. Scott Siddons, granddaughter of the great Siddons, appeared at the National with a fine company in Shakespeare's plays. Kate Bateman, John Owen, Sothern, and many other celebrated actors and actresses made the amusements for the winter delightful, the theatres being crowded every night.

General and Mrs. Grant were the recipients of much attention; you met them everywhere. General John A. Rawlins,

General Dent, Mrs. Grant's brother, General Badeau—later General Grant's biographer—General Comstock, General Horace Porter, General O. E. Babcock, all members of General Grant's staff, often accompanied the general. General Grant's friends had presented to him the house on I Street, owned and occupied by the late Matthew Emery. The large parlors of that palatial mansion were inadequate to accommodate the numbers who were eager to pay their respects at every recurrent reception day of Mrs. Grant. All their children were at home then and the survivors of that time remember the charming household. With General and Mrs. Grant in the centre, Fred, the eldest son and the most like his illustrious father, Ulysses, Jr., Nellie with her sweet face, her long hair hanging down her back and her beautiful eyes as gentle as those of a gazelle, and Jesse, the youngest, they are immortalized in the painting by Cogswell, known as "Grant and His Family."

In the Grant home on I Street, I witnessed one historic gathering which will ever be most vivid in my mind. After the nomination of Grant and Colfax at Chicago, the committee appointed to wait upon them and notify them of their nomination was composed of J. R. Hawley of Connecticut, Lewis Barker of Maine, C. N. Riottet of Texas, Willard Warner of Alabama, J. M. Hedrik of Iowa, John Evans of Colorado, S. M. Cullom of Illinois, R. T. Van Horn of Missour, J. K. Dubois of Illinois, T. L. Tullock of Virginia, J. W. Holden of North Carolina, T. F. Lee of North Carolina, W. C. Goodloe of Kentucky, Valentine Dill of Arkansas, J. H. Harris of North Carolina, A. McDonald of Arkansas, B. F. Rice of Arkansas, H. A. Pierce of Virginia, and others. They came to Washington and it was arranged that Mr. Colfax should go to General Grant's house, and that the committee should call upon them there. Mrs. Grant kindly advised a few special friends, inviting them to be present. General Logan and I were among the fortunate number. We reached the Grant home about eight o'clock, or a little after. Mr. Colfax, his distinguished mother, Mrs. Matthews, and his half-sister, Miss Matthews, arrived soon after followed by Mr. E. B. Washburn, Mr. Halsey of

New Jersey, and General Grant's staff—Generals Rawlins, Babcock, Dent, Badeau, and Colonel Comstock.

After exchanging greetings and pleasantries, General Grant was informed that the committee had arrived. He and Mr. Colfax moved to the rear of the parlor, and stood side by side while the committee was presented. Mrs. Grant and her venerable father, Mr. Dent, and Mrs. and Miss Matthews were not far from them. After the presentation, Governor Hawley, with all the power of his eloquence in his palmy days, made the speech on behalf of the committee, informing General Grant and Mr. Colfax that they had been chosen the standard-bearers of the Republican party for the campaign. General Grant had the same unpretentious bearing, so characteristic of him under all circumstances. His reply was very brief and that with much embarrassment, leaving Mr. Colfax, a fine speaker, to make the speech of acceptance for the nominees of the Republican party. The guests who were present stood about the group with rapt attention, feeling it a great privilege to have been present at such a ceremony. After it was over the party was invited into the dining-room where refreshments were served, and the company dispersed. Mrs. Grant was so cordial and unassuming, and received her guests with such simplicity of manner that she won all hearts. Every one went away quite as ready to be her champion as that of her husband, their chieftain.

While writing the names of the committee and the guests present that I remember, I am overwhelmed with the melancholy thought that so few remain of the conspicuous figures of that occasion.

The campaign of 1868 was probably the most enthusiastic of any since 1860. The ex-Union soldiers were everywhere wild with delight over the nomination of General Grant as the leader of the party. Every political demonstration was participated in by them. Flags, banners, patriotic music rendered by glee clubs and brass bands were the order of the day. The well-worn uniforms of the soldiers were donned for all such occasions, and it was not surprising that the November election witnessed the largest majorities ever polled by a party, nor that General Grant and Schuyler Colfax were elected overwhelmingly.[7]

When Congress assembled December 1, 1868, there was general rejoicing because it was thought there would be little trouble over reconstruction and other vexatious problems. The South felt that so magnanimous a conqueror as General Grant had shown himself would be their friend under the severe trials through which they must pass before they could again become a part and parcel of the compact they had tried to dissolve. You heard no mutterings from any quarter. Congress felt sure that now the die was cast, Mr. Johnson would not attempt further arbitrary action, but would probably finish his term in a quiet way. He gratified himself and vented his spleen on Congress for their attempted impeachment by pardoning every one he could, especially those who had been debarred from political rights because of participation in the rebellion. His proclamation covered such cases as those of Jefferson Davis, Slidell, Mason, Mann, and other exiles who hastened to return to the United States after having sought refuge across the seas.

He closed his career with a "Farewell Address," in which he arraigned all who opposed him and lauded himself in a most remarkable manner. After Congress reassembled, the Tenure of Office bill was repealed in time for Grant to make such changes as he thought important.

Reconstructive legislation continued, many of the States wishing to come back into the Union that they might reassume their relations to the Government and have representatives in both Houses of Congress; so, while they deemed Mr. Johnson powerless for harm, they pressed the work, well knowing that the new Congress, who would take their seats after the 4th of March 1869, would be so largely of one party that there might be delay in adjusting these questions. The opposition, recognizing this fact, in most cases acquiesced. At no time in the history of the Government have there been abler men in Congress than there were then. Among the senators were Sumner, Wade, Chandler, Morton, Fessenden, Conkling, Morgan, Sherman, Morrill, Voorhees, Trumbull, Anthony, and Wilson. In the House were Garfield, Colfax, Butler, Brooks, Bingham, Blaine, Shellabarger, Wilson, Allison, Cullom, Logan, Ames, Hooper, Washburne, Boutwell, Randall, and Voorhees. Such men were earnest, thoughtful, patriotic, and keenly alive to the interests of the country. They allowed nothing to pass that was in any sense questionable.

February 10, 1869 was a memorable day. It was gloomy and disagreeable, but that had no influence on the multitude that gathered at the Capitol to witness the counting of the electoral vote which was to declare Grant and Colfax President and Vice-President of the United States. Senator Wade of Ohio, vice-president of the Senate, and Mr. Colfax, then speaker of the House, were to preside over the joint session of the two Houses, which was to assemble in the House of Representatives. Tickets were necessary to procure admission to the galleries. By ten o'clock every available space was taken. The diplomatic gallery was occupied by the foreign representatives, including Sir Edward Thornton, Baron Gerolt, Blacque Bey, Mr. DeBille, and other distinguished foreigners who were much engrossed with American affairs. In the reserved galleries were Mrs. Grant, Mrs. Dent, Mrs. Sharp, members of General Grant's staff, Mrs. Matthews, Schuyler Colfax's mother, and his sister, wives and ladies of the Supreme Court, senators and members, and also many distinguished visitors in the city. On the motion of some member, permission was given to admit ladies on the floor in the rear of the members' seats. In a brief time every available spot was occupied. At twelve o'clock the House was called to order and the opening prayer was followed by some minor motions incident to the morning hours. The hour-hand pointed to one o'clock; the sergeant-at-arms, General Ordway, announced the presence of the Senate and their desire to be admitted. Preceded by Colonel Brown, sergeant-at-arms of the Senate, the whole body filed in and took the seats provided for them. The imperturbable Ben Wade, ascending the speaker's platform, took the presiding officer's chair with Mr. Colfax on his right. As soon as all were seated Mr. Wade took up the gavel and called the joint House to order. The clerk then proceeded to call the roll of States. As soon as the first contested State was reached, a discussion arose and the Senate withdrew to discuss the question separately.

After an hour and a half the Senate returned to continue the count. During the absence of the Senate, the members of the House discussed also the question of rights of States to cast their votes where an irregularity was charged, some of the members exhibiting much feeling. They had not gone far when they again got into a wrangle over the State of Georgia, General Butler leading in the attack upon Mr. Wade who, in the generosity of his heart, had recognized the gentleman from Massachusetts, not anticipating the muddle to which it would lead. A second withdrawal of the Senate was necessary and while they were out they determined that such proceedings should not continue, as it looked at one time as if the time prescribed by the Constitution might elapse before they could finish their work from which untold complications might arise. Consequently, upon the renewal of the motions by General Butler, a number of members arose to the defence of Mr. Wade and Mr. Colfax seized the gavel and restored order, declaring that the sergeant-at-arms would be called to his assistance if the disorder continued. After some further discussion the count was finished and the joint assembly adjourned.

General Logan was much excited over what he termed discourtesy to the revered Mr. Wade. It seemed to him outrageous that any member of that body should embarrass and confuse the venerable statesman in the closing hours of his long and faithful career. General Logan's castigation of Butler in as strong terms as parliamentary rules would allow elicited prolonged applause and contributed much to restoring order, securing for Mr. Wade the respect and consideration due to him. On adjournment it was most interesting to see the groups of men discussing the proceedings of the day, and to hear their denunciatory remarks on those who had attempted to delay the count and annoy Mr. Wade.

We were then living at Willard's Hotel. That evening about eight o'clock there was a knock on our parlor door, and in answer to the command to enter Mr. Wade walked in and, extending his hand to General Logan, he said: "Logan, God bless you; I have come here to thank you for coming to my rescue to-day when they attempted to crucify and mortify me. My blunder was in recognizing any one, after which I could do nothing but bull it through." He had his umbrella in his hands, and emphasized every word by striking it on the floor. In all respects he was a quaint figure, but so earnest and enthusiastic that he commanded the admiration of every one who came in contact with him. We prevailed on him to sit down and the memory of that visit will abide with me forever. He spoke with much emotion of his long service for the cause of human liberty. He said he retired to private life to spend the remnant of his days contentedly in the consciousness of having performed his duty to the best of his ability. He spoke most affectionately of Mr. Lincoln and was grateful his lines had been cast in the same epoch and that he had been able to do something to further the cause for which Mr. Lincoln had been martyred.

We heard much that winter of *Alabama* claims, the great methods of arbitration in international affairs, and other questions signifying that we were entering upon a wonderful era in human affairs; that, with the close of our rebellion, came a new order of things which was to mark the greatest progress in republicanism.[8]

Congress met the first Monday in December 1868. The gloom following the assassination of Mr. Lincoln by a madman, immediately upon the dawn of peace after four long years of fratricidal war, still hung like a pall over Washington. To this melancholy event was added the personal sorrow of very many who wore the habiliments of mourning for loved ones lost during the war. Mr. Johnson was naturally a serious man and was so overwhelmed by the grave responsibilities resting upon him in the trying position in which he was placed that it seemed as if the pall would never lift. Mrs. Johnson was an invalid and could do nothing to brighten the home of the President. Fortunately their daughters, Mrs. Stover and Mrs. Patterson, were typical Southern ladies with rare accomplishments, fascinating manners, and fine conversational powers. They appreciated keenly their social rank and were anxious to do everything possible to make the White House attractive and to have every one feel that it was the people's house, which they occupied temporarily. Therefore they extended a very cordial welcome to all who were entitled to be received.

In both houses of Congress there were many of the most distinguished men of the nation. In the Senate Hamlin, Sumner, Conkling, Fenton, Fessenden, Frelinghuysen, Booth, McDougall, Simon Cameron, Chandler, Howard, Kellogg, Morrill of Vermont, Morrill of Maine, Wilson, Boutwell, Bayard, Morton, Williams of Oregon, Yates, Trumbull, and others made it one of the ablest bodies that ever convened in any country. In the House there were Washburn, Logan, Cullom, Judd, Arnold, Singleton, Wentworth, Henderson, Farnsworth, Cook, Sherman, Schenck, Garfield, Grow, Shellabarger, Bingham, Archer, Thaddeus Stevens, Clymer, Williams, Colfax, Voorhees, Davis, Banks, Butler, Wheeler, Wood, Slocum, Brooks, Frye, Blaine, Hale, Boutwell, Allison, Wilson of Iowa, and a score of others who were leaders of men and statesmen in every sense of the word.

Before the Christmas holidays the breach between the President and Congress had widened so seriously that it was evident that the last days of Mr. Johnson's administration were to be full of friction and unpleasantness between himself and his party. As if in sympathy with the political situation, January 1, 1869 was one of the gloomiest of days; a cold rain fell all the night before and continued during New Year's Day. Every preparation, however, had been made for the reception at the White House.

The Marine Band, under the leadership of the well-remembered Professor Scala, was in its accustomed place. The President, his daughters, Mrs. Stover and Mrs. Patterson, and Miss Cohen of Tennessee, assisted by one or two of the ladies of the cabinet, received the callers. Secretary Seward presented the Diplomatic Corps and their ladies, all of whom appeared in regal costume; the gentlemen were in full court dress, wearing all their orders. Stately Sir Edward Thornton and gracious Lady Thornton led the column in which followed M. Bethemy, the French minister; M. Blacque Bey, the Turkish minister;

Baron Gerolt of Prussia and his lovely wife and beautiful daughters; Mr. DeBille, the Danish minister and his charming wife; Don José Antonio Garcia of Peru; and the whole list of the distinguished diplomats then in Washington. This was Mr. Seward's last appearance at a New Year's reception and, as many looked upon him as the last of Mr. Lincoln's cabinet, they felt a pang of regret that in so brief a time every representative of that administration should have gone out forever. The diplomatic corps was followed by the Supreme Court, headed by Chief Justice Chase, Associate Justices Nelson, Clifford, Davis, Miller, Strong, Swayne—all now gone to another world with the majority of the throng that surged through the White House that dreary day.

The cabinet was well represented, Secretary Stanton alone being absent. Secretaries Welles, McCulloch, Browning, Stanberry, P. M. G. Randall were there, each contributing his best efforts to the pleasure of every one. Very few of the Senate and House appeared—Senators Sprague, Dixon, Doolittle, Grimes, Trumbull, Ross, and a few others attended; of the House there were even fewer who paid their respects.

The army, led by General Grant and a long list of military officers, presented an imposing appearance, as also the officers of the navy following Admirals Farragut and Porter. There were then a number of officers of both branches of the service in Washington who had but recently been relieved from active duty. The bureau officers, different organizations, and privileged persons had scarcely passed the President when a fearful crowd from the streets pushed their way in, their feet muddy, and their clothing dripping with the rain in which they had been standing outside. The President encouraged their coming and very soon the reception became a motley surging crowd to the disgust of dignified people.

Mr. Johnson's cabinet, Mr. Seward, Mr. McCulloch, Mr. Stanton, Mr. Welles, Mr. Browning, Mr. Randall, and Mr. Stanberry were all men of national reputation. Their families were, without exception, charming people who enjoyed conforming to all the social requirements of their positions. They gave dinners, luncheon parties, afternoon and evening receptions, and made their guests feel they were pleased to see them.

No one ever heard the wives of those officials say they were "bored to death by callers" or that they "despised society." Their entertainments were beautiful and on a scale of magnificence equal to those of the moneyed kings of to-day, who claim to rival Belshazzar's feasts in their extravagant entertainments which are, as a rule, ordered from caterers and decorators and have few personal touches displaying the taste of the hosts or anything that betrays the delightful hospitality of a real home.

The most refined people came to Washington every winter, because of the opportunity to meet celebrities. It was a pleasure to take these visitors to pay their respects to officials and their families, of whom all loyal Americans were justly proud. Every one was assured of a cordial welcome, the recipients appreciating the honor conferred upon them by those calls. No one was made to feel he was an intruder; neither did any one presume upon the courtesy extended to him. If the cabinet ladies felt their duties irksome, they were too well bred or too diplomatic to betray their feelings.

Chief Justice Chase, in his then considered palatial home on the corner of Fifth and F Streets, gave royal dinners and parties. His daughters, Mrs. Kate Chase Sprague and Miss Nettie Chase, both fascinating and brilliant women, presided over the home of the chief justice and made it one of the most attractive in the city. Here eminent statesmen and learned men and women of the time were dined and entertained with lavish hospitality. Justices Miller, Strong, and Swayne, and their attractive families gave many social functions in their spacious homes, where one met persons who were interesting and celebrated on account of their achievements.

It may be imaginary but when one recalls the resplendent social affairs given by Sir Edward and Lady Thornton, the French minister, the German minister Baron Gerolt, Mr. DeBille, the Danish minister, Mr. Zamacona, the Mexican minister, the Garcias of Peru, and others of the Diplomatic Corps, one feels that diplomatic hospitality was more brilliant and frequent than it is in these days of boundless prosperity and greater cordiality between all nations and the United States.

Many of the senators and members of Congress were men of wealth for that epoch who entertained lavishly in their own homes. It was rare that their dinners were cooked by caterers. They lived well every day and a dinner was to them merely a question of what guests they desired to invite. Mr. Sumner's dinners, as I have already said, were famous. The most delicious viands lost their flavor when compared with the intellectual feast that all enjoyed who sat at his board. Mr. Hooper, his most intimate friend, vied with Mr. Sumner in dinner-giving and in the choosing of brilliant people. The Frelinghuysens, with three lovely young ladies in the house, General and Mrs. Butler with their charming daughter Blanche, afterward Mrs. Ames, were delightful hosts who enjoyed having their friends. General and Mrs. Grant, Admiral and Mrs. Porter, and very many more gave superb dinners and receptions that were no less resplendent than those given every winter since. There was a charm about the dinners given in those days which, it must be admitted, does not characterize such gatherings now. They were less formal but there was more sincere cordiality than is manifested in latter-day social functions.

On account of the political imbroglios which Mr. Johnson was unfortunate enough to precipitate, the state dinners, though given punctiliously, were not especially enjoyable. With the President out of harmony with his party, no amount of feminine tact could keep the sparks from flying, especially when the poles were in such close proximity as a dinner-table necessitates.

However, President Johnson's daughters, with consummate tact, decided to give a brilliant and memorable social function in the White House which would not be clouded by any political collisions or awkward coupling of guests. The grandchildren of President Johnson, Frank Johnson, Andrew Stover, Sallie and Lillie Stover were all very attractive. Mrs. Stover, a most charming woman, conceived the idea of converting the staid old mansion into fairy-land and filling it with the fairies that inhabit every city, in this way hoping to avoid the unpleasant meeting of political rivals. Invitations of the most formal character were issued two weeks or more before the affair was to occur. Every child honored by one was in a great state of excitement lest his costume should not be gorgeous enough for such a grand occasion. Indulgent mammas exhausted every resource in designing and providing the bewildering fairylike garments which were often provided with wings that the children might have the true resemblance to elves. The decorators made the corridors, east room, and parlors bowers of vines and flowers that the little creatures might disport themselves in a veritable fairy-land.

Professors Marini and Bates prepared the grand promenade, fairy dances, and music for the occasion. "Mammas" and "papas" were invited to accompany the children, so that the company was very large. The children of the White House received their guests in the blue room, thence passing into the green room, the doors of which were closed so that none might enter the east room before the procession. The hours were from six to eleven. It was nearly seven o'clock when Frank Johnson and Sally Stover headed the procession, keeping time to the lovely music. After them came the numerous couples who had assembled in the blue and green rooms and who were to take part in the dance in the east room.

A more enchanting scene was never witnessed in the White House. Nellie, Ulysses, and Jesse Grant, the Barneses and McCullochs, the Wallachs, the Blairs, children of the Diplomatic Corps, and many others from the families of officials and citizens made a bright picture with their gay dresses and pretty faces, while their merry laughter rang out above the strains of delightful music. At the proper time President Johnson, surrounded by fairy queens, led the way to the state dining-room, where the long table, spread with every delicacy, refreshed them after they had danced and promenaded to their hearts' content. The Italian minister, Chevalier Cerruti, although a bachelor, had given a charming children's party previously, he himself crowning Nellie Grant queen of the evening. Thus the little people had that winter two wonderfully pretty parties.

The winter was so full of stirring events that it passed

quickly, and yet every one was impatient for the 4th of March and the inauguration of General Grant and Schuyler Colfax as President and Vice-President. Mr. Johnson, his family, and cabinet longed to be released from the continual bickerings and warfare between the President and Congress that had reached and passed the pitch of an "impeachment trial" of the President by Congress. The trial only failed by one vote to result in conviction, but to all intents and purposes convicted the President of bad faith to his party, and placed him in a humiliating position before the nation, causing him and his family to long for the seclusion of his home in Tennessee.

General Logan had made an engagement for both himself and me to accompany Colonel Charles L. Wilson of Chicago, editor of the *Journal* of that city, to visit the battle-fields of Virginia and the city of Richmond in March 1868. Colonel Wilson came on accompanied by his niece Miss Anna Wilson and the young lady to whom he was engaged, Miss Farrar of Boston. However, it so happened that there were such important matters before Congress that General Logan could not go. The colonel, however, insisted that I with my two children, our daughter Dollie and baby son John A. Logan, Jr., should carry out the plan of our visit.

We arrived in Richmond on a cold bleak day in March, to find the hotel in a very wretched condition. As it was so soon after the war, we were prepared to find evidences of the rebellion everywhere. The colonel had great difficulty in finding an equipage to drive over the battle-fields around Richmond. He particularly wanted to go to Libby Prison, and to inspect the fortifications that had afforded defence for the capital of the Confederacy for so many long months. I shall never forget the poor horses, the well-worn carriage, and the miserable-looking white man, accompanied by a boy about thirteen years of age, who sat on the box. We had, fortunately, brought lap-robes, cloaks, and warm robes, expecting the weather to be disagreeable. Driving about over the battle-field, we saw the colored people picking up the bullets and pieces of shell which afforded them quite a livelihood immediately after the war. Foundry men had established agencies around all these fortified cities to buy up exploded shrapnel-shells, broken cannon and Minie balls, and every species of old iron that was so abundant on these battle-fields. Driving about from place to place, we were greatly interested, and realized more than we ever could have, had we not visited the city immediately after the war, the horrors through which the people of the Confederacy had passed. I remember hearing the poor little boy, who was so thinly clad that he had little to protect him from the inclemency of the weather, call out to the driver: "Well, it isn't so miserably hot to-day, is it?" At the same time his teeth were chattering in his head with the cold from which he was suffering. We were not long in finding that we could do without one of the lap-robes, which we insisted that the poor child should wrap around his shivering body.

During this trip we visited the churchyards and cemeteries at Richmond, Petersburg, and other points made historic by the struggle which had taken place in and around these cities. In the churchyard near Petersburg we saw hundreds of the graves of Confederate soldiers. These graves had upon them small bleached Confederate flags and faded flowers and wreaths that had been laid upon them by loving hands on the occasion of their Decoration Day.

Upon our return General Logan was much interested in our account of what we had seen and I remarked to him that I had never been so touched as I was by seeing the little flags and the withered flowers that had been laid on these graves. At this General Logan said that it was a beautiful revival of the custom of the ancients in thus preserving the memory of the dead, and that he, as commander-in-chief of the Grand Army of the Republic, would issue an order for the decoration of the graves of Union soldiers. Colonel Wilson, heartily approving of the plan, said that he would be glad to exploit it in his paper in Chicago. General Logan sent for General Chipman, then adjutant-general of the Grand Army of the Republic, and dictated Order No. 11, for the first decoration of the graves of Union soldiers that ever took place in the United States, as follows:

HEADQUARTERS GRAND ARMY OF THE REPUBLIC,
Adjutant-General's Office, 446 Fourteenth St.,
WASHINGTON, D. C., *May* 5, 1868.

General Orders }
No. 11. }

I. The 30th day of May 1868, is designated for the purpose of strewing with flowers or otherwise decorating the graves of comrades who died in defence of their country during the late rebellion, and whose bodies now lie in almost every city, village, and hamlet churchyard in the land. In this observance no form of ceremony is prescribed, but posts and comrades will in their own way arrange such fitting services and testimonials of respect as circumstances may permit.

We are organized, comrades, as our regulations tell us, for the purpose, among other things, "of preserving and strengthening those kind and fraternal feelings which have bound together the soldiers, sailors, and marines who united to suppress the late rebellion." What can aid more to assure this result than by cherishing tenderly the memory of our heroic dead, who made their breasts a barricade between our country and its foes? Their soldier lives were the reveille of freedom to a race in chains, and their deaths the tattoo of rebellious tyranny in arms. We should guard their graves with sacred vigilance. All that the consecrated wealth and taste of the nation can add to their adornment and security is but a fitting tribute to the memory of her slain defenders. Let no wanton foot tread rudely on such hallowed grounds. Let pleasant paths invite the coming and going of reverent visitors and fond mourners. Let no vandalism or avarice or neglect, no ravages of time, testify to the present or to the coming generations, that we have forgotten as a people the cost of a free and undivided Republic.

If other eyes grow dull, and other hands slack, and other hearts cold in the solemn trust, ours shall keep it well as long as the light and warmth of life remain to us.

Let us, then, at the time appointed, gather around their sacred remains, and garland the passionless mounds above them with the choicest flowers of spring-time; let us raise above them the dear old flag they saved from dishonor; let us in this solemn presence renew our pledges to aid and assist those whom they have left among us, a sacred charge upon a nation's gratitude —the soldier's and sailor's widow and orphan.

II. It is the purpose of the Commander-in-Chief to inaugurate this observance with the hope that it will be kept up from year to year, while a survivor of the war remains to honor the memory of his departed comrades. He earnestly desires the public press to call attention to this order, and lend its friendly aid in bringing it to the notice of comrades in all parts of the country in time for simultaneous compliance therewith.

III. Department Commanders will use every effort to make this order effective.

By order of— JOHN A. LOGAN,
Commander-in-Chief

Official:
WM. T. COLLINS, *A. A. G.* N. P. CHIPMAN,
Adjutant-General.

After much discussion and investigation as to the time of the year when flowers would be in their greatest perfection in the different sections of the country, it was decided that May 30 would probably be the most appropriate time when this ceremony should take place. General Logan's anticipations were fully realized by the universal observance of the day in every State in the Union. The exercises were characterized by patriotic addresses, recitations, music, and ceremonious decoration of the soldiers' graves with flowers. Almost all loyal people participated in the observance of the day devoted to the perpetuation of the memory of the heroic dead.

May 30, 1868 was a beautiful day. Most extensive preparations had been made for the decoration of the graves of the soldiers buried at Arlington. There were a great many ex-Union soldiers in and around Washington at that time, and they seemed to vie with each other in their efforts to make the occasion a memorable one. The probabilities are that a greater number of ex-Union officers and soldiers took part in the ceremonies than have since participated. Among those occupying seats on the platform during the ceremonies were General and Mrs. Grant, Mr. Dent, Mrs. Grant's father; Secretaries Fish, Rawlins, Borie, Boutwell, and Cox; Postmaster-General Creswell; Sir Edward Thornton, the British minister; Senators Nye and Warner; Treasurer Spinner; Mayor Bowen; General Sherman; the venerable Amos Kendall; Hon. Mr. Laflin of New York; Hon. Sidney Clarke of Kansas; the Swiss consul-general; Mr. John Hitz, Doctor L. Alcan of Paris, and others.

General Logan subsequently succeeded in getting an appropriation for the publication of the reports of the ceremonies of Memorial Day, and also in making the 30th of May a national holiday. Since his death there have been many who have claimed for themselves or their friends the authorship of Decoration Day, but the story I tell here contains the true facts as to the origin of Memorial Day. It was conceived by General Logan, his sympathetic nature being deeply touched by what we had told him that we had witnessed in the cemeteries of Virginia. He said that it was strange that a people who were so loyal to their country as had been the Union soldiers and their friends should not have been the first to inaugurate this beautiful ceremony, and that it must be attributed to the fact that they were so engrossed in taking up their vocations in life that they had not had time to indulge in sentiment. He said it was not too late for the Union men of the nation to follow the example of the people of the South in perpetuating the memory of their friends who had died for the cause which they thought just and right. General Logan had infinite satisfaction in the thought that he was the author of Decoration Day.[9]

CHAPTER 7

Confidants to the First Family

As THE FLIGHT of time brought the 4th of March nearer and nearer, committees were formed and the most extensive preparations ever conceived were made for the inauguration of Grant and Colfax. Experts and artists from New York and other large cities were brought to suggest schemes and designs for decorations and the arrangement of the programme.

General Grant being the greatest military hero who had ever been elected President, and there being so many ex-soldiers in Washington at that time from all parts of the country, it was determined that the military display should be greater than it ever had been on previous inaugural occasions. State and local organizations made extensive preparations; everybody in and around the capital city was on the alert for weeks before the 4th of March. The local committees were untiring in their labors. The citizens were most generous in their subscriptions. Consequently, no grander scene could be imagined than was presented, nothwithstanding the day was stormy and that it rained very hard at night.

The committee on the part of the Senate was composed of Hon. Richard Yates of Illinois; A. H. Cragin of New Hampshire; and T. C. McCreary of Kentucky. They attended to the details of the arrangements of the Capitol, while the numerous committees for every part of the ceremony succeeded in having everything perfect. The procession was magnificent. It began with the grand marshal, General Alexander S. Webb, and his efficient staff composed of prominent military officers, members of General Grant's staff and others. Then the carriages with the President and Vice-President elect and the committee. Then the outgoing President and the committees, followed by an unusual quota of distinguished officials—judges, senators, governors, ex-senators, ex-governors, and many other noted visitors. Then the various organizations—military, masonic, and civic to the number of thousands, while the numerous bands played martial airs with much enthusiasm. The whole of the space, including the park east of the Capitol, was literally packed with people. The waving banners of the various organizations here and there made it a gay panorama. The usual ceremonies of swearing in the Vice-President by the Chief Justice took place in the Senate chamber at the constitutional hour of twelve o'clock. The Senate chamber was packed to suffocation. The diplomatic corps, in full court dress, presented an imposing appearance, while the galleries were filled to their utmost capacity. Mrs. Grant, her children, and father Colonel Dent, and Mrs. and Miss Matthews, mother and sister of Mr. Colfax occupied front seats in the reserved galleries. The diplomatic gallery and that reserved for ladies looked brilliant with their complement of well-dressed beautiful women. Every movement was chronicled by the vigilant reporters, who occupied their accustomed places in the gallery reserved for them.

Vice-President Colfax was as pale as death while taking the oath, and seemed deeply moved in assuming the responsibility of the office of Vice-President and, as he occupied the chair a few moments his pallor became even greater. After Chief Justice Chase had pronounced the last word which made Mr. Colfax the legal Vice-President of the United States, the Senate arose and, preceded by Chief Justice Chase, the President-elect, Vice-President, and Supreme Court filed out of the Senate chamber in order according to rank through the corridor to the rotunda, and out through the bronze doorway to the platform always erected before the east front of the Capitol for the ceremony of administering the oath to the President by the Chief Justice, and from which the President delivers his inaugural address. The day was inclement, but, as General Grant's address, like most of his state papers, was very short, the people were not long exposed.

Nothwithstanding the multitude of people massed in front of them and on every side, so interested were they that absolute silence prevailed. The deep voice of Chief Justice Chase reached to the very outside of the crowd. General Grant's great diffidence almost overwhelmed him and he could be heard only a few yards from where he stood. No one could have believed that the shrinking, unpretentious man stammering through the well-prepared address had commanded thousands of men and conquered as many more. After the close of the address, and when all within reach had congratulated and blessed the President many times over, the procession again re-formed and escorted the President to the executive mansion, the bands playing all the triumphant familiar airs they knew. Reaching the White House they were received most formally, without the luncheon and other hospitalities the outgoing President uniformly extends to his successor. General Grant did not remain that night in the White House, but returned to his home on I Street.

The north wing of the Treasury was just nearing completion at that time, so that the committee made arrangements to have the reception and inaugural ball in the new building, occupying all the floors. Immediately over the entrance hall were the reception-rooms of the President, Mrs. Grant, the Vice-President, and the ladies of his family, all communicating, while other rooms furnished ample accommodations for the cloak-room. The magnificent marble or east room was the main dancing-hall. It was furnished and elaborately decorated, as was the whole building. The bronze gallery running round this room made a grand place for the music and spectators. The decorations in this room were the finest of all, the soft tints of the Pyrenees, Siena, Egyptian, Tennessee, and Vermont marbles contrasting exquisitely with the bright colors. The whole effect was superb.

There was a very great crowd and, but for the solidity of the building and the perfect management it might have been most uncomfortable. About ten o'clock President Grant entered the reception-room assigned him. He was accompanied by Senator Morgan of New York, and one or two others; Mrs. Grant was escorted by General George H. Thomas. Mr. and Mrs. Colfax came in together. Horace Greeley, Julia Ward Howe, Governors Jewell of Connecticut, Oglesby of Illinois, Curtin of Pennsylvania, Fenton of New York, and innumerable others, including many army and navy heroes were there, among them that illustrious Illinois soldier Major-General James H. Wilson, whose daring as a cavalry-officer placed him in the front rank of officers of that arm of the service. The capture of President Jefferson Davis, as he was fleeing from Richmond, was the crowning glory of his brilliant career. I remember seeing a group of such men as Porter, Farragut, Du Pont, Dahlgren, and Rogers together, while Generals Sherman, Logan, McDowell, Meade, Burnside, Hancock, Thomas, Sickles, and a host of others recalled the stirring events of the war so recently over. Celebrities from every part of the country were among the numbers who were glad to honor General and Mrs. Grant by their presence, making the inauguration ceremonies of 1869 the most notable up to that time in the history of the Government. The 5th of March found the city full of weary people who felt themselves almost too fatigued to take their departure for home after the procession, ball, and ceaseless tramping about.

The day before the inauguration an event occurred in General Grant's office in the War Department that few knew about, which reflected great credit upon the generosity of some of our patriotic and worthy citizens. The house occupied by General Grant on I Street had been given him by some friends when he was General of the Army. He was about to move into the executive mansion, many thought for a residence of eight years at least. His successor as General of the Army was the next most renowned soldier of the Union army, General W. T. Sherman. A committee composed of A. T. Stewart, Hamilton Fish, B. F. Field, W. H. Aspinwall, Judge Hilton, Solon Humphrey, and William Scott had been chosen by the subscribers to present this house and the furniture to General Sherman. They had negotiated with General Grant and had arranged that Mr. Hoyt and General Butterfield should take General Sherman to General Grant's office at an appointed hour. When they all met, the committee handed General Grant sixty-five thousand dollars. He, in exchange, gave them the deeds, bills of sale, and documents, making an absolute conveyance to General Sherman of the property on I Street and all thereunto belonging. Then the committee gave General Sherman the subscription list, informing him that a check for the balance of the subscriptions, in all about one hundred thousand dollars, would be sent to him at an early date. General Grant was delighted that General Sherman was so soon to have the house, and Sherman was completely overcome by the unexpected kindness of his friends. When the little group separated each felt supremely happy, the donors knowing they had done a graceful thing and the recipient feeling that his services had been appreciated. General Sherman lived a longer period probably with his family about him in this house than anywhere else, and enjoyed more uninterrupted pleasure here than in any other house he ever occupied.

In a few days after Grant's inauguration the question of the cabinet was settled by the appointments of Hamilton Fish as Secretary of State, vice [successor to] Mr. Washburne, who was transferred to the French mission, and of Mr. George S. Boutwell as Secretary of the Treasury, vice Mr. A. T. Stewart, resigned. Notwithstanding the fact that Chief Justice Chase decided that the transfer of his business to trustees made Mr. Stewart eligible, many lawyers held it did not. General Grant, desiring to avoid any technical questions on the subject, accepted Mr. Stewart's resignation, which Mr. Stewart enclosed with the opinion of Chief Justice Chase. General John A. Rawlins, long his faithful adjutant-general in the field and after the war, was made Secretary of War. Adolph Borie of Philadelphia was appointed Secretary of the Navy, but occupied that position only a few months. General Jacob D. Cox was made Secretary of the Interior, General John A. Creswell Postmaster-General, and Judge E. R. Hoar Attorney-General.

Everybody applauded these appointments, and the political skies seemed clearer than they had been since the assassination of Mr. Lincoln. Few persons knew that Senator J. F. Wilson of Iowa, then a member of the House and one of the impeachment committee, was very strongly urged by President Grant to accept the position of Secretary of State. He even consented at one time to consider the matter favorably but, subsequently learning that Mr. Washburne desired to name a number of the appointees to the diplomatic service, he reconsidered his promise and declined to have any connection with the cabinet, after which Mr. Fish was chosen at the request of Senator Morgan, Mr. Conkling, and other New York friends of President Grant. Had Mr. Wilson accepted this position, who can tell the effect upon the policy of the administration? Cuba might have been one of our strongest allies and a prosperous republic before the expiration of President Grant's second term.

Upon reflection it will be remembered that very early in Grant's administration the Cuban question came up as one of the most important of the time. I recollect that many earnest and prolonged conferences were held as to the duty of the United States in the matter of the various troubles in that unfortunate island. Mr. Fish bitterly opposed any recognition of Cuba by the United States and finally carried his point, notwithstanding the urgent solicitation of many prominent citizens, senators, and members of Congress to the contrary. General Grant entertained a strong desire for negotiations but was ever handicapped by the fear of the cry of dictator, knowing that the mercurial temperament of the people all over the country was ready to start such a sensation, should they be given the slightest foundation in the line of any desire for the acquisition of territory.

Upon the appointment of four of his staff to clerical duty in the White House there was another spasmodic outburst of clamor against the military. Generals Porter, Babcock, and Badeau and Colonel Dent were looked upon with much suspicion when it was announced that they were to be secretaries to the President. It was considered most unwise that applicants for appointments should be obliged to file their applications through the executives of the respective departments, who in turn sent them to the President through these secretaries. There was especial sensitiveness on the subject of uniforms being worn about the White House. There were then a great number of officers of the army and navy in Washington, some on duty and some on leave of absence. The mutterings of Congress frightened many of them who, to avoid attracting attention, secured the passage of a resolution permitting officers on duty or leave in Washington to wear citizens' dress. When the Navy and War Departments presented themselves to President Grant at the White House, there was a large number of distinguished officers in the company that assembled in the east room to pay their respects, which must have made Grant feel that he would be ably sustained by friends whom he had trusted in darker days and who had never been found wanting.

The pressure, unfortunately as great as ever, for appointment in the civil service was the one great drawback to his peace of mind. The applicants would not be satisfied and kept up their importunities in and out of season. Mr. Wade, who would have been President had Andrew Johnson been impeached, called upon President Grant after he had been in the executive mansion some weeks and congratulated him, and the President replied that he was not sure the Presidency was a thing to be desired, on account of the annoyances that hedged about the incumbent as a result of the impossibility of satisfying the demands of all his friends. Mr. Wade advised him to be master of the situation, to please himself, and to let those who were disappointed murmur as they wished. He said, for himself, he was delighted to go into retirement and, feeling that he had done his duty faithfully, he had no regrets but that of leaving his friends. The parting between these two men, who had both played so conspicuous a part in national affairs, was most touching.

President Grant was unfortunately situated, because of the number of men whom he knew to be eminently qualified for the various positions, and the comparatively few positions to fill. His cabinet were [*sic*] equally embarrassed in the matter of choosing among the multitude, who came favorably indorsed by men who had been with Grant through the war. Many were the heart-burnings and, as a matter of fact, many mistakes occurred in the selections that had finally to be made. Subsequent troubles brought upon the administration by the action of these appointees caused President Grant great suffering and vexation of spirit and involved him in difficulties that it required a long time to outlive.

In the reorganization of the Senate, Reverend J. P. Newman, pastor of the Metropolitan Church, was made chaplain; Mr. George Gorman of California was made sergeant-at-arms. Mr. Blaine was re-elected speaker of the House, and immediately confronted a galaxy of as able men as were ever in that body. His first duty was to solve a most difficult problem in assigning the chairmanships of the committees, with such men to choose from as Logan, Garfield, Banks, Schenck, Dawes, Allison, Windom, Holman, Brooks of New York, Williams, Orth, Myers, O'Neil, Shellabarger, Wilson of Indiana, Wilson of Iowa, Butler, Lochridge, Bingham, Stoughton, Paine, Wheeler of New York, Ingersoll, Cook, Cullom, Farnsworth, Frye, Hale, Judd, and a legion too numerous to mention. Mr. Blaine was then young and vigorous, and probably the most promising statesman of the nation. His administration of the speakership was, without doubt, the most brilliant in the history of Congress, spanning the most important epoch of the nation. There were then, perhaps, more critical occasions when the great skill, knowledge, and quick perception of the speaker were necessary to avoid serious trouble than during any other period. Mr. Blaine was ever ready for any emergency, at times displaying diplomacy, tact, and a memory that had been unequalled by any other parliamentarian.

I remember once listening to some debate upon postal matters wherein Tucker of Virginia was criticising the action of the post-office authorities for throwing out matter deemed unmailable on account of its political character. Mr. Blaine was in the chair. As quick as a flash he beckoned some one to the chair and took his place on the floor. As soon as Tucker had finished, Mr. Blaine addressed the chair, saying: "If the gentleman from Virginia will permit, I should like to ask him a question." Mr. Tucker assented. Mr. Blaine continued: "Were you not attorney-general for the State of Virginia during the administration of Henry A. Wise as governor of Virginia, and did not you decide that a post-office official in the State of Virginia had committed no offence by the destruction of copies of the New York *Tribune?*" This question Mr. Tucker admitted to be quite true, and thereby lost the whole point of his argument in the case then under discussion. That evening we were dining with Mr. Blaine, and as I sat on his right I remarked to him that I was astonished at his memory. He told me that at the time of Tucker's decision he was publishing a paper up in Maine and remembered writing an editorial on the subject, but that he had quite forgotten the whole thing, and had never thought of Mr. Tucker being the former attorney-general of Virginia until attracted by his utterances. It flashed through his mind that he must be the man and, seeing his opportunity to disconcert and defeat him, he determined to make the inquiry. Such remarkable instances of his great ability were of frequent occurrence. Before the close of the first session the House of Representatives had reason to be proud of its speaker and to congratulate itself upon having elected James G. Blaine.

Immediately after the inauguration ex-President Johnson returned to his home in Tennessee, where in a speech he repeated his eulogy upon himself and his anathemas against the Republican party. Mr. Seward returned to Auburn, New York, where he spoke in glowing terms of President Grant, prophesying that his administration would be a blessing to the country. The remainder of Mr. Johnson's cabinet went to their respective homes. In a brief time everything was adjusted to the change of administration and the affairs of the nation proceeded as if nothing had occurred.

Among the callers at the White House soon after the occupancy by President Grant and his family was General Robert E. Lee, who came to Washington to visit his wife's kinswoman, Mrs. Kennon of Tudor Place, Georgetown. Mrs. Kennon was the niece of George Washington Parke Custis, father of Mrs. Lee, and occupied for many years her home in

Georgetown. Her husband was on board the ill-fated *Princeton* at the time of the explosion of the Stockton gun during Tyler's administration, when so many distinguished persons who were members of the excursion party lost their lives. The greeting between Lee and Grant was very cordial, but General Lee could not have been otherwise than embarrassed; hence he remained but a short time.

One of the first appointments made by President Grant was that of General James Longstreet as surveyor of the port of New Orleans as a recognition of the reconstructed Confederates. They were warm personal friends, the memory of their happy days at West Point having survived the stormy days of warfare, and President Grant desired to show his magnanimity and good faith in his wish to encourage those lately in rebellion to renew their loyalty to the government. General Longstreet, who had nobly stuck to a bad cause, and more nobly acknowledged his error when defeated, was therefore a fitting representative of his section. General Longstreet has since occupied other honorable positions and always to the credit of himself and the United States. I saw not long since in the newspapers a most interesting description of a banquet given in Atlanta, where a meeting between General Sickles and General Longstreet was the initiative of a most enthusiastic and delightful reunion of survivors of the two great armies. The speeches were eloquent, the music fine, and the picture of Sickles and Longstreet clasped in each other [*sic*] arms, with tears trickling down their cheeks, must have touched the sternest hearts. General Mosby was appointed by President Grant, as also a number of others. Thus the great conqueror became the great benefactor of those whom he had conquered, and was the first to inaugurate sectional harmony and the rebuilding of the devastated Southern States, culminating recently in the celebration of the fiftieth anniversary of the battle of Gettysburg, July 1, 2, and 3, 1863, by a reunion of the Blue and the Gray, furnishing a spectacle never before witnessed in any other country. The policy of General Grant doubtless opened the way for the reunited country which exists to-day, and it is not too much to say that the nation owes General Grant a debt of gratitude, not only for his brilliant military achievements, but for his wisdom and magnanimity which won back to the Union those who were in rebellion against its preservation.

The White House at that time was not what it is to-day. During the Civil War Mr. Lincoln permitted every one who desired to see him, whether through curiosity, friendliness, or on business, to have free access to the executive mansion, and as a result the wear and tear on everything in the house was something frightful. The excitement which attended Mr. Lincoln's assassination brought great throngs, who were not refused admission to pay their respects to the sacred remains of the dead while they lay in state in the east room. When Mr. Johnson and his family succeeded Mr. and Mrs. Lincoln in the staid old mansion they found everything in a shabby condition. Be it said to the credit of Mrs. Patterson, who directed Mr. Johnson's household affairs, that she did the best she could to make the White House habitable without occasioning great expense to the Government. She had the carpets, curtains, and upholstery cleaned, remade, and put in place with as much economy as if she had been paying the bill out of her own purse. The style of furniture, draperies, etc., was out of date, and was never beautiful in either style or color. The dear lady could not accomplish very much with the small appropriation that was made for the repairs in the White House. Congress had at that time a very different idea of the necessities of the home of the President from the one it holds to-day. Americans had not arrived at an appreciation of the gorgeousness of European palaces and the requisites of the home of the ruler of the country. When President and Mrs. Grant moved into the White House, March 5, 1869, they consequently found it in a very deplorable condition, to say nothing of its hideous appearance. I remember well the bright green curtains with gay trimming which used to hang in the state dining-room. Congress was more generous in its appropriation for the repairs necessary at this time than it had been previously. General O. E. Babcock was authorized to negotiate for many changes, refurnishing and redecorating during the summer of 1869.

The relations between General Logan and President Grant

were so intimate that we were constantly summoned to the White House for formal and informal dinners, lunches, and receptions. I was very familiar with the economies and efforts of Mrs. Grant to utilize everything that could be retained in the executive mansion, and to make it as attractive with as little expense as possible. General Babcock had exquisite taste, and had a wonderful ability in the line of duty to which he had been assigned. Mrs. Grant was so gentle, so kind, and so gracious to every one, that she doubtless received more people than any of her predecessors. She was the same thoughtful, generous, devoted wife and mother, whose gentleness and loyalty to her family and friends made her equally beloved with her husband by the whole nation. After General Grant's election to the Presidency and their final establishment in the White House, she was still the unpretentious, sincere friend of the unfortunate. Among the first guests invited to the executive mansion were her old associates whom she had known in her early days of adversity. Nothing she could do for these dear friends, who had been so much to her before fortune had smiled upon them, seemed onerous. Her only grief was that the President could not provide each one of the many with lucrative positions, and thereby improve their conditions in life. Many sought her aid and were never turned away impatiently. She at least made an appeal for them. Every member of President Grant's cabinet had stories to tell of Mrs. Grant's kind heart. Every Christmas the asylums, hospitals, and charitable institutions in Washington received donations from Mrs. Grant, while the members of her family and her friends and their children were most generously remembered. She was the veritable "Lady Bountiful" in more than one household. Her greatest fault, if she had faults, was her extreme leniency. She could never discipline either her servants or her children, her kind heart always suggesting some excuse for misdemeanors or neglect of duty. She was never so happy as when planning entertainments and indulgences for her children and their multitude of friends. The basement of the White House was reserved for the boisterous games of the boys who were always with "Buck" and Jesse, Fred, the elder, being then at West Point. Nellie, and her companions, had full sway on the upper floor. Scarcely a Saturday passed without a large theatre-party of children from the White House and the homes of the cabinet officers, especially if the amusement column of the newspaper contained anything attractive for children.

President and Mrs. Grant entertained constantly. There were always guests staying in the house, for whom entertainments were given. They were especially fond of having young people with them. They entertained more distinguished people with scions of royalty than any other occupants of the White House. Among them were the Duke of Edinburgh, Earl de Grey, Lord Northcote, and the young Prince Arthur of England, the Grand Duke Alexis of Russia, King Kalakaua of Hawaii, and the first Japanese and Chinese ministers after the signing of the Burlingame treaty. We were present at the state dinners and receptions tendered these celebrities, and have since sat at the table of royalty more than once, and are proud to say that in no wise did the latter surpass in bounty, elegance, and good taste the entertainments of President and Mrs. Grant.

It must be remembered that the Joint High Commission, composed of more distinguished men than had ever served on such a commission, was in session in Washington during that winter. The usual official state dinner was given, of course, but, in addition to that, President and Mrs. Grant gave a reception in honor of Earl de Grey and his associates. Mrs. Grant was assisted by Mrs. Sharpe, Miss Washburne, Miss Pelt, and myself. The appointments of this reception surpassed anything that had previously been given in the White House. Lady Thornton, with her tall, spare figure and dignified dress, accompanied the aristocratic Lady MacDonald, whose brunette complexion and dark hair were in striking contrast with the blond hair and fair complexion of her chaperon, Lady Thornton. In contrast to them was the superb figure of Madame Catacazy, magnificently dressed and crowned with that beautiful head of hair for which she was so generally admired.

The whole Diplomatic Corps, the judges of the Supreme Court, members of the Senate, the House, and many other official dignitaries were in attendance on this rare occasion. The press was represented by Horace Greeley, David A. Wells, Horace White, Samuel Bowles, Charles Nordhoff of the *Herald*, Sands, Minturn, Marshalls, Halstead, Samuel Read, Gobright, Benjamin Perley Poore, and John W. Forney. The usual number of senators and representatives were in attendance, also a large contingent of the army and navy.

A few evenings later Hon. Zachary Chandler of Michigan, who occupied one of the most beautiful homes in Washington on H Street between Fourteenth and Fifteenth, gave a very large reception to the commission, many of the persons above enumerated being among the guests who were glad to honor our British friends. Members of the cabinet also gave dinners and receptions in honor of the commission, all of which were brilliant affairs and must have made a very favorable impression upon the British members, as the son of Lord Northcote subsequently married Miss Edith Fish, daughter of Secretary Fish.

Neither the President nor Mrs. Grant could ever have been considered a fine conversationalist; no one, however, partook of their hospitality who was not charmed by them both, because of their sincere and unpretentious cordiality. President Grant was full of sly fun, and particularly enjoyed a joke at Mrs. Grant's expense, and often perpetrated one himself. Her frankness and pronounced opinions frequently gave him opportunity to turn what might sometimes have proved an embarrassing situation, particularly when her views were in contravention to those of a guest or host, Mrs. Grant never remembering individual characteristics or histories. Her noble nature would never have permitted her to wound any one, but she often failed to remember that Mr. and Mrs. So-and-so had been twice married, were or were not temperance leaders, Protestants or Catholics, and of such other personal tastes or opinions as to make it dangerous to express oneself too frankly. The President at such times would lead her on to her own undoing, and then chuckle over her embarrassment, as one has seen brothers do when teasing their sisters. The absolute harmony of their domestic lives was ideal. The boasted domestic bliss of our ancestors in the early days of the republic furnishes no history of a happier or more united pair than the General and Mrs. Grant.

From the hour of Grant's entering upon his duties as the President of the United States the political caldron began to boil; and, while the Republican party which had elected him was greatly in the majority, there were the same rivalries among men that have always existed, and the same vexatious problems in regard to national affairs which had to be settled.

Reconstruction of the States late in rebellion was, by no means, the smallest of these problems. Smarting under the whip of adversity and failure, the people of the South naturally resented the advent of Northern men into the Southern States. They resented the tendency of these men to occupy representative positions when the majority of the support of their ambitions was the colored race, so lately the slaves of these same Southerners. The colored men themselves were not without ambitions and were numerically in a majority in many localities, and this majority was greatly increased by the disenfranchisement of those lately in rebellion. Therefore they became candidates for representative positions, as well as places of trust. Conflict between these two elements was inevitable, and waxed hotter and hotter in the States where the negroes were in greatest numbers.

It may have come from prejudice acquired in my youth in regard to the colored race, but I must confess that when I first visited Richmond and, on going into the Capitol, saw the negro members of the House and Senate of the Virginia legislature occupying the places that were once filled by the great men of Virginia, the spectacle was repulsive to me. I could readily understand that a true Virginian could not do otherwise than resent the conditions that had brought about such a situation. The débris and the desecration that had almost destroyed that beautiful capitol made one heart-sick, and I turned away with unspeakable disgust and the feeling that it would take a much longer time than it really has taken to adjust political affairs in the late Confederate States.

The tragedies of the early days of reconstruction are matters of history and are not a part of my story. I make this digression to recall the chaos which confronted President Grant, who had had previously no sort of experience in legislative or executive affairs beyond those of a military character. Reports of outrages in almost every State south of the Mason and Dixon line, the evident wrong on both sides, and the responsibility for the protection of human life weighed heavily upon the chief executive. Grant appreciated that he was without power to issue orders as he had done when he was in command of a great army.

All the winter of 1869–70 we were subject to daily startling reports of public scandals, defalcations, and high-handed outrages. The reckless extravagance practised during the war had so demoralized the money-making people of the country that they were ready to organize any sort of scheme out of which they could expect a fortune. In addition to this, many men who had lately been in the service had gone West and were undertaking stupendous enterprises for the development of the then Far West. They were asking subsidies from Congress to build railroads and carry on various projects that would expedite the advancement of the new States and Territories west of the Mississippi River. President Grant was so trustful of his friends that he was oftentimes greatly deceived and placed by charlatans in unenviable positions. Contractors whose occupation was gone had to turn their attention from furnishing supplies for a great army to industrial undertakings which had to be watched to avoid criticism and national scandals.

General Logan was then a member of the House and, having been elected commander-in-chief of the Grand Army of the Republic and a representative-at-large from the State of Illinois, he had an innumerable constituency who made insatiable demands upon him. It required all of his time and much of my own to attend to his correspondence and to obtain information from the Treasury Department in regard to finances, customs, revenues, and the various branches of the Government that belong to the Treasury Department. From the War Department he had to obtain information about military affairs, the army, and the various military posts throughout the country; from the Navy Department, about the navy, its organization, the position of the various squadrons, and personal information as to the whereabouts and condition of the officers and seamen; for the Department of Justice, the information to answer all sorts of inquiries as to prisoners and the possibility of having them pardoned, and personal inquiries as to the condition of cases being prosecuted by the Government. From the Interior Department he had to find out about back pay and pensions and the various tracts of land subject to entry under the Government; also all about Indian reservations, Indian posts, and other important facts in reference to the various tribes of Indians. From the Department of Agriculture General Logan had to secure information in regard to agriculture and horticulture, the cultivation of our rich farming lands, as well as the distribution of seeds, plants, and agricultural reports; from the Smithsonian Institution, all sorts of information in regard to scientific matters. General Logan was also supposed to obtain for his clients what they wished to know in regard to fish and fisheries and the furnishing of spawn for the planting of the streams with the various fish that would thrive in the waters of certain localities. All this, together with the extensive personal correspondence of his constituents and the members of the Grand Army of the Republic of the whole nation, made a stupendous task which was not lightened in those days by stenography and typewriting. Many of General Logan's correspondents were grossly insulted if it were intimated that any of these letters were written by a clerk. They were supposed to be written by General Logan himself.

To satisfy these unreasonable demands, I cultivated the art of counterfeiting the general's penmanship and signature, so that many thought they were receiving letters from the general which I had written out and signed. In fact, the general had only time to sign the most important ones, and I must not forget to add that a voluminous correspondence was going on all the time in regard to local political affairs. More than once we appreciated that "brevity is the soul of wit," especially when these correspondents were rather long-winded. I remember one letter, which we took the trouble to measure, was written in a very close, fine hand on foolscap paper. When pasted end to end it reached the incredible length of thirty feet by actual measurement.

So intimate were the relations between General Logan and his constituents and the members of the Grand Army of the Republic that they thought he could accomplish everything which they desired. Not infrequently they had to be disappointed, and to reconcile them at long range to their disappointment and hold their friendship required skilful diplomacy which often taxed one's strict adherence to the truth.

We had removed from Willard's Hotel into a large brownstone house which formerly stood near the corner of New York Avenue and Fourteenth Street. Thus we were very near the White House. General Butler's residence on I Street, Zachary Chandler's on H Street, Speaker Blaine's in the row on Fifteenth Street between H and I Streets, General Garfield's near the corner of I and Thirteenth Streets, made it convenient for these dignitaries to come to our house, or have General Logan go to theirs, to consult in regard to many important measures before Congress. These consultations were often held after an informal dinner in one house or another and were most delightful affairs. After dinner the gentlemen retired to the library or parlor, and there could indulge in the freest possible expression of views on public affairs without the fear of interruption or of the omnipresent newspaper reporter.

It may be imagination, but from knowledge of the way in which affairs are handled at the present time I believe that public men really gave more time to their public duties then than they do now. I further believe that there were fewer instances when members and senators paired with other members and senators and went to attend to their personal affairs during the session of Congress. I know one thing, that General Logan was so conscientious in regard to his duties as a representative and senator that he rarely absented himself from the halls of Congress unless he was confined to our home by illness. It was an unusual thing to hear that it was impossible to have a quorum in the House or Senate on account of absentees who had to be summoned by the sergeant-at-arms before the public business could proceed.

General Butler was then a member of the House. He used frequently to boast of his great friendship for Grant and at the same time insist that he ran the administration. President Grant facetiously said to a friend one day: "I understand that Butler thinks that he runs the administration. He comes up here with a dozen names for some appointment, and I can not see my way clear to give him more than one of the number for which he asks. After explaining all this to him, he goes away very well satisfied. It is a very different thing with Logan. He comes here with a dozen names which he wishes me to appoint to positions and, after listening to his pleas and demands for some time, I try to provide for at least ten or eleven. Generally, he goes off with ten or eleven appointments, and I hear that he tells his friends he is sorry he has no influence with the Grant administration." [1]

President Grant had as much confidence in General Logan in politics as he had in military affairs, and when he was worried over anything he generally sent for him to come to the White House to talk over issues in Congress which were under consideration.

There were a few men who had been conspicuous in the Confederacy, either in the army or in Mr. Davis's cabinet, who had been elected to represent their people either in the House or Senate. They had not lost any of their Southern fire or prejudice, and occasionally indulged in the most violent criticisms of the Grant administration and of officers in command of posts in the South. Grant knew that he could always depend upon General Logan's coming to the rescue, and more than once General Logan came home in a great state of excitement after having defended the administration or some officer who was in command of a military post in the South.

Mrs. Grant was ably supported on all social occasions by Mrs. Matthews and Mrs. Colfax, the mother and the wife of Vice-President Colfax. Both Mrs. Matthews and Mrs. Colfax were charming, graceful women who appreciated their position and the obligation they owed to the people who had elevated Mr. Colfax to the second highest position within their gift. They realized that, should anything happen to President Grant, Mr. Colfax, by provision of the Constitution, would slip into the very highest position in the land. They were untiring in their efforts to be agreeable. They not only gave the social functions required of the Vice-President, but many more, because of their extensive acquaintanceship with people from every State in the Union, Mr. Colfax having previously been speaker of the House of Representatives.

The majority of the ladies of the cabinet were eminently fitted to grace their positions as wives of cabinet officers. Mrs. Hamilton Fish of New York, as the leading lady of the cabinet, was one of the most superb women of her time. In imagination I can see her to-day as she appeared on all occasions, the personification of dignity, graciousness, and cordiality. Her manner put the timid at ease and restrained the overpresumptuous. Notwithstanding her age, she was so vigorous mentally and physically that every one considered her much younger than she really was. Her style of dress was regal without the slightest suggestion of inappropriateness. She had mastered the manual of etiquette in her youth, and found, when she came to Washington, there was nothing new for her to learn, except the relative rank of officials and the Diplomatic Corps at the national capital. Her experience as a member of the best society and as the wife of Hamilton Fish, in the various positions he had held in the State of New York, fitted her to preside over the home of the Secretary of State. She was ably assisted by her daughters, Mrs. Benjamin and Miss Edith Fish, subsequently Mrs. Northcote, wife of the son of Lord Northcote. Mrs. Fish was punctilious in the observance of all the duties of the wife of the Secretary of State and next in rank to the wife of the Vice-President.

One morning Washington was thrown into a spasm of horror over the stigma brought upon society by the marriage of Senator Christiancy of Michigan to an obscure young German girl occupying an insignificant position in one of the departments. The disparagement between their ages and positions being considered appalling, a tremendous hubbub was raised. Senators' wives were indignant and vowed ostracism of the poor, unfortunate girl who dared to enter the sacred social senatorial circle as the wife of a man old enough to be her father, if not her grandfather.

Never a word came from Mrs. Fish, the recognized leader in social affairs. Mrs. Grant's position being fixed by Thomas Jefferson, the author of "Etiquette at the American Court," was not supposed to venture as to what was to be done with the offender against the dignity of the senatorial coterie.

While the excitement was waxing hotter and hotter, Mrs. Fish's carriage stopped at our door one Thursday morning at about ten-thirty o'clock. The footman came to the door, rang the bell, and handed Mrs. Fish's card to our servant, the footman saying: "Mrs. Fish's compliments to Madame Logan, and Mrs. Fish will be obliged if Madame Logan will grant her an interview about an important matter." I directed the servant to have Mrs. Fish shown into the parlor at once, and I came down to greet her, as I was naturally flattered by so early a call from Mrs. Fish, whom I honored and loved. She made quite sure we were alone, and then said: "I have come to talk to you about the Christiancy affair." [2]

I replied: "Dear Mrs. Fish, I shall be delighted to follow you in the matter," her motherly smile assuring me that no ill boded the poor little unsophisticated victim of remorseless criticism and injustice. She then said: "I am glad you will agree to join me in a quiet vindication of the inoffensive girl who has been so mercilessly criticised. I want you to go with me this afternoon (senatorial day) to call on Mrs. Christiancy and, if she is not too frightened and will see us, we will simply pay her the respect due a senator's wife, saying nothing about the excitement, invite her to call on us, and come away." I said: "I shall be glad to go with you, notwithstanding the fact that it is Mrs. Christiancy's place to call on me first. She probably does not know her duty, and I am sure will be grateful for the recognition."

We went to call about four o'clock and found Mrs. Christiancy in very unpretentious quarters, evidently much embarrassed by the notoriety which had been given her on account of Senator Christiancy's position as United States senator. She was a shrinking, modest young woman, who betrayed the fact that she was as guileless as a child. As soon as she recovered from her shyness, her face brightened up, and with innate grace she expressed her gratitude for the honor done her. After the announcement that Mrs. Fish had called on Mrs. Christiancy, and that Senator and Mrs. Christiancy had dined with Secretary and Mrs. Fish, no further adverse comments were made about the incongruous marriage of the doty senator.

Mrs. and Miss Boutwell, the wife and daughter of the Secretary of the Treasury, were plain, New England women of great refinement and reticence. The Boutwells then lived in a noted boarding-house on Twelfth Street, kept by the no less noted Mrs. Rines, where many of the most distinguished men of the nation and their families lived for years. There were few millionaires in official life in the '60's. Apartment houses were unknown. A majority of officials and their families lived in more or less pretentious boarding-houses and paid quite as extravagant prices for their rooms and board as are paid for the far more comfortable apartments of to-day. They had not the privacy and convenience offered by the furnished housekeeping apartments, now so numerous.

General John A. Rawlins, Secretary of War, lived in a modest house on the corner of M and Twelfth Streets. Mrs. Rawlins, like her husband, had very poor health. They had four children, the care of whom occupied much of Mrs. Rawlins's time.

George M. Robeson of Trenton, New Jersey, was appointed Secretary of the Navy. He was a widower at the time of his appointment, but afterward married Mrs. Aulick, widow of Commodore Aulick. Mr. Robeson rented a commodious house on K Street, formerly occupied by Secretary Stanton of Mr. Lincoln's cabinet. Both the Secretary and Mrs. Robeson were fond of society and understood the art of entertaining royally. They had travelled extensively and had always lived handsomely. Mr. Robeson was a veritable *bon vivant*. Soon after the 1st of January they began a series of entertainments which were long remembered by the fortunate guests who were honored by invitations to them. Later on Secretary Robeson built a large house on Sixteenth Street, where they continued their lavish entertainments. While Secretary Robeson was Secretary of the Navy, reverses overtook these hospitable people, and the auctioneer's voice was heard in the drawing-room, library, dining-room, and chambers of this pretentious home, crying: "Who bids?" for this, that, or the other many valuable treasures that the Secretary and Mrs. Robeson had collected. Secretary and Mrs. Robeson, like legions of others who live for a period in Washington society, finally passed on with none of the multitude whom they had entertained following them in their exit, when the clouds of adversity had overshadowed their pathway.

General George Williams of Oregon was appointed Attorney-General, greatly to the delight of his beautiful and ambitious wife, whose elevation from obscurity on the frontier to the wife of a United States senator had inspired her with an ambition which was destined to be her undoing. They moved into a large house on Rhode Island Avenue near Connecticut Avenue, close to where Saint Matthew's church now stands. In this gorgeously furnished house they lived in great splendor, notices appearing daily in the newspapers describing Mrs. Williams's rich gowns and elaborate social functions. Mrs. Williams became so elated over her sway that she undertook to change the time-honored rules of etiquette at the national capital. She induced Mrs. Grant to call the ladies of the cabinet together in the White House to consider the changes she deemed necessary. At the same time Mrs. Grant insisted that it was foolish and could not be done, but gratified Mrs. Williams's whim by calling the ladies together for a confidential talk about social affairs. The majority, in fact all but Mrs. Williams, agreed with Mrs. Grant that they had no power to change Jefferson's code of official etiquette. Mrs. Williams said she, for one, would not make the first call on the families of senators. She very unwisely so informed many of the senators' wives and insisted they must call first on her, as the wife of the Attorney-General. This provoked the indignation of the senatorial ladies and many of their husbands, among them Senator Matthew H. Carpenter of Wisconsin.

Chief Justice Salmon P. Chase died, and General Williams's name, on account of his ability as a jurist and man of high character, was sent to the Senate as the proposed successor of Mr. Chase. The moment the Senate went into executive session Senator Carpenter made a violent speech against the confirmation of General Williams's name, making many charges against Mrs. Williams, accusing her of numberless peccadilloes, acceptance of presents without General Williams's knowledge from persons who had cases before the Department of Justice, presumption, and other undesirable qualities in the person of the wife of the Chief Justice. General Williams's confirmation was defeated, the real trouble originating in Mrs. Williams's arrogance toward the wives of senators who joined Carpenter in his determination to humiliate Mrs. Williams. Therefore, notwithstanding General Williams's masterly ability and distinguished statesmanship, they eventually retired under the whips of outrageous criticism.

Mr. Columbus Delano of Ohio was made Secretary of the Interior. Mr. and Mrs. Delano were wholesome, ingenuous people. They appreciated the honor which had been conferred upon Mr. Delano by his appointment as a member of President Grant's cabinet. It is possible that Mr. Delano was too honest a man to contend with the insidious cormorants who have ever besieged the Interior Department and, like many of his predecessors and successors, was unable to escape the entanglements of scandals that have ever pursued the Secretary of the Interior. Mrs. Delano was a motherly, unassuming, loyal wife and mother, who made no attempt to introduce changes in the mode of etiquette in Washington. She tried to conform to all the rules laid down for the members of the cabinet and their families. She gave all the entertainments, discharged all the duties supposed to be obligatory upon the ladies of cabinet officers' households, and into them she put real hospitality and pleasure. She extended a hearty welcome to her callers, repaid their visits as soon as she could, and acknowledged every courtesy extended her with a grace born of innate refinement.

The latter-day ungracious manner of receiving calls, and the almost universal custom of returning visits by sending cards through the mail or by footmen, was almost unknown. If the ladies of the cabinet and the wives of other officials felt it a tax upon their strength and time to receive callers once a week, they never made themselves disagreeable by expressing their distaste for their duties.

General Horace Capron of Illinois was chosen commissioner of the Agricultural Bureau, then a bureau of the Interior Department. General Capron, in addition to his fitness for the position on account of his knowledge of agriculture, hailing as he did from the great Prairie State with its wonderful agricultural resources, was a most accomplished and patriotic man, who soon elevated the bureau and its important work to a high place on the list of bureaus and, doubtless by the methods he introduced, paved the way for its becoming a department. Mrs. Capron was a lovely woman. Their house on N Street, near the corner of Twelfth, became worthy of being added to the official list. Their receptions were largely attended, proving their popularity. During the visit of the Japanese embassy at this time it was discovered that the Japanese visitors were really a commission sent to secure teachers and agents from every department of the Government to go to Japan to teach the Japanese Western civilization. The Japanese also desired to learn data connected with every phase of a republican government, as well as finance, agriculture, and various industries.

General Capron accepted an appointment under the Japanese Government and went to Japan to teach them agriculture. Many other Americans returned with the visitors to engage in initiating these Orientals in American methods of doing things, which probably partly accounts for the rapid advancement of the Japanese.

Hon. John A. Creswell of Maryland was appointed Postmaster-General. He was an eminent lawyer, and his administration of the Post-Office Department was the most successful of any up to that time. He was a man of ambitions, and his beautiful house on the corner of Eighteenth and I Streets is still the property of Mrs. Creswell. In this palatial home General and Mrs. Creswell gave superb dinners and receptions and extended to all of their guests a warm welcome. General Creswell had occupied a prominent position in the State of Maryland; therefore Mrs. Creswell had much experience in the matter of entertaining and, being a person of unusual amiability and charm, won the admiration of every one.

Every member of the cabinet and his family delighted to carry out all the usual schedule of social affairs and, as the city was full of visitors from every city in the Union, it was probably as brilliant a winter as ever was passed in Washington. I can not think that it is an imagination when I say that all officials of the Government worked more assiduously than they do to-day. It might have been because of the fact that there were all sorts of matters that had to be attended to promptly. Absenteeism from the cabinet or any other branch of the Government was a very rare thing, and I shall always believe that every one did his part nobly. But for the jealousies and political rivalries, it would have been one of the most delightful winters ever known in Washington.

Admiral and Mrs. Porter were among the hospitable entertainers in the city in their handsome home on H Street. Admiral and Mrs. Dahlgren were for some time at the navy-yard. Mrs. Dahlgren, with her genial disposition, literary taste, and unusual intelligence, made their entertainments among the most popular in the city. The receptions of Professor Henry of the Smithsonian Institution and his interesting family were especially charming, as they had something out of the usual to show from the wonderful scientific collections under his supervision. Hon. Alexander and Mrs. Shepherd gave lavish entertainments. I regret that space forbids a more extensive description and enumeration of social affairs which were once so attractive in Washington.

CHAPTER 8

Memorable Years in the Senate

WHILE AFFAIRS socially were moving so smoothly there were many important matters arising in Congress. There was a proposition to remove the capital to Saint Louis, as a more central location for the capital of the United States than that of the District of Columbia. General Logan championed the movement for the removal of the capital, on the ground that the present location was made at a very early time in the history of the Government, and the vast area west of the Alleghanies had not been considered by white men and was only inhabited by the various tribes of Indians and aborigines that were to be found in what subsequently became the States of Illinois, Wisconsin, Michigan, and the great territories that have added many new States to the galaxy of the Union.

While the movement may have been abortive, and from a historic point of view justly failed, it had the effect of arousing a spirit of pride in the citizens of the District of Columbia, and caused them to become active in the introduction of improvements of all kinds, especially in the municipal government. They succeeded in organizing a Territorial government for the District and in appointing a governor and a secretary of state and in organizing a Board of Public Works, who deserve great credit for the transformation of the city of Washington from a slow-going Southern city of magnificent distances and void of every evidence of beauty and progress into the progressive and beautiful city of to-day. But for the indomitable courage, unfailing energy, and patriotic devotion of such men as Alexander Shepherd, Crosby S. Noyes, J. W. Douglas, A. B. Mullett, Kilburn Claggett, and others, the movement for the removal of the capital to the West might have succeeded, and Washington would never have attained its great beauty and attractiveness. The Board of Public Works employed skilful engineers who levelled the perpendicular hills and filled up the deep chasms that had made Washington unattractive and impracticable. Pennsylvania Avenue being the first street in the city to be paved with modern paving, the completion of the work was an event fraught with so much importance that it was celebrated by a great carnival.

This seemed to be the beginning of the prodigious work of the Board of Public Works and those in authority in the Territorial government. Washington had been fortunate in having secured years before, as superintendent of the botanical gardens, that wonderful genius William Smith, the great Scotch horticulturist. Previously the botanical gardens had done little else than furnish plants, seeds, and floral specimens for the members of Congress. William Smith had become greatly interested in L'Enfant's wonderful plan for the capital of the United States, and had, as far as he could, planted trees along the streets and avenues of the city. The Board of Public Works interested him enthusiastically in their scheme to beautify Washington and in a few years they had accomplished such wonders as to make a proposition for the removal of the capital seem ridiculous and again confirmed forever the action of the earlier commissioners in making Washington the immovable capital of this great country.

This question created the most intense interest, and the galleries of Congress were crowded day after day. Be it said to the everlasting shame of the then citizens of Washington and of many representatives in Congress, that they heaped such ignominy upon Governor Shepherd and his associates that he departed from Washington a heart-broken man, and sought a home in old Mexico, where he lived until his death a few years ago. Others of his associates were accused of limitless graft, and their families have since had a great struggle for existence. Time has vindicated these men but, alas, too late for them to have had the satisfaction of knowing that their herculean achievements had at last been appreciated.

Another question that was all-absorbing was the reduction of the army to a peace basis. It might have been easy to solve the problem of mustering out regiments and officers down to the peace standard, but to do so without readjusting the salaries of those that were to remain would have created universal resentment. Therefore General Logan, as chairman of the committee on military affairs in the House, had to work very hard and call into conference men interested in the army and its requirements, who were both in and out of Congress. Personally, he had no desire to reduce the salary of the General, Lieutenant-General, and the officers of higher rank, but as it was deemed necessary to reduce the pay of commissioned and non-commissioned officers, it seemed unfair to allow the officers of higher rank to retain the same pay they received during the war. These men, however, had most gallant records and made many friends who, looking at it from a personal standpoint, were anxious, as far as possible, to keep up these officers' pay to the war standard. This question can be said to have been among the first to bring about a break of friendship between General Logan and General Sherman, who was then General of the Army.

There were quite a number of military men in Congress whose constituents demanded that a reduction of the army should be accompanied by a reduction of the salaries of the higher officers of the army. General Logan felt that the private soldier, non-commissioned and subordinate officers were not receiving too much pay, but that the higher-rank officers' pay was greatly out of proportion when compared to that of the lower-grade officers. Therefore, he began to scale the salaries from the General of the Army down and reported a bill providing that the General should receive $12,000 instead of $19,000 a year; the Lieutenant-General, $10,000 instead of $14,000; the major-generals, $8,000 instead of $10,000; brigadiers, $5,000 instead of $7,000; colonels, $3,500; lieutenant-colonels, $3,000; majors, $2,500; captains (mounted), $2,000; captains (foot), $1,800; first lieutenants, $1,600; second lieutenants, $1,400; the pay of the non-commissioned officers and privates to remain unchanged.

General Sherman wrote a long letter to the committee, bitterly complaining of the injustice of General Logan's plan, but the schedule was received with so much favor, as being eminently just, that General Logan carried his point, and his bill providing for the reorganization of the army on a peace basis was adopted.

All this meant a great deal of work. At that time I was so occupied with hunting up facts about the armies of every country and the rules which had governed our army from the time of the Revolution that I had little time to do anything else. I really enjoyed making researches for the general, so that he could take up the question when not engaged at the Capitol, and thus I enabled him to get at the very best possible basis upon which to report his bill.

In the midst of the discussion of the army bill reports of scandalous conduct on the part of members of Congress were rife. From time immemorial there have always been delinquents who have, by their improper and dishonest practices, brought harsh criticism down upon public men. Many Northerners had gone South and established homes in the different States lately in rebellion, some investing their all in these homes and business enterprises, which they subsequently were forced to defend with unparalleled heroism. Unfortunately, some of these men were very unworthy, and removed to the South thinking that they would have a greater opportunity for political preferment, and to become conspicuous in public affairs, than they would ever have in the North. They expected to profit by the ignorance of the colored people, and in that way to monopolize the offices—both State and national. There were many of these "carpet-baggers" in Congress, and some of them were a disgrace to that body and to their country. It began to be whispered that some of these gentlemen were selling their appointments to cadetships at West Point and Annapolis, and that one member from North Carolina—one Whittemore, who posed as a Republican and an honest man—had sold a cadetship to West Point for the paltry sum, as I remember it, of three hundred dollars.

Charges were made before the military committee. General Logan investigated the matter thoroughly, summoning before the committee all persons who were supposed to have had something to do with the transaction. He succeeded in bringing before that committee indubitable evidence of the truth of the accusation. Led by General Logan, the committee reported the matter fully to the House with the recommendation that Whittemore be expelled. General Ben Butler was a conspicuous figure at this session. He was very fond of antagonizing men like General Logan, but he did not understand General Logan as well as he thought he did. Whittemore went to Butler and begged Butler to defend him on the floor of the House. I shall never forget the scene, as I sat in the gallery and watched the proceedings the day the Whittemore case came up. Every inch of space on the floor and in the galleries was occupied. General Logan, as chairman of the military committee, soon after the morning hour addressed the speaker to make his report on the case. He had not gone far with his remarks and the reading of the report when General Butler arose in his place and attempted a defence of Whittemore. General Logan had been advised that Butler would probably do this, so he quietly hunted up the statute which forbids a member of Congress to act as attorney for another member in any case before the House. He merely asked Mr. Butler whether he wished to be considered the attorney of Mr. Whittemore. Without hesitation Mr. Butler replied that he did wish to be so considered, whereupon General Logan read the clause of the statute mentioned, which fell like a pall on General Butler and the whole House and galleries. Butler stammered a disclaimer, explaining that it was a matter of sympathy on his part. General Logan followed this up by a scathing rebuke to a man who would undertake to apologize for a criminal who had violated the law, and who, as a member of Congress, had disgraced his State. One of the general's greatest gifts was that of eloquence as a prosecutor, and perhaps no greater arraignment of a criminal has ever been heard in the House of Representatives. His plea for the preservation of the honor and integrity of the members of the House has never been equalled. General Butler withdrew from the floor of the House, but got little sympathy from his friends on account of his downfall in the attempt to defend Whittemore. Whittemore was driven from the House in disgrace as he should have been.

I may be wrong and may overestimate General Logan's keen sense of honor and integrity in representing the people, but I can not help feeling that if those who came after him had been as strong champions of the preservation of the honor of members of the House and Senate as was General Logan, there would not have been the very many scandals that have reflected upon our national and State legislators in these later years.

In the month of April General George H. Thomas died. He was mourned throughout the whole nation as a gallant soldier. Memorial services were held throughout the country. General Logan, being the commander-in-chief of the Grand Army of the Republic, caused a meeting to be held by the Department of the Potomac in Masonic Hall, which was then the largest auditorium in the city. The hall was profusely decorated with mourning, draped flags, and other evidences of the grief of the nation at the untimely death of this great soldier. General Logan was the orator of the evening, and paid a glowing tribute to the memory of General Thomas, forgetting, in his grief at the nation's loss, the personal differences which had existed between him and the dead soldier, thus giving another illustration of the unusual magnanimity and nobility of his own character.

On April 30 General Logan called the attention of the House to the conspicuous ingratitude with which the memory of General John A. Rawlins, late Secretary of War under Grant's administration and the faithful adjutant-general of General Grant during the Civil War, had been treated, in that his remains were still lying in a vault in the Congressional cemetery, eight months after his death and had not had honorable burial. He asked that a suitable place be selected, suggesting that General Rawlins's remains should be taken to Arlington and interred in that cemetery. Others joined in suggesting that a monument also be erected to General Rawlins. General Logan felt very deeply on this subject, as he always recognized in General Rawlins one of the most gifted men in the army and one of the most earnest patriots of the Civil War. As a result of this movement General Rawlins was buried in Arlington and a full-length statue of him was erected on the south side of Pennsylvania Avenue in Market Space, where it still remains.

The session was a very long one, and I remained in Washington until June, before taking the children to our home in Carbondale, Illinois. General Logan was very late in reaching home but found plenty of work awaiting him. The candidates for the local offices of representative and senator were clamoring for him to come to help them in their campaign for election to the legislature. Political feeling ran high in the State and General Logan was busy canvassing. He was much embarrassed by the continued importunities of men desiring appointment to official positions. They believed Grant would not refuse him anything he might ask for his friends. He realized better than they did that there was a limit, and that there were innumerable petitioners for everything within the gift of the President. He tried, however, to do all he could for every applicant.

General Logan's friends insisted that he should enter the senatorial race before the legislature met on January 1, 1871. Ex-Governor Palmer and General Oglesby were also candidates. A majority of the candidates for both houses were men of high character and, if elected, would know no bosses or any power but the dictates of their own consciences and the maintenance of their principles in the selection of a United States senator. Their choice for United States senator would be based absolutely on their desire to elect the men whom they believed would serve the best interests of the great State of Illinois.

The three most popular candidates had splendid records in the Civil War. Two had occupied, with great credit to themselves and the State, the highest position within the gift of the people of Illinois. General Logan was then in Congress from the State at large, and therefore could be said to be enjoying honorable reward for his services. He was disinclined to accept the nomination of Congressman-at-large, preferring the position of United States senator. He had resigned his seat in Congress to go into the army, and felt that after five years of hazardous service in the army he had earned the position he desired. Therefore he finally agreed to take his chances in the senatorial contest. He went to Washington December 1 for the beginning of the session. Returning to Illinois for the Christmas holidays, he decided to go at once to Springfield, the capital, to be present when the legislature met, and to enter the contest. We had adopted Miss Kate Logan, a distant relative, one of the talented and beautiful Logan sisters, aunt of Commander George Logan of the United States Navy. She was a fascinating girl with a charming manner and a fine, highly cultivated voice. We begged General Logan to let us go with him to Springfield, and, as it was hard for him to refuse any request from me, he consented. He secured a suite of rooms for us on the second floor of the Leland Hotel, kept by that prince of landlords, Mr. Horace Wiggins, who was untiring in his efforts to make us comfortable. The general had a suite of rooms on the first floor as headquarters, where men congregated to talk politics and discuss their plans.

I consulted Mr. and Mrs. Wiggins and told them I wanted to change the aspect of our rooms to make them as nearly homelike as possible. Our daughter, Dollie, was in school in Cincinnati; Baby John A. Logan, Jr., was with us in the hands of a good nurse, but I wanted him to be in our rooms much of the time. Mr. and Mrs. Wiggins obligingly took a personal interest in everything and very soon we had a large drawing-room with plenty of easy chairs, sofas, a piano, and other appointments found in a home. The citizens of Springfield gave us a warm welcome. Many ladies called and extended invitations for luncheons, dinners, teas, and receptions. We reciprocated by inviting them to spend much time with us in our rooms at the hotel. Kate sang and played by the hour, and our drawing-rooms soon became the rendezvous for a majority of the members and senators and young people of Springfield, who entered with enthusiasm into the spirit of the good time. I wish I could recall some of the good stories that were told or hear again the peals of laughter they provoked. They all enjoyed themselves. Every night it was long past the midnight hour before the happy parties broke up and our guests sought their rooms or homes in the city.

Among the members and senators were some of the ablest men in the State. In those days men who were incorruptible and independent in every sense of the word accepted nominations for the legislature. They had the courage of their convictions and were not subservient to the influences of corporations, trusts, or combinations. The majority were not self-serving, but patriotic, far-seeing men, loyal to their trusts and faithful in the discharge of their public duties. The most solemn among them enjoyed coming to our rooms, sitting in an easy chair listening to good music, stories, and anecdotes, or telling stories themselves. General Logan led them on by his own jocular disposition into forgetfulness of the passing of time. The newspaper correspondents—friends and foes—came and went at their pleasure. There was nothing going on that they were not permitted to know all about; hence they could not in conscience write anything disagreeable or indulge in criticism.

Colonel Clark E. Carr of Galesburg, Illinois; General T. O. Osborne of Chicago; General Thomas Scott; General Berry; Colonel William L. Distin; Colonel Beardsley of Rock Island; Judge R. S. Tuthill; Colonel E. S. McCook; Colonel R. N. Pearson; Colonel Rowett S. D. Phelps; Cadet Taylor; General Shaffer; Captain Isaac Clements; and a host of others were in and out continually, doing far more effective work in influencing voters than if they had adopted the methods that are said to have been in vogue in later years. It was a new feature in politics, and I can not refrain, egotistical as it may seem, from incorporating the report of one of the correspondents in the *Evening Post* of January 6, 1871:

The levees which Mrs. Logan is constantly holding in her parlors in the Leland have not been properly "written up," but their interest is certainly sufficient to justify mention. The *Tribune* has gazed into Parlor No. 26 from the standpoint of a humorist, and the *Times* from the standpoint of a clown; and it is high time that the public is permitted to see it as it is. It may readily be admitted, to begin with, that it is one of the phenomena of this exciting struggle—one of its very pleasantest and most grateful features. Here, directly over the headquarters of the general himself, is a levee always in session presided over by Mrs. Logan herself, who is assisted by her husband's younger brother and his handsome cousin, Miss Logan. In this room all are welcome and all are graciously received, and to this room almost all the members of the first, second, and third houses have beat a retreat at some time during the heat of the contest. It is where they go to escape for a moment from the fetid atmosphere of politics. In Parlor No. 26 politics are not among the refreshments. It is an oasis of peace in a desert of wrangling. It is a retreat, a neutral ground which the combatants of both sides fly to, to get their soured hearts sweetened with music and their bewildered brains cooled by sensible conversation.

Mrs. Logan is a native of Missouri, transplanted to southern Illinois—a small, fragile lady with an attractive mobile face, a mass of turbulent black hair and sharp eyes selected to match it, a wide experience of the social world, a good fund of information, abundant wit, and a ready tongue freighted with complaisance and suavity. She certainly impresses very favorably all who come within her influence. Having accompanied her husband in the field, she is acquainted with camp life in its varied phases. At Belmont and Fort Henry, at Donelson and Vicksburg, she hovered on the edge of battle, and kept her eye fondly on one particular flag. Is it extraordinary that she should follow his fortunes with equal fidelity now? And is it anything less than infamous that her fair name should now be made the subject of insults in the Chicago *Republican*, whose editor, when a correspondent in the field, broke free bread at her table for weeks together and rode her husband's horses and drank gratuitously of the commissary whiskey? Strangers and lifelong enemies are safe from the outrageous calumnies of this young man; it is only those whose guests he has been that he assails.

Mrs. Logan dresses neatly and plainly: a black silk, edged with satin, point laces, a silken knot at the throat, and a gold chain. Her parlor is an exchange of suavities; she never herself introduces the subject of politics, but, if asked, has no hesitation in confessing that she is strongly prejudiced in favor of Logan, and in stating tersely why she thinks he ought to be sent to Washington. She is never aggressive or intrusive on this point, but is fearless and confident and exercises her woman's right of speech with such persuasive tact that there is no doubt whatever that she has made some votes for the coming man. Doubtless a round dozen of gentlemen from the unpaved districts have crossed that charming threshold, confident that they were for Oglesby or "neutral," who have ever since worked steadily for the swarthy little general, and haven't any idea what changed their minds. The fascinations are so thoroughly disguised that even the Oglesby man is disarmed in their presence, but he feels their potency.

This evening, about supper-time, Oglesby and Mrs. Logan, old acquaintances, met in the hall and after an exchange of compliments, a dialogue ensued, somewhat like this:

Mrs. Logan: "Ah, general, I fear you are forgetting the oldschool politeness that used to become you so well; you have not called on me."

Oglesby: "Well, madam, the fact is that I am afraid to subject myself to your blandishments. You are making trouble here; I am afraid I might leave your presence a Logan man."

Mrs. Logan: "Now, general, don't joke; I would like to see you sociably; you would meet a good many pleasant people at my rooms; it would do you good."

Oglesby: "I am not sure about that. I wish you would leave town, Mrs. Logan. You see I am forgetting my politeness. But I really think it is an unfair advantage."

Mrs. Logan: "Not at all. You are suffering one of the disabilities of bachelorhood, as you ought. It seems to me obvious that General Logan should have the senatorship. He has not received any promotion since the year he volunteered for the army, and you have been governor ever so long. Now, general, you see you can be senator next time—or what do you say to Congressman-at-large?"

Mrs. Logan was as gracious as could be, and the fact that she did not mean to be impertinent rendered the last proposal exceedingly cunning, and the old soldier smiled a broad, deep, long, thoughtful, profound, and penetrating smile and withdrew, promising to think about it.

On January 17, 1871, at twelve o'clock, the two houses met in joint session. The vote was as follows: Senate—Logan, 32; T. J. Turner (Democratic candidate), 18. House—Logan, 101; Turner, 70; William H. Snyder, 2. Logan was then declared duly elected United States senator, vice Richard Yates, for six years from the fourth day of March, 1871.[1]

A committee visited General Logan and announced the

good news to him, when he appeared before the assembly and addressed them as follows:

Mr. President, and gentlemen of the Senate and House of Representatives:

I find myself at a loss for appropriate language to express my high appreciation of the distinguished honor you do me in conferring upon me the position of United States Senator, and I can only assure you that my heart wells up with gratitude to you; and, through you, as their representatives, I desire to convey my grateful acknowledgments to the people of Illinois. It is very gratifying to me that I have been chosen with such unanimity by political friends as to leave no serious wounds to be healed. The contest has been one marked with a degree of kindness of feeling among political friends that is very unusual, but highly commendable. The greatest respect has been and is entertained for the ability, integrity, and generosity of those who sought the same position at your hands.

To the interests, prosperity, and happiness of the people of this State I am allied by the closest ties. Born in the midst of this people, I have passed with them through the storms of adversity and the sunshine of prosperity. Their interest is my interest; their prosperity is my prosperity; their hopes and aspirations are mine. All I have ever been or will be, I owe to the people of this State. They have sustained me beyond that which I had a right to expect. For that I owe to them a debt of gratitude that I fear I shall never be able to pay. Whether I shall come up to the standard fixed for me by my friends, or their hopes and anticipations be dashed to the earth, must be left to the future to disclose. I shall, however, enter upon my duties, giving whatever of abilities and energy I may possess to the promotion of the interests of our whole country, but especially shall I devote myself to the interests of that constituency which I shall immediately represent; and trusting implicitly in Divine Providence to guide me in the right direction, I hope to succeed in making you a faithful senator. Again thanking you, with all the warmth of my heart, for your partiality in conferring upon me this great honor, I, for the present, bid you farewell.

It is a melancholy fact that with all our boasted progress along all lines of civilization the question of the election of a United States senator should have degenerated to its present level, and it is one of the incomprehensible questions why this should be. It would be considered disloyal to suggest that there has been a decadence of patriotism and that men of meaner minds have been destined to represent the people in the legislatures of the various States, that money has taken the place of higher motives, and that a majority are prompted to seek these positions by a desire to advance their pecuniary interest, expecting to receive a reward from wealthy and ambitious men for their support of these parties for the position of United States senator. They ignore altogether the very necessary qualities of patriotism and integrity so essential in all members of the United States Senate.

General Logan took his seat March 4, 1871. He soon found that election to the Senate multiplied instead of decreased his work. He was ambitious to comply with every legitimate request of the people of the State, and to co-operate with senators in their advocacy of measures for the general welfare of the country and nation. His comprehension of all subjects, and his—up to that time—tireless energies enabled him to perform stupendous labors.[2] His personal relations with every member of the Illinois delegation were most cordial, notwithstanding his intense loyalty to his party.

In May, 1871, in connection with the delegation, he secured an appropriation of eighty-five thousand dollars for the improvement of the Illinois River and Hennepin Canal. Every movement for the development of the resources of his State claimed his faithful vigilance and earnest labors.

My own social duties were quadrupled, and I was determined that I should not be found ignorant of, or remiss in, the discharge of them. In addition, hordes of the people from the great State of Illinois and especially from Chicago, were continually arriving in Washington. A majority of them hastened to find us and to claim our time to assist them in accomplishing the object of their visit, whether it was sight-seeing, seeking appointments, or a glimpse of society. General Logan knew that he could rely on me to assume the role of guide and chaperon and to secure the introduction to every sanctum of the capital which they wished to enter. He usually brought me a long list of engagements he had made for me to contribute to the pleasure of his visiting constituents.

Early in May I returned to Carbondale, as the general had concluded, after conferring with many of our friends, that it would be a wise thing for him to remove to Chicago. There existed at that time a sentiment in regard to the geographical location of the homes of senators, and Chicago claimed that it should be the residence of one of the senators from Illinois. General Logan had bought a house in Chicago sometime before, which a friend had been occupying, intending to go to Chicago to practise law, if he had not gone into politics in 1866. We had always lived in southern Illinois, and it was a tremendous wrench to take our goods and gods away from Egypt, and to take up our abode in a great city. After Congress adjourned the general went to Chicago to have our house put in order for us, and I took charge of the packing, making good-by visits, and trying to reconcile these old friends to the change we were about to make. My part of it was no small task, and I had to explain over and over again "the reasons why." Finally, in August, we shipped our goods and bade good-by to friends who were very dear to us.

Our house in Chicago was located on Calumet Avenue, just north of the Twenty-second Street depot of the Lake Shore, about the middle of the block, with detached houses on the north and south sides of us. The houses fronted west, the rear facing the lake. We had broad lawns that extended down to the track of the Illinois Central Railroad, with no division fences, and it was a most beautiful location. Here we spent many happy years during the interim between the sessions of Congress. I was obliged to dispose of this home after General Logan's death, and have since had the painful experience of seeing it fall before the march of the resistless commercialism of Chicago.[3]

We had not gotten our home settled when that fearful holocaust of October 9, 1871, swallowed all of Chicago north of Twelfth Street to Lincoln Park. We had friends calling on Sunday evening, when we heard the continuous ringing of the fire-bell and went out on top of the house, where there was an observatory, to try to locate the fire. In the northwest we saw the heavens lighted up by the flames, which were consuming the wooden houses and lumber in the lumber districts of northwest Chicago. It seemed many miles away; so, after watching it for hours, we descended to our rooms, our friends departed, and we retired. In the early morning we were awakened by a great confusion in the street and looked out upon our front lawn to find the whole of the block from Twenty-first to Twenty-second Streets occupied by every conceivable article of merchandise. Men, women, and children were crying and wringing their hands, having come from the fire district to our locality as a place of safety. The alleys in the rear of our barn were full of tremendous trucks loaded with goods. We hastily dressed and came out to open our doors to welcome these frightened and stricken people. On General Logan's going to the alley to see what he could do there, he found that the goods which J. V. Farwell & Company had rescued from the fire were being piled high in the rear of our barns. He quickly had the coachman open the doors and, in a twinkling, almost every inch of space in the barn and its loft was occupied by cases of priceless laces and rare imported goods. Our first thought was that all the supplies would be cut off, as the gas-house on the north side had been exploded, and the gas was escaping from every main all over the city. We realized that we should be in total darkness when the sun went down. I hurried over to Twenty-second Street and bought from our grocer and butcher large quantities of supplies, including boxes of candles which we had to use for many days. We had no candlesticks, but in their place found that empty bottles served every purpose.

I shall not attempt to describe the horrors of many days and nights. I joined the army of people residing south of Twelfth Street who were, without exception, gathering together all they could get to take to the churches that were being used for hospitals and for sheltering homeless people. They had gone into old barns, residences, churches, and houses, and every place that furnished a roof for the people that had fled from their homes. General Logan and General Sheridan had had much experience in such catastrophes during the Civil War, and they rendered valuable service by assuming direction of the armies of men who were tearing down houses, and using the fire department as much as they could in breaking the fire line. Almost every one was worn out, and some were so exhausted that there was nothing to do but to lie down wherever they could get shelter. The patriotic and noble State of Illinois responded within a few hours with train-loads of provisions and supplies of all kinds for the immediate relief of the victims of the fire district. The world knows the generous response that came from all over the globe and of the long and tedious months when armies of men, women, and children had no resource but to visit the relief depots and have issued to them their daily supplies. When we look at Chicago to-day, we realize the situation during those unhappy early days of October, 1871. About one hundred persons, and tons of goods of delicate and valuable character were in our house for more than two weeks. We had to have as many cooks as could be utilized in a private kitchen, and the range was going from early morning until late at night to furnish meals for these friends who had been deprived of their homes and abiding-places. The memory of meeting the survivors of families that had been swept by the flames from their homes through the darkness of that Sunday night will abide with me forevermore. We found men broken and weary, weeping like children because they knew not where their families were. We found women crying for their babes; babes crying for their mothers; wives in tears over the loss of their husbands and their homes. Hand-presses of Chicago and the newspaper presses of the neighboring towns and cities were busy publishing the names and location of persons, hoping in this way that their friends and families might learn of the whereabouts of their loved ones. Hundreds of families were reunited in this way who had not known for days how many of them were alive. The hospitality of the districts not included in the fire, and that of the towns and homes within miles of Chicago was taxed to its utmost. Many died and were borne to their last resting-places unattended by any member of their family, and but for the records that were kept, and the stories that were told before these poor creatures died, their fate would never have been known. Bodies were recovered from the tunnels and in out-of-the-way places where the victims had succumbed in their attempt to escape from the smoke, darkness, and confusion that reigned supreme for the hours between sundown Sunday night and Monday morning.

General Logan was more deeply impressed with the horrors of the Chicago fire than with anything he had ever experienced. His prodigious efforts in Congress as soon as it assembled in December 1871, told the story of how deeply his great heart was stirred by the misfortune of his beloved city of Chicago. Through his efforts the Government did very much to enable the city to rise from its ashes. Probably Chicago would not be the city it is to-day but for this unutterable calamity which may have been a blessing in disguise. It roused an indomitable spirit in the men of that generation and those that have followed them which has never been exceeded by mankind.

In November 1871, we returned to Washington and removed to No. 8 Grant Place, to a house occupied by Major and Mrs. Hayden, brother of Professor Hayden of the geological survey. The members of the Hayden family and ourselves being the only occupants of the house, it was more like our own home would have been than anything we had previously had in Washington. The house was new and well appointed, and Mrs. Hayden was a delightful housekeeper; hence we had all the comforts of a home without any of the cares and the indispensable vexations attending housekeeping. Katie Logan was with us, and we had a very delightful time on account of her wonderful musical genius. Every evening our parlors were crowded with friends who came to enjoy her music.

General Logan on his entrance into the Senate was made chairman of the military committee, greatly to the disgust of General Ames, who had been chairman of that committee prior to General Logan.[4] General Logan was also second on the committee on judiciary, second on the committee on appropriations, and second on the committee on privileges and elections. The amount of work which devolved upon him as a member of these important committees was something prodigious. He had very little time for recreation and constantly devoted himself to his duties. To the labors of the committees was added a voluminous correspondence, as he was commander-in-chief of the Grand Army of the Republic, and had so lately occupied the position of Congressman-at-large from the State of Illinois that his constituents did not relinquish their claim upon him, but desired him to attend to everything in which they were interested. The collection of pensions, back pay, and bounty, and the inquiries which followed the passage of his bill for the establishment of the geological survey also augmented the work of the daily grind very much. Naturally, I could not see my husband working day and night without also doing what I could to share in the burdens of the drudgery attending the detail of proper attention to these various interests.

Among the first things that confronted him was the contested election case of Ransom and Abbott of North Carolina. Abbott was a Republican and had demanded the throwing out of the votes cast for Ransom, which would have given him (Abbott) the majority of the North Carolina legislature, and secured for him a seat in the United States Senate. General Logan, though a steadfast Republican partisan, differed with the committee in his opinion of the case. Upon its submission to him, he asked for a delay of one week before making the report of the committee. He had, in a way, scanned the evidence and thought that to throw out Ransom's votes would be an outrage in view of the facts then existing. There seemed to be no evidence that any fraud had been perpetrated in the election of those members of the North Carolina legislature whose votes Abbott demanded should be thrown out. It further seemed from the evidence that was before the committee that, even if Abbott's demands were acceded to, he was not the choice of a majority of the legislature.

The amount of work that General Logan put on this case was beyond description. He came home one evening telling me that he had asked for the delay in submitting the report, but had previously sent his clerk to the Library of Congress to get such authority as parallel cases afforded, or cases bearing on these contested elections. The mail-wagon brought to our house that evening five bags of books from the Library of the Senate and the Congressional Library. These books were journals and reports of law cases. To read each of the cases and at the same time attend to the duties of each day would have been impossible. When General Logan had anything very important that he desired to do and wanted to be sure he made no mistake about it, he always asked me to hunt up the information for him, for he insisted that he could trust me implicitly to give him the facts of a case without perverting them, as is often done by secretaries who are more anxious to please their chief than to disappoint him in not finding material he desires.

Three days and three nights we stayed in the back parlor, which was the general's office, working on this case, with the exception of the few hours that General Logan had to go to the Senate to be present during the session. We had our meals served in our rooms, and never went to bed during the three days and nights except for an hour or so in the early morning. While he was at the Capitol I ran over these various cases, wrote on slips of paper what they were and the points upon which they bore, and marked for him the paragraphs that were most important. When he came in, as soon as we had our dinner he would take these volumes and read only the paragraphs which I had marked for him. Notwithstanding the digest which I had prepared, it was almost impossible to have his report ready for the meeting of the committee at the end of the week. We had no such helps in those days as stenography and typewriting; all this work had to be done by writing it out in longhand, and after deciding which cases had the strongest bearing upon the position he had taken he wrote out his report, giving the authority, the case, the page, and the paragraph in support of his decision. When he asked for the delay in the submitting of the report, it was to prevent the committee from making a favorable report on the case and casting out Ransom's votes. When he had made his argument before the committee he changed the whole feature of the case, and an adverse report was made upon the side of Abbott and in favor of Ransom.[5] Naturally we were pretty well worn out for a week afterward, but we were young in those days and soon recovered from the over-taxing of our mental and physical strength.

January 1, 1872, President and Mrs. Grant gave the usual New Year's reception. There were most elaborate preparations made for the reception, as there was at that time a greater number of officers of high rank of the army, navy, and marine corps in Washington than have ever been there at one time before or since. The Diplomatic Corps was represented by distinguished men, as Washington had been considered an important post during the long years of the Civil War.

New Year's Day was bright and clear, and at an early hour—as the reception was to begin at ten o'clock in the morning—the streets were full of carriages en route to the White House. Mrs. Grant had invited the ladies of the cabinet and the Supreme Court and the wives of the more prominent members and senators. I was fortunate enough to be included on this list, and I shall never forget the remarkable splendor of the occasion. Every member of the Diplomatic Corps was in full court dress, wearing innumerable decorations. They were accompanied by ladies who, it seems to me now, were very superior in their gracious manners to those whom I have met in later years. The ladies' jewels were quite as dazzling as those of the orders worn by their husbands. Sir Edward and Lady Thornton; Baron and Madame Gerolt—who set the magnanimous example of giving the French fair such articles as she had been unable to use in the German fair for the relief of the wounded and unfortunate of the Franco-Prussian War—accompanied by her beautiful daughter, who subsequently took the veil in the Convent of the Visitation at Washington; the distinguished Spanish minister and his brilliant wife, wearing flame color and yellow, and resplendent diamonds half veiled by her rich Chantilly; Count Marquis de Chambrun, many years an attaché of the French legation, with his charming wife, a descendant of Lafayette; Madame Catacazy, wife of the Russian minister, with her great beauty heightened by her wealth of golden hair, who created such a sensation by her magnificent dress and diamonds, represented the Diplomatic Corps.

The ladies of the cabinet who were not assisting in the reception accompanied their husbands and sustained themselves admirably as representative American women.

In the throng there were such distinguished persons as Gail Hamilton—Mrs. Blaine's cousin—Sydney Hyde, Mary Clemmer Ames, Miss Foote, John W. Forney, Ben Perley Poore, and many other representatives of literary circles, while Senators Fenton, Conkling, Chandler, Bayard, Morton, Ferry, Howard, Drake, Carpenter, Thurman, Edmunds, Frelinghuysen, Fessenden, William Pitt Kellogg, and hosts of others represented the Senate. Of the House, there was Wilson of Iowa; Frye and Blaine of Maine; Hawley of Connecticut; Pomeroy of Kansas; Farnsworth and Burchard of Illinois, and many others whose names are associated with the stirring events of that era.

To this brilliant galaxy were added our army, navy, and marine corps, all in the full-dress uniforms of their respective branches of the service, wearing all the medals and gold lace to which they were entitled. Almost all of them were accompanied by wives or daughters who, not wishing to be outdone in expressing their appreciation of the occasion, had worn their most beautiful costumes, many carrying magnificent furs.

The mantels of all the reception-rooms, the red, blue, green, and east rooms, were banked with most gorgeous flowers, while palms and pots of flowering plants were distributed in every available spot. The brilliant lights of the crystal chandeliers made it a veritable fairy scene. The well-known Marine Band, led by Professor Scala, with their red coats and blue trousers heavily trimmed with gold lace, played in the corridor and added much to the gayety.

President Grant was most democratic in his manner, and had given instructions that none who came to pay their respects should be excluded from the White House. Consequently, an hour after the programme had been finished a long line of citizens and visitors, two abreast, passed through the White House, halting only long enough to speak to President Grant. It was after twelve o'clock when the last one had been gratified by a welcome to the White House.

Secretary Fish had the customary breakfast for the Diplomatic Corps, foreign relations committees of both houses, and other distinguished guests, who did full justice to the bounteous buffet feast. It was then the custom for persons receiving on New Year's Day to furnish refreshment, and it has been said that there were barrels of egg-nog used every New Year's Day in Washington. I regret, sometimes, that the good old custom of New Year's receptions with their accompaniment of beautiful ladies, flowers, music refreshments, and cordial greetings has passed away. It seems that one should be able to make this day a happy one, to renew old acquaintances and make new friends, to start the year as it should be started—with good cheer.

The New Year's reception was the beginning of the social season, and was rapidly followed by state dinners and receptions in the White House, in the homes of the cabinet, in the homes of the Diplomatic Corps, justices of the Supreme Court, members of both houses of Congress, and prominent and wealthy people of Washington. As I remember it, no administration has exceeded that of President and Mrs. Grant's in hospitality. President Grant was very fortunate in choosing members of his cabinet who seemed to realize that they had to make acknowledgment of the honor which had been conferred upon them in some way besides the daily routine of properly discharging their official duties. There were hosts of beautiful women in Washington at that time who had been well-trained for the positions they occupied. Social events seemed less attended by commercial features than they are to-day. Men and women apparently laid aside everything for the purpose of greeting their friends and making them feel that they had time enough to devote to their entertainment.

As if to emphasize their welcome of General Logan and myself to the senatorial circle, we had many invitations for dinner, President and Mrs. Grant inviting us for the first state dinner of the season, notwithstanding the fact that the letter "L" was low down on the alphabetical list. Members of the cabinet and senior senators and their wives included us among their guests for the first dinners after New Year's Day. Those were delightful functions and we enjoyed them to the full.

Mrs. Kate Chase Sprague presided over the home of Chief Justice Chase. There could not possibly have been sisters more unlike each other than were the Chase sisters, not only in personal appearance but in disposition, talents, and characteristics. Nettie, though of a plainer face, was one of the most gentle, modest, retiring, and lovable characters that one could possibly imagine. Their mother had died when they were both quite young. Kate was the elder; hence, when she was in her teens she was mistress of her father's house, and presided over the executive mansion while he was governor of Ohio. Her remarkable beauty attracted much attention. Her famous Titian hair, peach-blow complexion, graceful figure, and bewitching manners seemed to have especially fitted her for the position which she was destined to occupy.

Soon after Mr. Lincoln's inauguration Mr. Chase was chosen Secretary of the Treasury and took up his residence in Washington in a commodious house on the corner of Fifth and E Streets, N. W., which was then considered an eligible part of the city. It was not long before his daughter Kate became the leader in society. Her inborn diplomacy enabled her to harmonize the discordant elements then existing in Washington and to capture the Diplomatic Corps, who were extravagant in their admiration of her brilliant conversational powers and incomparable beauty. Her devotees were innumerable, and no queen ever held a more imperious sway than did Kate Chase. Legions of suitors sought her hand, apparently without touching her heart. Finally Governor Sprague, the multimillionaire merchant of Rhode Island, joined the ranks of suppliants for her favor.[6] After their marriage Mr. and Mrs. Sprague departed for Europe. The newspapers were full of reports of the lavish expenditures of Mrs. Sprague. Her wardrobe was equal to that possessed by crowned heads—priceless jewels and laces were added to her collection, and excesses of all kinds characterized the honeymoon of this ill-mated pair. Before their return home hints were given in the press that the old house of Sprague Brothers was approaching failure. Governor Sprague, however, was elected to the United States Senate. At the beginning of the session they took up their abode with Chief Justice Chase, and Mrs. Sprague resumed her accustomed sway as the wife of a senator.

Late in January, at the height of the season, sorrow came to us through the death of the illustrious Eliza Logan Wood, elder sister of our adopted daughter, Kate Logan. She had been one of the most brilliant actresses of her day. She played all the many roles in legitimate drama for a female tragedian. She was the daughter of Cornelius Logan, one of the celebrated actors of his time. She was once a great favorite in the South and West, and on her benefit nights she was often the recipient of rare and valuable gifts. On one of these occasions a wealthy Southern planter, residing in the interior of Georgia, travelled many miles on horseback to see Miss Logan act, accompanied only by his faithful negro boy servant. The planter and his servant attended the play. He was enthusiastic over Miss Logan's acting and was most anxious to convey to her some expression of thanks for the pleasure which she had afforded him. Taking a card from his card-case, he wrote above his address the words: "To Miss Eliza Logan, with the compliments of ———" and, pinning it upon the coat-sleeve of his faithful negro valet (worth at the then market price two thousand dollars), bade him present himself to his new mistress. The slave presented himself at the stage-door, and the management advised Miss Logan of his presence. She was much amazed, and, not knowiing what to do with him during her nomadic career, resolved to return him. The following morning Miss Logan returned the slave to his owner, with an autographic letter couched in such terms that the planter was more than satisfied. This is probably the only instance in this country when a human being was ever presented to an artist as a token of esteem.

Miss Logan was so successful that she took care of her mother and sisters and when she was married had a large fortune in her own right. She married Mr. George Wood, retired from the stage, and continued to reside in New York until her death, January 15, 1872.

General W. W. Belknap had succeeded General John A. Rawlins as Secretary of War. He and his bride—for he had not long been married to his second wife—took up their residence on Lafayette Square in a house that was long considered a fatal place of abode on account of the tragic events that had taken place in and near the plain red brick, three-story building that was removed to make place for the present Belasco Theatre. This house had been occupied by Secretary William H. Seward at the time of the assault upon him when Mr. Lincoln was assassinated. Mrs. Belknap's death cast a shadow over the gayeties of the official circles.

In March a great sorrow came into our own household through the death of our adopted daughter, the talented and beautiful Kate Logan. Early in the month she expressed a desire to make a visit to her mother, who resided in Philadelphia. She had been such an assistance and had won so many friends that we were loath to do without her, but we appreciated her loyalty and devotion to her widowed mother, and therefore consented to her going. She had been in Philadelphia only a few days when we received a telegram that she was dangerously ill from peritonitis. I hurried to her bedside, and the moment I saw her I knew that death was near. I telegraphed to General Logan and to Doctor J. M. Woodworth, superintendent of the Marine Hospital Service, to whom she was engaged. They came at once and immediately secured the ablest skill in the profession, and everything that was possible was done to save her life, but all to no avail. She died in my arms, surrounded by her family, among them her brothers, Thomas A. Logan of Cincinnati, and C. A. Logan of Leavenworth, Kansas. Her father, Cornelius A. Logan, the distinguished tragedian, and other members of her family were buried in Cincinnati, at Glenwood Cemetery, and so it was decided that her remains should be taken to that city. It was a long, sad journey, and cast such a shadow over our home, which she had made so bright by her gracious manners and lovely voice, that we could not rally for some time. I withdrew from further participation in social affairs during that session of Congress.

CHAPTER 9

1872: A Time of Troubles

POLITICALLY excitement was running high. Rivals of President Grant were busy in the manufacture of all kinds of charges against and abuse of his administration. Unfortunately, some of his appointees had not conducted themselves as they should, and he was held responsible, though totally ignorant of their misdeeds. James G. Blaine was ambitious to be nominated for the Presidency, and it was said that he had used the speakership in every possible way to secure delegates to the national convention which was to nominate the candidates for President and Vice-President. There was never a more bitter campaign than that conducted before the holding of the national convention. President Grant's friends—General Logan among them—were so outraged at the methods that had been used that they allowed themselves no respite day or night in their defence of the administration. It is probable that General Logan's defence of President Grant against the attacks of Senator John B. Gordon of Georgia, and other ex-Confederates who were then in the Senate, together with those of the Sumner-Schurz coterie, has never been equalled in fervor and vehemence. To General Logan probably belongs greater credit in rendering service to President Grant in the halls of Congress than to any other man.

At no time in the history of the Government has there been a greater number of able men in Congress than there was in the early seventies. Unhappily, ambition all too often attributes evil to the motives of rivals. Grant was naturally the only barrier in the road to the White House to each of the men ambitious to occupy it. He had reluctantly accepted the nomination for President in 1868, realizing that he had no training for an executive position. The Republican party would not listen to his objections, knowing that his name was a synonym for a victory. He had conscientiously and wisely administered the affairs of the Republic, and had advanced the United States to a high place on the roll of nations. Yet he and his followers were the targets against whom the shafts of the designing were levelled. Grant was held responsible for every act of his appointees—the whiskey-ring scandals, sale of arms to the French, and nepotism. It was said that he might have averted the grasshopper scourge in Kansas had he been equal to the position of President! Charges against the administration by the coterie determined to destroy Grant and able defence of him and his administration were heard daily in Congress. The galleries of both houses were crowded to suffocation with men and women eager to hear the eloquent men of both sides engaged in the discussions. Meanwhile conventions were being held in every district of the country to elect delegates to the national convention to be held at Cincinnati, in June, 1872.[1]

The imbroglio between Charles Sumner and President Grant was especially bitter. Mr. Sumner was one of the most learned men in the Senate. He was commanding in his personal appearance—tall and straight as an arrow. His head was large and covered with heavy hair; his eyes were dark and expressive. He spoke with great earnestness. He had made a national and an international reputation by his opposition to slavery, and had suffered bodily injury at the hands of the slaveholding Brooks of South Carolina which, together with his unwavering demand for the abolition of slavery, made him the idol of the Whigs and Abolitionists.

A person once told Grant that Sumner did not believe in

the Bible. Grant replied: "That is because he did not write it himself." Sumner had been elected to the Senate four times, first succeeding Daniel Webster, and had rendered splendid service to his country. All loyal people regretted exceedingly that the controversy between him and President Grant should have arisen. It was apparent to observers that Mr. Sumner's influence and powers were waning. He had brooded over his unfortunate marriage and separation from the widowed daughter-in-law of his old and cherished friend, Mr. Hooper of Massachusetts and, in addition, it broke him down to be obliged to endure the daily relentless excoriations of brother senators with whom he had previously been on most intimate terms. He died March 12, 1874, never having regained his wonderful mental and physical vigor.

Carl Schurz supported Mr. Sumner in his attacks upon President Grant and the administration. He was a German revolutionist of 1848 and had had a most remarkable career in the United States. He had been teacher, newspaper correspondent, editor, and as a reward for his support of Mr. Lincoln in the convention of 1860, was made minister to Spain, a position he soon resigned to enter the service during the Civil War. He was made brigadier-general of volunteers, and was assigned to a command in the army. He was in the battles of Chancellorsville, Gettysburg, and other engagements of the Army of the Potomac. He lived first in New York, then Wisconsin, and from there went to Missouri, from which State he was elected to the United States Senate to succeed General John B. Henderson. He was most intense in the advocacy of any measure of which he approved and in the denunciation of anything which he opposed. He used effectively weapons of sarcasm and ridicule.

But he was no match for Senator Conkling in this line of debate. Schurz had dubbed Senator Conkling "The Powter Pigeon of the Senate," but Conkling was probably the author of the cognomen "Mephistopheles" which had been conferred upon Schurz in virtue of his peculiar physiognomy. It is needless to add that Carl Schurz was not re-elected to the Senate from Missouri, but he was subsequently appointed Secretary of the Interior by Mr. Hayes. He was a very remarkable man but could never quite get over his revolutionary ideas. He was wont to say that the Roman punch was the life-saving station in Mrs. Hayes's temperance dinners. Mrs. Schurz and her daughters were among the most charming women that have ever been in Washington. I was especially fond of Mrs. Schurz, who was so serious-minded that she had no appreciation whatever of a joke and was often shocked by the easy manner of the ladies who received at the White House. Propriety and dignity were her chief characteristics. She could not bear to see the line of ladies assisting at a reception in the least irregular, and was constantly calling them to order, greatly to the annoyance of some and the amusement of others. She was a stately German matron whose kindness knew no bounds, and who was so sincere in her profession of friendship that you felt perfectly at ease in her company. The daughters were charming young women but they left Washington when they were quite young, and I trust have married well, as I am quite sure they were equal to any position they might undertake to fill. Mr. Schurz wrote in his *Memoirs* a voluminous history of his life and times and died only a few years ago in the city of New York.

Days and weeks were consumed in the debates in both houses over the charges of mistakes and misdoings of the administration. Among other things, there was a great scandal created about the Crédit Mobilier, which meant that Oakes Ames of Massachusetts, who had organized a company inside of the company which built the Union Pacific Railroad, had sold its stock to members of Congress, many of whom were so afraid that their names would be mentioned in connection with it that they denied having made the purchase or knowing anything about it. Those who admitted having bought the stock as an honest investment of their own money in what promised to be a legitimately profitable venture suffered nothing whatever. General Logan, who had invested in the stock, suffered no discredit because, when he discovered that Congress would be asked to pass additional legislation in the interest of the Union Pacific Railroad, he returned his stock to Mr. Ames. The truth is that Mr. Ames was a very much persecuted man. He had patriotically put his fortune into the Union Pacific Railroad to save it from failure and received for this courageous and noble venture on his part condemnation and almost ostracism. He was only vindicated in after years, when the whole facts in connection with the matter came to light.

In the midst of all this the Japanese embassy arrived.[2] Congress made an appropriation for their entertainment, which sum was to be expended under the direction of General Myers, then quartermaster of the United States army, on duty at Washington. Among the social features of their entertainment a grand reception was given in the Masonic Temple, then the only hall in Washington spacious enough for such affairs. General Logan was on the committee for their entertainment and was very much interested in all the arrangements. A magnificent banquet was laid in a room adjoining the reception-room of the Masonic Temple. The main hall was used for the reception and had been decorated profusely with flags of all nations, palms, flowers, and colored globes for the gas-burners, as electricity was not known in those days.

The President and Mrs. Grant, all the members of the cabinet, and everybody entitled to be present on state occasions came to welcome this interesting Oriental delegation. Many were disappointed that the ladies of the Japanese party were not present, but at that time they were not permitted by their own people to mingle in society as they do to-day. A commodious house in Georgetown had been secured for their accommodation, where every luxury was provided. The "little yellow men of the East," however, were the keenest observers of everything and lost no time in asking questions and gaining such information as they had been authorized to secure. They engaged the services of many teachers, artisans, agriculturalists, financiers, and political economists and returned to Japan, having recruited quite an army of educators in Western civilization. This was the beginning of the friendly relations between the United States and Japan.

Soon after the visit of the embassy, the first Japanese minister made his appearance—Mr. Mori and his interesting family, who has been succeeded from time to time by other most interesting diplomats. Mr. Yoshida, one of the early ministers from Japan, became so much interested in the United States and its progress that his family adopted many of our customs. When he came to Washington he brought his bride, who had the most gorgeous gowns, made up in true Japanese style. Mrs. Grant was very fond of Madame Yoshida and insisted upon her attending many of her receptions. Madame Yoshida was a most agreeable, sensitive lady, and was naturally much distressed over the curiosity manifested by ill-bred people in her dress, coiffure, and appearance. One evening, at one of Mrs. Grant's receptions, Madame Yoshida wore one of the gorgeous gowns of her trousseau. Some one had the rudeness to take hold of it to feel the quality of the rich brocade of which the gown was made. She was so much distressed over it that she confided her feelings to her husband. He went to the French dressmaker, Madame Soulé, and told her she was to go up to the legation and see if she could not change Madame Yoshida's gowns into regular court-dress, so that she might appear in European dress at the next reception. Madame Soulé was much elated over the order, and at the next reception Madame Yoshida appeared in one of her rich gowns which had been converted into a regular European court-dress.

The Yoshidas were here many years, making visits to Japan and returning. General Logan and I were dining at their home one night, when Associate Justice Field sat on Madame Yoshida's right and I sat next to Justice Field. The Justice was a very agreeable conversationalist and Madame Yoshida had learned to speak English quite well. Justice Field said: "Madame Yoshida, how many children have you?" She replied: "I have two American and one Japanese children," at which Justice Field smiled. Quickly realizing the fact that she had made a mistake, she said: "Two born in America, and one in Japan. One is named Ulysses Grant, and one other Roscoe Conkling." They were hospitable entertainers, and when you went there to a dinner they had many favors at your plate, which was then the custom. I said to Madame Yoshida at one time: "It will be necessary to have an express to take the beautiful things you have given us to our home." She laughed heartily over it and said she would send them to the house by her servant if I so desired. Fancy boxes, beautiful carved ivories, and all kinds of exquisite and dainty favors, besides the menu-card, were laid at our plates, and you would have committed a grave offence if you had not taken them with you. One felt quite ashamed to leave the dining-room with hands so full of souvenirs of the occasion.

Soon after March 4, 1872, I returned to our home in Chicago for the summer, General Logan going directly from Washington to the convention in Philadelphia, where, after a stormy time, Grant and Wilson were nominated for the Presidency and the Vice-Presidency. The national committee met soon after the adjournment of the convention and made a programme for the conduct of the campaign. General Logan was booked to speak almost every day until the election, having appointments in Indiana, Ohio, Maine, Kansas, Nebraska, and Iowa, in addition to the many made for him in the State of Illinois, a State which he had ever a pride in carrying. Indiana was always a battleground between the Republican and the Democratic parties, and it required much labor to carry it for the Republican party.

After my father's second marriage, he desired to go west. He was appointed an assessor under the Internal Revenue Bureau and removed to Provo, Utah. Early in August, when the campaign was at its height, I received a telegram from Doctor Taggart, a friend of ours, who was the collector of internal revenue at Salt Lake City. He said that my father was dangerously ill from meningitis and desired that I should come to him. Knowing how dependent he was upon me after my mother's death, and how unhappy he was to be seriously ill so far away from us, I communicated with General Logan at once, to ask his permission to join my father. It was impossible for him to accompany me on account of his duties in the campaign, but I insisted that I could go alone, and hence it was arranged. I set out upon the journey a few hours after receiving the telegram. At that time the arrangements were not as perfect as they are now. Persons travelling over the Union Pacific Railroad were obliged to change cars and get their sleeping-berth at Omaha. Following the directions of the agent in Chicago, I went into the depot at Omaha to find the Pullman office to secure the tickets for the section which I supposed had been assigned to me. There were many passengers in the room in line before the window of the Pullman office. Realizing that I would have no chance to reach the window for some time, I sought one of the officials on duty in the depot. He knew General Logan very well and at once busied himself to secure my tickets. He stood up on a chair and called to the Pullman agent, saying: "What is the number of Mrs. Logan's section in the Salt Lake car?" After some delay the agent responded: "Number twelve." The official then escorted me to this car, and I was soon with all my belongings ensconced in section twelve. The official probably knew more about the matter than I did, because he said to me: "No matter who claims this seat, you sit still. Nobody will dare to take hold of you." I was rather uncomfortable for fear there was something wrong about the seat but made up my mind to follow his instructions. A little while afterward two Englishmen came into the car and deposited their numerous pieces of "luggage" in number eleven, directly opposite my section. They were muttering to each other and manifesting much displeasure over something that had occurred, but fearing that I might in some way have disconcerted their plans, I looked out of the window steadily for some time. It seemed to me a long time before everybody was assigned to his proper place in the car.

Finally we were off and, in my great anxiety, I realized that it was to be a long and tedious journey, relieved only by the enjoyment of the magnificent scenery as we reached and crossed the Rocky Mountains. In order to have a better view, I retired to the observation car. There being a vacant seat next to my neighbor, number eleven, I sat down. The gentleman said: "I beg your pardon, are you Mrs. John A. Logan?" I replied in the affirmative. He said: "I speak to you, madam, to apologize for our seeming discourtesy, but you will pardon me if I tell you that you have one of our sections. I am afraid that we manifested much displeasure when we found that we both had to occupy one section, whereas we expected to have two." I told him I was very sorry, but that I was not aware of the fact that I had displaced them. He replied: "Oh! it is all right now, because we have learned of your sad journey, and we wish to apologize for what may have seemed rudeness." They proved to be English officers of the army and navy making a journey around the world. They were delightful gentlemen, and we grew to be very good friends before we reached Salt Lake. I noticed that the naval officer had a copy of "Lucille," which he read very assiduously. Upon my remarking that I was very much attracted by the literature which he seemed to enjoy, he told me all about a very serious love-affair which he had had just before leaving England, and that he was trying to pull himself together a "bit" by this journey. I reminded him that "there are just as good fish in the sea as ever were caught." I shall never forget their great courtesy and attention during that long and weary journey. I invited them to make themselves more comfortable by depositing part of their luggage on one of the seats of my section. They were to stop in Salt Lake to learn something of the wonders of that famous city, and therefore attended me to the hotel.

Doctor Taggart met me soon after my arrival and relieved me by saying that my father was better, but that he was still very ill. He told me that he had made arrangements for me to go to Provo on the stage-coach. The stage line at that time was under the management of Gilmer and Saulsbury, men from Illinois and, of course, I felt quite sure that I would have every care and attention. The railroad only extended a few miles out of Salt Lake, where we were met by a stage-coach. At the terminus of the railroad there was nothing but an empty freight-car for a depot, and a few tents and cloth houses, where it seemed to me there was nothing but gambling-places and whiskey saloons. Near the car which was used as a depot were a number of barrels upon which were laid some boards. Around them men were gathered playing cards. Imagine my dismay when I descended from the car to go into the stage to see all these men pick up their bottles and cards, put them in their pockets, and get into the stage! I knew no one, but I was obliged to go to my father. I shall never forget the absolute silence that prevailed in that coach. The men were as polite and as considerate as they could possibly be, and spoke never a word until we reached the first station where the horses had to be watered. Doctor Taggart had evidently told the driver who I was and where I was going, for I shall ever remember the gallantry with which he came to the door and asked me if I would have a drink of water. He then said: "I think you would enjoy riding on top of the stage if you would not mind sitting by me." It was a great relief, and I accepted his invitation with much gratitude. He had watered his horses and assisted me up to the box on top of the stage. He had the reins tied to the brake, the passengers were all in, and we were about ready to start, when he darted into the house and returned with an umbrella in his hand. It was a very hot day, and nothing I could do would induce him to surrender that umbrella to me, but he drove his horses and held the umbrella over me all the way to Provo. We went to a dizzy height over mountains, and crawled along the sides of precipices. If he had made the slightest mistake, we might have been dashed hundreds of feet to our death. I was scarcely seated on top of the coach before I could hear the men inside cracking jokes, laughing, and enjoying themselves hugely. It made a deep impression on me, realizing, as I did, that their silence was their way of expressing their profound respect for a lone woman. Rough as they were, they still retained the innate instincts of gallantry of American men toward women.

It was nearly five o'clock when I reached Provo, and was again embraced by my dear old father. He improved rapidly after my arrival and, after spending ten days with him and seeing him convalescent, I decided to return home. After he had improved and was quite on the road to recovery, he wanted me to meet his Mormon friends of the city of Provo. Among them were many of the highest intelligence and refinement, and I used to enjoy hearing them talk. I remember one Bishop Dusenberry, an Englishman, who was as fine a looking man as I have ever seen. Though a bishop of the church, nothing would induce him to practise polygamy. He had one wife and lived handsomely in a substantial house surrounded by beautiful grounds. Though he was loyal to the tenets of the church, I discovered in conversation that his bank account was kept in England, and I jocularly remarked to him one day: "Bishop, I expect some day to hear that you have renounced Mormonism and gone to England." He laughed quite heartily and replied: "What makes you think so?" I said: "Because I understand the greater part of your fortune is deposited in the Bank of England, in London." He again laughed and replied, "Don't you think that it is in a very safe place?" thus avoiding a direct reply to my remark.

Knowing General Logan's position, the friends of my father lost no time in paying me every respect, bringing me fruits and flowers, and in every way manifesting their great admiration for my husband. I could but admire the courage that had enabled these people with their teams and wagons to cross the great American desert and hew their way over the Rocky Mountains to the great valley of Salt Lake in the Territory of Utah at a time when pioneers had to brave every conceivable danger, including that of hostile Indians. They surely could never have succeeded in making this great valley blossom as a rose and in establishing homes that are as comfortable as those of other sections if they had not been sustained by the fanaticism of their remarkable religious faith. I felt more resigned to my father's living in this part of the country after having seen and known that these people were full of kindness and generosity.

After my return home I frequently accompanied General Logan in the campaign, to look after his health and to entertain his friends so that he might be able to snatch a little rest between his engagements. In this way I met the representative people from every part of the country, and, being anxious to spare General Logan all that I could, I confess to having carefully studied the histories of the different States and as far as possible to have informed myself as to the exact position of every man in politics. I tried to find out all I could about their relations with their own people so as to enable General Logan to put a correct valuation on their services to the party. Naturally, there were many pleasant things in connection with these visits to different towns and cities, and I have no recollection of any disagreeable episode. I came to think in those days that a man's politics were akin to his religion, and that most men were moved by motives of patriotism and an honest desire to serve the best interest of their respective States and the nation at large.

I shall always feel that Henry Wilson added little to the influence of the ticket. He was known to be an honest and faithful New England senator, but he had little knowledge of the people or of the interests of the middle-west, north-west, and western States. He had spent his life in Massachusetts and, while it was never necessary to defend his reputation, it was hard to arouse enthusiasm for a man of neutral character. The world knows the result of the campaign and of the sad death of Vice-President Wilson.

As an outcome of the savage attacks of Sumner and Schurz on General Grant and the leaders of the regular Republican party, what they called the Liberal Republican party was organized by such ambitious newspaper men as Whitelaw Reid (our late ambassador to England), Horace White, Alexander McClure, Henry Watterson, Samuel Bowles, Murat Halstead, and a number of disgruntled Republicans, who held a convention in Cincinnati, May 1, 1872, and after three or four days' farcical sessions nominated Horace Greeley for President and B. Gratz Brown, ex-Governor of Missouri, for Vice-President. One might be forgiven for saying that this was a cruel attempt on the part of ambitious young men who had nothing to lose and all to gain if they could succeed in electing "Father" Greeley President of the United States. The whole attempt was so abortive and so ludicrous that it gave Thomas Nast, then at the meridian of his power as a cartoonist, an opportunity to inflict the most cruel blows upon Mr. Greeley. One caricature which caused great amusement was a cartoon of Mr. Greeley as the candidate for President, with a placard on the tail of his coat marked "B. Gratz Brown," which was all that was said of Mr. Brown as the Vice-President. How Mr. Greeley and Carl Schurz and men of their great ability could have been so foolish as to express their willingness to participate in this gigantic Falstaffian effort to capture the Presidency I do not profess to know. Mr. Greeley canvassed the country and made a most feeling appeal to the people who, he thought, ought to support him for the Presidency. Notwithstanding the fact that Mr. Greeley and Mr. Brown were indorsed by the Democratic convention held in Baltimore on July 9, 1872, this indorsement did not at all increase the possibility of their election. Even Mr. Greeley's letter of acceptance of the Democratic nomination and his appeal to the people failed to make any serious impression.

In the midst of the campaign Mr. Greeley was summoned to his home on account of the serious illness of Mrs. Greeley, which proved fatal. This sad event so affected Mr. Greeley, in addition to his great disappointment in not being made President, that his mind gave way and he was sent to a sanitarium, where he died. The whole episode was so pathetic as to touch the heart of the country. President Grant and his entire cabinet, together with many noted men of the North and South, attended the funeral. Mr. Greeley had gone on the bond of Jefferson Davis, that Davis might be released from prison. This act, while it lessened his influence in the North, made many friends for him in the South, where he had previously been hated on account of his advocacy of the freedom of slaves. He was one of the most remarkable men of his time, and should never have been induced to depart from the position of a great editor for which he was so eminently fitted. He was earnest, tender, and guileless, and was in no sense a man suited to the handling of the vexatious problems of politics. As has often been said before, his death may have saved him from a more cruel fate—that of ridicule.[3]

Notwithstanding the bitter warfare that had been waged against General Grant, he was elected by an overwhelming majority, as were also a majority of the nominees of the Republican party for members of Congress.

We returned to our apartments in November, 1872, I to take up the usual routine of looking after my children, acting as secretary to General Logan, receiving and entertaining friends who were daily growing more numerous, and discharging my social duties. These were not at all distasteful, because, as I recall now, society women, or rather the families in the official homes of the capital, made a great effort to make themselves a reputation for refinement, cordiality, and intelligent appreciation of the positions of their husbands and what was required of themselves to discharge their duties as wives and daughters. A majority of the senators and members lived in hotels and boarding-houses, for at that time Washington furnished very meagre accommodations for congressional and other official families. The schools were poor, and those who could possibly arrange for their children to attend boarding-schools away from the city did so. Almost without exception the ladies felt that they must welcome to Washington visitors who were entitled to consideration. They felt that they must, on the days assigned to the Supreme Court, the Senate, the House of Representatives, the speaker, the army, and the navy, receive all who did them the honor to call. These receptions began about two o'clock and were not supposed to end before half-past five. During these hours hundreds of calls were made, and they were not, as to-day, considered a bore and a drudgery. Most hostesses made every preparation for their afternoons at home, wearing beautiful gowns, inviting their friends to assist them in preparing tables where refreshments were served, and decorating their rooms with flowers. They extended a hospitality that made every one feel that their call was appreciated. There were many bright women, and often before you entered a drawing-room you could hear the peals of laughter and the bright conversation of the happy people within. The hours being early, it was possible to make a great many calls in the afternoon and to reach home in time to welcome my husband after the adjournment of Congress and the official duties of the day were over. Monday was the day for the Supreme Court, Tuesday for the House of Representatives, Wednesday for the cabinet and the speaker, Thursday for the Senate, Friday for the army and the navy, and Saturday afternoon for the White House. The mistress of that mansion always made extensive preparations for her Saturday afternoons. The Marine Band played as at an evening reception and every room was beautifully decorated with plants and flowers. It gave an opportunity for the wife of the President to extend invitations to some of the wives of members of the Supreme Court, Senate, House of Representatives, army and navy, and citizens and visitors in Washington to assist her at these receptions. The recipients never forgot this compliment, and it helped to make fast friends for the President of the husbands of these women who had had these little attentions.

Latter-day wives of Presidents seem to have forgotten that it is in their province to extend such courtesies, or do anything to acknowledge the honors that have been paid their husbands and themselves by their elevation to the highest position within the gift of the people. It is impossible for any lady in the White House to go through the long list of persons entitled to consideration if she confines herself to the regulation state dinners, the four evening receptions, and the occasional musicale or garden-party. People are so quick to discover whether the invitation is sent through a desire to do one an honor or whether it is a grudging discharge of a disagreeable duty. The only way to account for the difference in treatment accorded guests in the White House latterly and in the olden time is by recognizing the fact that money is now more highly considered as a standard. It has been interesting to contrast the *menus* served in the state dining-room to his guests by President Arthur with the bowls of punch and gingersnaps that have been served in the corridor of the White House by caterers after musicales within the past few years. Not that one accepts these invitations expecting a feast, yet one feels a pride in having whatever is done in the White House either well done or altogether omitted.[4]

Allowing for the Christmas holidays, any session beginning December 1 and closing on the 4th of March is very short, and there is little time for the passage of many bills that must fail altogether if they are left on the calendar March 3 of the last session of a Congress. Therefore, those interested work prodigiously at these last hours. March 3, 1873, was the close of the Forty-second Congress and, though many of the senators and members had worked heroically, the calendar was far from being exhausted. Work in the departments was also greatly in arrears, as possibly a larger number of bills had been introduced in Congress, and more important matters laid before every department, than had ever before been done in the history of the Government.

March 4, 1873 was probably the most inclement inauguration day within the memory of any American. The thermometer had fallen below zero, a thing previously unknown in this climate. The militia from many States almost perished with the cold while they were en route, and they arrived in Washington to find inhospitable temperature and few preparations for their accommodation. The decorations of the city were frozen stiff and looked dismal with their coats of ice and sleet, which had fallen the night before. The cadets from West Point and Annapolis were nearly frozen in line, many dropping out on account of their inability to stand on their feet, and, though they were taken back to their academies as speedily as possible, they left a number behind in the hospitals of Washington, while others were borne to the hospital on their arrival at West Point and Annapolis, fatal pneumonia claiming several in each corps.

The procession was the poorest display ever seen on such an occasion. Senators Logan, Cragin, and Bayard were the committee on the part of the Senate, supplemented by a large committee of distinguished men. Governors of many States with their staffs were present. The weather spoiled their splendor, their feathers and gold lace yielding to the frost in the air. Helmbold, of patent-medicine fame, was then in Washington with a famous four-in-hand mouse-colored team of horses which he drove attached to a superb landau with light lining.[5] He insisted that the committee should allow him to use this turnout to convey President Grant and the committee to the Capitol for the inauguration, and back to the White House. The committee accepted his offer, and on inauguration day Grant, together with the Senate committee—Logan, Cragin, and Bayard—drove to the Capitol and thence to the White House in this beautiful equipage. Another though less pretentious outfit conveyed Vice-President Wilson to the Capitol. A commendable but futile effort was made by the shivering throng on either side of Pennsylvania Avenue to cheer the President, Vice-President, and distinguished men whom they recognized in the procession.

The crowd assembled in the park on the east side of the Capitol were packed close together in front of the rotunda steps, which were covered over to serve as the platform upon which the President takes the oath of office and delivers his inaugural address. These people were better able to resist the bitter blast that had been wildly blowing for forty-eight hours, beginning the day before the inauguration, than were those who held exposed positions on the avenue. Fortunately, the ceremonies were brief. The Vice-President proceeded to the Senate chamber to adjourn that body to wait for the President's message, while President Grant and the committee resumed their seats in the carriage to return to the White House.

We had in our employ at that time a faithful colored man servant, Louis Davis, who has occupied the position of trusted messenger in the Interior Department almost ever since. He insisted upon taking our little son, John A. Logan, Jr., who was then eight years old, to the inauguration, promising to be very careful of him. He took the child up to the Capitol and stood beside the general who occupied the place of committee-man near Grant. After he had finished the inaugural address, President Grant noticed the boy and, Jack being a great favorite with him, he said to General Logan: "Bring Jack in the carriage as we return." Louis, overhearing President Grant, preceded them to the carriage. Imagine General Logan's surprise when he saw Louis sitting on the box beside Helmbold with Jack on his knee! The President laughed heartily and insisted upon his being left there. When they arrived at the White House, President Grant took Jack by the hand and led him into the reception-room to be welcomed by Mrs. Grant. When they adjourned to the state dining-room for the luncheon which Mrs. Grant had provided for the large party accompanying the President, he insisted upon taking Jack with him.

It was a red-letter day in the dear boy's life, and he used to tell it to all of his school friends with a good deal of satisfaction. It spoke volumes for the kind heart of General Grant. Jack was always proud of being a favorite with the President and Mrs. Grant, who never forgot him at Christmas, but always sent him some beautiful Christmas gift. He was her champion and made many speeches in eulogy of Mrs. Grant, which were reported to her and caused her to be very strongly attached to him as long as she lived.

The afternoon was spent by everybody in trying to get warm. The inaugural committee had made most extensive preparations for the inaugural ball. They had built a temporary marquee on Judiciary Square. It was magnificently decorated and extensive enough to have accommodated the thousands whom the committee expected would attend the ball. A superb banquet had been provided and hundreds of waiters secured and the committee on music had provided many bands. The weather abated not a whit or tittle and, as night came on, it seemed to grow colder and colder, and yet every one felt they must carry out the inaugural programme.

We had as our guest Miss Nina J. Lunt of Chicago. Mr. E. B. Wight, representative of the Chicago *Tribune* had invited Miss Lunt and our daughter, then in her teens, to go to the inaugural ball and, while Dollie was not in society, we thought it might be an event she would like to remember as long as she lived. Therefore we gave our consent to have her go with Mr. Wight. After they had gone, and before we could reach them, we became very anxious indeed, because of the growing intensity of the cold. Mr. Wight was very careful, and through his influence in newspaper circles, was able to get them a most comfortable position, and they suffered no inconvenience or ill-effects from this, our daughter's first experience at an inaugural ball. Like all young people, she was so enthusiastic about all she saw and the interesting people who were present, that she was unmindful of the cold.

The President and Mrs. Grant and Vice-President Wilson, who was a widower, arrived at about half past eleven o'clock. Mr. and Mrs. Fish, Secretary and Mrs. Boutwell, Secretary and Mrs. Belknap, Secretary Robeson, Postmaster-General and Mrs. Creswell, Attorney-General and Mrs. Williams, Secretary and Mrs. Delano, accompanied by Mr. and Mrs. John Delano, were in the Presidential party, while the Diplomatic Corps, led by the Dean Blacque Bey of Turkey, Sir Edward Thornton, the Marquis de Naoville of France, Mr. and Madame Mori of

Japan, and the Peruvian minister, all in full court dress—as on the occasion of all inaugural balls, the ladies wearing their most gorgeous gowns—attended the ball, and the grand promenade was given. The marquee not being heated, it became so cold that one lady was seized with a congestive chill and died in the room. This sad event, in addition to the intensity of the cold, from which everybody was suffering, cut short the ceremonies of the evening. The food on the tables in the banquet hall was congealed, the coffee almost freezing into a *frappé*. Men and women in evening dress sought their heavy wraps to keep from perishing while they waited for their conveyances to take them to their abodes. Drivers of vehicles of all kinds were almost frozen, and great confusion reigned inside and outside the temporary building. Musicians were unable to play their instruments, the mouthpieces of some of the smaller instruments being frozen, and the festivities ended unceremoniously. The great crowd which had come to Washington for the inaugural ceremonies left the city as rapidly as they could get trains to carry them away.

The newspaper men and women then in Washington were among the most brilliant of the guild. All the metropolitan newspapers had bureaus in Washington, presided over by a coterie of men who were the equals, if not the superiors, intellectually of the men at the head of the bureaus of the metropolitan newspapers of to-day. Among them were such men as Whitelaw Reid of the New York *Tribune;* J. B. McCullough [McCullagh] of the Saint Louis *Democrat;* Alexander McClure of the Philadelphia *Ledger;* Horace White, Mr. Sheehan, of the Chicago *Times;* Murat Halstead, L. A. Gobright, E. B. Wight, George A. Townsend, J. Russell Young, subsequently librarian of the Congressional Library, W. Scott Smith, Eli Perkins, Charles Lanman, Don Piatt, Ben Perley Poore, E. V. Smalley, Mark Twain, Frederick Douglass, and a host of correspondents who have made enviable reputations in their calling. Among the women reporters who wielded influential pens as correspondents of important newspapers were Mary Clemmer Ames, Mrs. Lippincott, Mrs. H. M. Barnum,

Mrs. Olivia Briggs, Mrs. Coggswell, Mrs. and Miss Snead, and Miss Mary E. Healey.

General Grant soon nominated his cabinet, retaining those who had served during his first term, with the exception of the Secretary of the Treasury. The members of the cabinet were: Hamilton Fish, Secretary of State; William A. Richardson, Secretary of the Treasury; W. W. Belknap, Secretary of War; George M. Robeson, Secretary of the Navy; Columbus Delano, Secretary of the Interior; John A. Creswell, Postmaster-General; George H. Williams, Attorney-General. Congress resumed its treadmill routine, with now and again outbursts of criticism and vituperation heaped upon President Grant.

On March 9 our friend Doctor John P. Taggart of Salt Lake City, telegraphed General Logan that my father had passed away from a return of the meningitis from which he had suffered the summer previous. There were three of my mother's children with my father in Utah, and we realized at once that there was no alternative but for me to again return to Utah. It was impossible for General Logan to leave his post of duty, and we had no one whom we could send who could attend to matters and who understood affairs as I did. Consequently I made the second long, sad trip to Utah, to bring my father's remains home to be interred beside my mother in the cemetery at Marion, Williamson County, Illinois, and to assume the care and support of the three children left unprovided for. I do not even now like to recall that melancholy journey, or the multiplied cares which I had to assume, and which could never have been borne but for the unfailing tenderness and encouragement of my devoted husband. He was perfectly willing to share everything we had with my minor brother and sisters, who by my father's death had become double orphans. We had taken a furnished house on Capitol Hill when I returned to Washington, in November previous, for the session of Congress which ended March 4, and as soon as it was possible took the children and returned to our home in Chicago.

CHAPTER 10

Chicago and Washington
1873

IT WAS QUITE late in the summer before General Logan reached home, as the extra session of the Senate which convened after the inauguration, March 4, 1873, had been protracted much longer than had been expected. The children were out of school, and we were all settled in our lovely home, 2119 Calumet Avenue. The rear of our house overlooked the lake and, the broad lawns of the block being undivided by fences, those who lived in this square had the benefit of a beautiful park in the front and back of their homes. Consequently we found it unnecessary to go away in summer.

General Logan had worked very hard in the campaign, which was scarcely over when the last session of the Forty-second Congress began. He had really had no rest from the day he took his seat in the Senate in 1871. We had a number of friends in the West who begged us to come to Colorado. Through the death of my father my cares had multiplied so greatly that it was impossible for me to leave home. I urged my husband to go, however, and after much hesitation he went. While there he joined a party of capitalists, who were making prospecting tours over the mountains and along Cripple Creek, hunting for gold and silver mines. They discovered some "rich indications."

General Logan always insisted upon putting up his quota of expenses for these prospecting expeditions and promptly drew upon the small savings we had in bank. All went merrily while he remained and helped to furnish the "stake," and he was considered one of the partners, on an equal footing with the others. Finally General Logan had to come home on account of urgent affairs. After his return the others frequently drew upon him for funds to continue the prospecting, which was being made by these "true friends," who "were anxious to strike a bonanza on General Logan's account," because he had done so much in securing for them lucrative appointments. Letters came regularly, saying they had not yet struck a "rich vein," but the *indications* were good, and they required only fifty or one or two hundred dollars more, as the case might be, to insure success. General Logan was one of the most trustful men I have ever known. He simply would not believe in the infidelity of a friend until indubitable evidence forced him to see what was plain to every one else. He could ill afford the demands made upon him but could not bear to disappoint these supposed faithful friends. He became very sensitive over the matter and did not like to have me inquire "how much fodder the mules needed," when letters came requesting remittances. Finally he became suspicious and declined to send more money. Soon afterward there was great excitement over the discovery of the "Morning Star" mine by the parties with whom he had been associated. They telegraphed him that they were very sorry but the discovery of the "Morning Star" had not been made until after the funds to which he had contributed had been exhausted, and therefore he was not a partner in the ownership of the great mine. He felt very badly over this treatment by men for whom he had done many acts of kindness, and no one dared mention the matter in his presence. He was subsequently very glad that they had ruled him out in the beginning, as all the world knows of the shocking imposition that was played upon General Grant and of all the scandal and trouble which ensued. These same men were the ones implicated in the swindle that brought so much sorrow to General Grant, and ended in a penitentiary term for at least one of them.

General Logan was very anxious to make money in a legitimate way, and therefore invested in mines in Colorado rather extensively, but the story was always the same.[1] He was too trustful and too honest to gamble in mining-stocks, and, as a consequence, we had enough beautifully engraved certificates of stock in mines, for which he paid cash, to paper a good-sized room, which were, of course, worthless. Everything that General Logan ever had he earned by hard work and, while he had many successes, he could not be said to have been born under a lucky financial star.

The year 1873 was the beginning of the revolutionary action on the part of strikers. I shall not soon forget that I one day received a letter from General Logan, who was then in Colorado, desiring me to go down to our bank to arrange some matters for him. I was so much afraid that, if I waited for the coachman to get the carriage ready, I should not have the package in time for the mail that I decided to go down on the street-car and forward from the bank the documents he wanted out of the safety-deposit vault. I was not aware of the excitement existing in Chicago at the time, and imagine my consternation when I found the streets full of strikers, with militiamen trying in every way to preserve order. I went into the bank and found the cashier standing at the window with a pistol lying on either side. I inquired what the trouble was, and he said that the strikers had threatened to sack the banks of Chicago; that they were obliged to keep the doors open during banking-hours, and consequently had had to provide themselves with arms to defend their deposits. It was the year in which such fearful destruction of property occurred in Pittsburg, and I have always felt, if those in authority had thought less of the consequences to themselves politically, and had caused the law to be executed and these men in Chicago punished, we should not have had such frequent repetitions of revolutionary action on the part of men nursing imaginary wrongs.

General Logan had assumed the burden of the care of the members of my father's family so cheerfully and willingly that I could not help worrying, greatly to his distress, over the rapidly multiplying expenses to which we were in consequence subjected. Hence I decided that it would be better for me not to try to go to Washington with the general for the meeting of Congress, December 1, 1873. For the first time since the general had re-entered Congress after the close of the war I remained away from the capital until after the holidays, which General Logan was to spend with us in our Chicago home.

Chicago was rapidly regaining her importance as a great city. The world had been so generous that the citizens no longer required the relief which had been extended them from the time of the fire in October, 1871. The Grand Pacific Hotel had been built and was one of the largest which had, up to that date, been erected in Chicago. For a long time it had been the custom of the two noted hotel-managers, Messrs. Gage and Drake, to have in November what they called a game dinner. It was always a wonderful affair and this fall it was especially notable on account of the unique manner in which it was served in the new Grand Pacific dining-room, which seated five hundred persons. The walls and every part were decorated to represent a forest. On all the tables they had different devices representing the various animals and birds that come under the head of game. I remember one especially fine stag which had been secured from the far west, and stood on a table in the centre of the room. The superb antlers that crowned the head of the animal attracted universal attention, as did a fawn and the head of a great bear, which were also among the decorations. There were specimens of the rabbit, squirrel, and the opossum, while members of the feathered kingdom were interspersed in all their glory in the decoration of every table. The beauty of the arrangement of birds' nests in artistic devices was beyond the description of an ordinary pen. These specimens were, of course, stuffed while on the menu appeared bear, venison, opossum, rabbit, and squirrel meat, followed by pheasant, turkey, goose, duck, guinea-keat, chicken, plover, quail, and reedbird. An example of every member of the entire feathered kingdom which is used as food was laid before the guests. There were many speeches and songs written for the occasion, and the "wee sma' hours" had approached before the happy party dispersed.

The indomitable spirit of Chicago was just as irresistible

then as it has been ever since, and it seemed as if a magician's wand had been employed to cause so many superb buildings and other improvements to spring up in such a short time as had elapsed since the fire of October, 1871. We had just come to Chicago when the fire occurred, and had been away almost ever since. We were very glad therefore to renew the acquaintance of the friends we had known before, and to make new friends. New Year's Day had not been as universally observed in Chicago as was the custom in Washington. Therefore I conceived the idea that, as General Logan would be at home for the holidays, I would celebrate New Year's Day by keeping open house.

January 1, 1874 was an unusually bright day for that climate, and we had the pleasure of receiving our friends continuously from ten o'clock in the morning until that hour at night. I had caused a notice to be given out that we should be glad to see our friends, and many came who were delighted to welcome General Logan and myself as residents of Chicago. I invited quite a number of young ladies to assist me, and some of them sang and played beautifully. To make this essentially a home affair, they furnished the music at intervals during the day instead of introducing hired musicians. We had a bountiful table from which our callers were served with whatever they desired. This was the last New Year's Day we ever had the pleasure of being in Chicago. The population of Chicago increased so rapidly that it became impracticable to observe the general custom of receiving on New Year's Day.

There were many magnificent homes on Wabash, Michigan, Indiana, Prairie, and Calumet Avenues, south of Sixteenth Street, which were not reached by the fire. They were occupied by courageous men who were foremost in the work of rebuilding Chicago. On the corner of Twenty-second Street and Calumet Avenue lived Mr. Daniel Jones and his interesting family. Mr. Jones was one of the pioneers of Chicago—a short, sturdy, active man, who took part in everything that contributed to the prosperity of his beloved city, and by his will many charitable institutions were greatly benefited.

Mr. L. Z. Leiter, the famous merchant, and his family lived directly opposite us.[2] Their children, like our own, were quite small and played together constantly. Mr. Leiter was a great study. He was methodical and indefatigable in his attention to his business. I used to see him go out of his house every morning at seven o'clock, to get into a buggy which stood in front of the door waiting for him. He seemed to return every day at one o'clock to give an hour for his luncheon, and then back to business, not to reach home until six o'clock. Day after day he proceeded in this routine. His family entertained by giving dinners occasionally.

Mr. Aldrich, subsequently a member of Congress, was on the other corner, while on our side of the street, on the corner of Twenty-first and Calumet Avenue, was the residence of the celebrated surgeon Doctor Gunn and his charming family. Mrs. Gunn was a lovely woman, who was very domestic in her tastes. Their sons and daughters received her constant attention and are now among the worthy citizens of the city of their birth.

Mr. and Mrs. A. B. Meeker, father and mother of Mr. Arthur Meeker, one of the enterprising men of Chicago, lived in our block; Mr. and Mrs. John Markley, Mr. and Mrs. John Alling of the firm of Alling & Markley, lived in adjoining houses to us and were among our most intimate friends; while that ill-fated public-spirited man John R. Walsh, with his splendid family, also resided within two doors of us. Mr. Walsh was a very tall, rather stooping man, whose keen eyes indicated the restlessness of his disposition. He was in every sense a self-made man, and it is a melancholy thought to recall the combination of circumstances which led to his undoing. If, in an evil hour, he did anything that could be construed as irregular, he paid a penalty too sad to contemplate. One thing is certain —Chicago owes him as much as any other man for its rapid advancement to its present greatness and for his generosity to the charities and philanthropic enterprises of the city. I can never believe Mr. Walsh did anything in his whole career which had not previously been done by others. I am quite sure he had no dishonorable intent in any act of his life.

Ex-Governor Bross, one of the proprietors of the Chicago *Tribune*, was our next-door neighbor on the north. Mrs. Bross was an invalid, hence their intellectual and charming daughter

Jessie did the honors of the house. She was interested in music and literature, and in all social matters. She subsequently married Henry D. Lloyd, the noted writer.

Mr. and Mrs. H. O. Stone resided near us. Mr. Stone was one of the earliest successful men of Chicago and came to the city when it was a wooden hamlet on the great prairie. He appreciated the possibilities of making Chicago the wonderful city it is to-day and joined heartily in the various movements to accomplish this end. He had married for his second wife the beautiful Elizabeth Yager of Saratoga, New York, who made his home very attractive. Mrs. Stone was gifted in the matter of dispensing hospitality and in providing entertainment for her friends. As a result, their house was one where society met most frequently.

Mr. and Mrs. Marshall Field were also near neighbors of ours. Marshall Field was of the Field-Leiter firm, merchant princes of Chicago from the days of the Civil War. In personal appearance Mr. Field was a French marquis, and no one could imagine that back of his suavity of manner there was that rigidly calculating nature which enabled him to change the discouragements and calamities of the fire into means with which to turn the wheels of prosperity and success. The first Mrs. Field was of slight stature, medium height, with dark-brown eyes and hair, and very fair complexion. Her manners were charming; her wit fascinating. She always had about her interesting people. She encouraged every artist who appealed to her for aid and her natural generosity caused her list of pensioners to be quite long. Unfortunately, the attractions of Paris won her away from her Chicago home and friends, and like the many who become infatuated with the illusion and unreal life of the French capital, she drifted into its current and died an untimely death in France, surrounded by people who had lived on her bounty while they encouraged her estrangement from her native land.

Mr. George M. Pullman was one of the foremost men of that matchless coterie who rehabilitated Chicago and pushed forward the interests of that great city years in advance of what it would have attained in the ordinary course of events.

Mr. Pullman was a man of unusually fine appearance—six feet tall, with a well-developed physique, a fine head, and dark-brown eyes which expressed his genial, generous disposition. He married in 1866 Miss Harriet Sanger, one of the most famous beauties of Chicago and the West. As soon as possible after the fire he built his palatial brownstone residence at the corner of Eighteenth Street and Prairie Avenue. In this mansion Mr. and Mrs. Pullman royally entertained the most distinguished visitors who came to Chicago, especially during the World's Columbian Exposition. Both host and hostess had travelled extensively and had legions of friends who were glad to accept their invitations. Artists in every line were sure of a warm reception and encouragement from Mr. and Mrs. Pullman, and more than one has been able to cultivate their special talent through the generosity of these kindly people. No movement in the line of progress, education, or charity was ever started in Chicago without a liberal donation and every encouragement from Mr. and Mrs. Pullman.[3]

Mr. and Mrs. Henry Strong and their family, Mr. and Mrs. Lester, the Armours, Mr. and Mrs. J. W. Doan, Mr. and Mrs. Spalding, Mr. and Mrs. Cobb, Mr. and Mrs. Norman Williams, Mr. and Mrs. John M. Clark, Mr. and Mrs. E. B. Sherman, Mr. and Mrs. Jerome Beecher, Mr. and Mrs. Enos Ayers, Mr. and Mrs. Dunlevy, Mr. and Mrs. Coolbaugh (Douglas's great friends), and Colonel and Mrs. John M. Loomis resided near us. Colonel Loomis attracted universal attention because of his love for riding on horseback with all the paraphernalia of an officer of the army. He could be seen any afternoon, mounted on his beautiful black horse with all the trappings of a colonel of the army, and his mounted orderly close behind him, riding along the avenues and through the parks of Chicago. Colonel Loomis was a noble and generous man, and had an illustrious record as a volunteer officer during the Civil War. Mrs. Loomis was in all respects a fitting companion for this noted man.

Many others of that remarkable generation were within a few squares of our door. I was glad of an opportunity to come to know them better and, as far as possible, to participate in their many schemes for the betterment of social conditions and the welfare of mankind.

When General Logan went to Washington in December, 1873, he removed from Willard's Hotel, where we had formerly lived, to 1114 G Street, where he found delightful accommodations in a private house. When we returned to Washington after the holidays were over, we went directly to these apartments where we remained for a number of years. Our host, Captain Havard, was a most interesting man. He was a Frenchman, and had served in the French army as a commissioned officer, but came to America at the breaking out of the Civil War. He was an officer in the Union army, and was wounded in one of the battles in Virginia. He was brought to Washington and nursed back to health again by a widowed lady who had removed from Virginia. He was a very scholarly and a most interesting man, and it was a great study to see him and his Virginian wife together, as her chief qualifications were those of a good housewife.

The calendar of the Senate was a long one, and General Logan soon became absorbed in the matters before that body. Among the questions to be decided was the settlement of the *Virginius* massacre, which was conducted so satisfactorily that General Grant received the thanks of the survivors. Congress also passed a resolution asking all foreign powers to take part in the Centennial Exposition which was to be held in Philadelphia in 1876, and made an appropriation of $1,500,000 to aid Philadelphia in carrying out the plans for the exposition.

In the discussion of the Louisiana imbroglio which took place at this time the ablest men in the Senate took a very active part.[4] Matthew Carpenter of Wisconsin made his famous review of the situation.

So much criticism had been made of the government of the District of Columbia under the territorial law, and so many charges of fraud and unjust rulings in the administration of its affairs, that Senator Thurman of Ohio introduced, in January, 1874, a resolution asking for the investigation of the affairs of the District of Columbia. Under this resolution Governor Shepherd was furnished with a list of questions as to the affairs of his administration, to which he replied. After a long and tedious discussion of the subject in Congress, the form of government was returned to that of commission, President Grant sending in the names of A. R. Shepherd, A. G. Cattell, and Henry T. Blow for commissioners of the district. These men failed of confirmation, and subsequently J. H. Ketchum of New York, Henry T. Blow of Missouri, and W. Dennison of Ohio, were appointed and confirmed. The commissioners discharged many of the employees who had held positions under the territorial government.

Among the important work of the committees of the Senate was the investigation of General O. O. Howard's administration of the Freedmen's Bureau. The trial culminated in the acquittal of General Howard in July, and he was ordered to take command of the Department of the Columbia, U. S. A., with headquarters in Portland, Oregon. J. S. Creswell, Doctor Purvis, and L. H. Leipold were appointed to take charge of and wind up the affairs of the Freedmen's Bank, which from the first had been a very ill-managed affair and caused lots of trouble to the colored people in whose interest it was supposed to have been organized.[5]

The question of the finishing of the Washington Monument was taken up, and a handsome appropriation made by Congress, which, together with private subscriptions, caused to be completed this matchless shaft to the memory of George Washington, first President of the United States.

It was no small thing at that time to be one of the leaders in the Senate, for that body was made up of men of keen minds and indomitable courage. Anthony of Rhode Island, a ponderous sort of a man, with all the alertness and intuitive grasp of a New Englander, was always on the watch and ready for discussions of every question that might in any way lessen the influence of New England. Roscoe Conkling was probably the handsomest man in the Senate and was most fastidious in his style of dress and manner. He was ever ready for a debate and made many enemies by the sneers with which he treated the remarks of brother senators with whom he disagreed. He was so intense in everything he did that he sometimes apparently forgot there was any other person in the Senate besides himself and seemed to feel that upon him alone rested the responsibility of averting all the evils that threatened the republic. His industry was prodigious, and the great State of New York never had a more able or faithful senator than was Roscoe Conkling. He eschewed all social functions, as his family were rarely with him, and was infrequently seen at receptions, even in the White House. He occasionally accepted invitations to dine with gentlemen but had few intimates. It was natural for him to be reserved, but no more faithful friend could be found than Roscoe Conkling when he once allowed himself to become attached to a brother senator.

In striking contrast to Senator Conkling was his colleague, Senator Fenton. He had a most genial disposition and agreeable manner. He had not the intellectual power of Conkling but probably accomplished more through his diplomacy. He had a charming family, consisting of his wife and the Misses Fenton, who were very popular in Washington.

The venerable Hannibal Hamlin of Maine was a tall man, who had become somewhat bent by the weight of years. He was mentally as keen as when in his thirties. He was uncompromising in his Republicanism and had no patience with colleagues who were ready on the slightest provocation to yield points of advantage to the opposition. He was not especially aggressive, but could be relied upon as one of the most faithful committeemen in the Senate. His spotless reputation as Vice-President while the war was at its height secured for him the respect and admiration of all his associates. Mrs. Hamlin was a typical New England woman. They had two daughters. One of them had married General Batchelder, at one time a splendid soldier. General Batchelder was appointed to some position out in one of the Territories, where he became very much demoralized and the marriage in consequence turned out badly, and Mrs. Batchelder returned to her father's home. Batchelder finally lost his position, came to Washington, and died friendless in an isolated quarter of the city. Mrs. S. P. Brown, who was a friend of the Hamlins, learned of Batchelder's death and telegraphed the news to Senator Hamlin. With characteristic promptness the old senator telegraphed back: "Bury him decently and I will pay the bill with pleasure."

Matthew H. Carpenter of Wisconsin has been described as a short, heavy-set, shaggy man, and that is probably a correct description. He had, however, a phenomenally large head, which was said to be full of brains. His record in the Senate shows that he was one of the most brilliant men in that body. He was relentless in his prodigious and fearless advocacy of the principles of his party.

Another intellectual giant and forceful man was Governor O. P. Morton of Indiana. His physical disabilities did not in any way affect his wonderful mentality. Living as he did in a border State, he was accustomed to being in a controversy all the time and was ever ready to defend the principles of his party and his own integrity. He had made an imperishable reputation as war governor of Indiana. His people were much divided in their sympathies between the North and South. Thomas A. Hendricks, Daniel H. Voorhees, and other intellectual giants of his State were equally fearless advocates of the principles of the Democratic party, and often defended the acts of the Confederacy in its efforts to destroy the Union. It is remarkable that Senator Morton, as governor of Indiana, was able to protect his State from being overrun by raiders under such men as Morgan, an imaginary line only dividing Indiana from the slaveholding States of Kentucky and Tennessee.

Simon Cameron of Pennsylvania was one of the most remarkable men in the Senate. Born in the last year of the eighteenth century, his experience covered many years of his country's history. As journeyman printer and editor, he worked his way into politics, and was for a long time adjutant-general of the State of Pennsylvania. Reaching the exalted position of United States senator in 1845, he was re-elected in 1857 for the term ending 1863. He took an active part in the nomination and election of Mr. Lincoln in 1860, and in consequence resigned his seat in the Senate to accept the position of Secretary of War under Mr. Lincoln. His reputation as a wonderful organizer led Mr. Lincoln to choose him for the then important matter of organizing the Union army. He was the author of the scheme to enlist the negroes, a movement which contributed much to the numbers and strength of the army. Mr. Cameron, like all successful men, had many critics, and surrendered the war portfolio for the ministership to Russia in 1862.[6] He had amassed a large fortune and could afford to give the United States her proper place among nations by supplementing the meagre salary of a minister to foreign lands with ample means from his private income. Diplomatic life was not congenial to him or his family, and he soon returned to his beloved native land. Notwithstanding the charges which had been made against him, he was elected to the United States Senate in 1867, and again in 1873. His increasing years and great desire to have his son, James Donald Cameron, succeed him in the Senate, caused him, as soon as he had consummated arrangements for his son's election, to resign for the second time his seat in the Senate. He was an unusually tall, spare man, with sandy hair and clear blue eyes that spoke determination. His energy was indomitable, his astuteness limitless. He was not a fluent speaker, but so positive and immovable when he had taken a position that he almost invariably carried his point. His prejudices were intense, his friendship steadfast, and while he may have failed in his relations with the Diplomatic Corps, the management of the political and national affairs of his own country was an art with him. His power in the Senate in no wise waned with the years.

John Sherman, cold and calculating, who, in rendering great service to his country as representative, senator, Secretary of the Treasury, and Premier, did not neglect to look after his personal interests, was one of the most active and efficient senators in the Forty-third Congress. His colleague, Allen G. Thurman, was one of the ablest men in the Senate. He had been a member of the House, and had served on the bench as a district and Supreme Court judge in his adopted State of Ohio. He was originally a native of Virginia and was one of the foremost men of the Democratic party. He was ever ready to join the men on that side of the Senate in defence of the measures that had been advocated and the policies adopted by his party.

Rumors of the great wealth of Stewart and Jones of Nevada had been heralded before they made their appearance in the Senate, and it was not long before they demonstrated that they were men of untiring energy and keen perception of the requirements of the nation during the progressive era that followed the close of the Civil War. They were both steadfast Republicans and devoted friends of President Grant.

Hon. William Pitt Kellogg was a native of Vermont but removed to the State of Illinois at an early age. From that State he was appointed Chief Justice to the Territory of Nebraska. At the breaking out of the war he returned to Illinois and raised a regiment, the 7th Illinois Cavalry. After the war he was appointed collector to the port of New Orleans. The bitterness toward him was so intense that his life was in jeopardy many times, but he bravely protected the persecuted citizens and upheld the laws while occupying this position. He was subsequently appointed governor of the State of Louisiana from which position he was elected to the United States Senate. No man has ever displayed more indomitable energy, sterling integrity, and dauntless courage in the discharge of the duties attendant upon the positions he held. In the Senate he was a fearless advocate of the supremacy of the law and of the protection of Union men in the States lately in rebellion.

On the other side of the chamber were such men as John B. Gordon, a man of imposing appearance and great ability. He was proud of the part he had taken as a Confederate officer during the rebellion and was generally the leader in criticising everything that was done by Federal officers in the South. His criticism of General Sheridan's handling of the troops in New Orleans caused an exciting debate between him and General Logan, which friends thought at one time might end in a personal difficulty, as both men were known to be of unflinching courage and intense partisan feeling. There has rarely appeared anything in the record of Congress so caustic as General Logan's arraignment of Senator Gordon. Gordon soon discovered that his policy would not result in anything good for his people or his party and had the grace to discontinue his personal assaults upon representatives of the Government.

Senator William B. Allison of Iowa had had a very long experience in the House of Representatives. He was a most conscientious and careful man and soon attained the position of chairman of the appropriations committee because of his great discretion. He had one serious fault that kept him from being a really great man, and that was his disposition to be non-committal on every subject. He was never willing to take the lead in the advocacy of any measure that had not been previously advocated by some other senator. His reputation for being non-committal was so well known that there were a great many stories told at his expense. Senator Ingalls of Kansas once said to him: "Brother Allison, you could walk across the Senate floor in a pair of wooden shoes, and you would not make any more noise than a fly crawling on the ceiling, so non-committal are you on all questions at all times." His State and the nation had implicit confidence in his integrity, his patriotism, and his steadfast adherence to Republican principles, but he was in no sense aggressive, and many times allowed golden opportunities for doing great service to his country to pass because of his timidity. Allison was a large, heavy man with dark hair and brown eyes. He was phlegmatic and conservative in every sense of the term.

Hon. John J. Ingalls was one of the most sensitive, nervous men that was ever in the Senate. His intellect was keen, his mind active, and he manifested his caustic disposition almost every day he appeared in the Senate. He could no more help being sarcastic and critical than he could help the color of his eyes. He was very thin and tall, with dark hair and sharp features. He was a fine lawyer, a forceful writer, and probably no man's utterances in the Senate were couched in more refined language or expressed in better style than those of John J. Ingalls. He was at one time accused of buying his election to the Senate. General Logan was on the committee on privileges and elections. We lived in the same house with Ingalls, and one morning, after the Kansas committee had called on General Logan, Ingalls came into the room and asked the general what the members of the committee had said. The general replied: "I am one of the jurymen, and I can't tell you what they said." I was standing near by, and, seeing Senator Ingalls's intense curiosity in the matter, I said: "Senator, I am not on the committee, and I am going to tell you what they said." He laughed and urged me to do so. "They say that you bought your election." "Nonsense," he said. "I hadn't money to buy a single vote, even if I had been so disposed. The truth is, I couldn't buy a yawl, if ships were selling at a quarter apiece." At this we all laughed heartily. He was my *vis-à-vis* for a long time at the table, and I used to be most uncomfortable at his philippics. His criticism of persons for whom he had a contempt was a thing to be dreaded. He was always so very kind to me, however, that I had great admiration for his ability. One day, after he had finished a tirade against somebody, I said: "Senator Ingalls, I want to ask a favor of you." He very gallantly replied: "Mrs. Logan, you could ask me nothing that I would not promise to grant." "It is this," I said. "Promise me that you will never speak of me save in kindness, whether I be living or dead." He got up from his seat, came round the end of the table where General Logan sat, and took my hand. "Why do you ask that, when you know that I could never speak of you except to praise?" he asked. He was a charming man in his family. Mrs. Ingalls was one of the loveliest characters I ever knew. Senator Ingalls's deference for her and his affection and kindness were in striking contrast to his sarcastic treatment of so many others. Kansas made a great mistake when she discontinued the services of John J. Ingalls in the Senate. In the house where we boarded they had a "Travel Club," and many of the senators and representatives who boarded in the house used to give papers or addresses at the evening sessions of the society. Senator Ingalls gave a most interesting paper on George Washington's birthday, which he commenced in this language: "George Washington, the father of his country, and said to be the father of Judge Blank of Indiana, etc." You can imagine the consternation with which this announcement was received, but the senator went right on with his beautiful address as if he had said nothing out of the way.

Zachary Chandler of Michigan was another formidable man in the Senate. He was ponderous in appearance, with a very large head covered with dark hair. He was so positive in his manner that every word he uttered seemed to come from an unchangeable determination in his mind. He was a big man with a big heart, fierce as a lion as an antagonist but true to his friends, toward whom he was gentle as a lamb. The probabilities are that in all his public life he was never more outraged than over the part which he was deceived into taking in securing Grant's acceptance of Belknap's resignation before people understood the great scandal which was Belknap's undoing.[7] Chandler was so honest a man that he could not conceive of a public official, especially a man with such a record as Belknap had as a soldier, playing the part of which he was accused in the matter of commissions on the sale of post-traderships. He knew no such word as timidity, and was always ready to join in the advocacy of measures supposed to be in the interest of the public welfare. His record as a senator and as Secretary of the Interior is without a stain.

Meanwhile, in a political way, excitement was waxing hotter and hotter, and the most stupendous charges were being made against President Grant and his administration, while the prominent men of the Republican party ably defended them.

On July 1 General John A. Creswell of Maryland, Postmaster-General and one of the most efficient and distinguished members of any cabinet, resigned. Eugene Hale of Maine was appointed his successor, but for some reason, after considering the matter, declined the post-office portfolio. Marshall Jewell, a prominent Republican of Connecticut, was appointed and confirmed as Postmaster-General.

As soon as Lent was over society began a series of entertainments. Members of the cabinet, senators, and citizens of Washington rivalled each other in magnificence of their luncheons, dinners, and receptions. It was rumored that there was to be one of those unusual events in the White House in which everybody takes a personal interest. Nellie Grant was to be married to Algernon Sartoris of England. In the early springtime of 1869 Secretary and Mrs. Borie had decided to take a trip to Europe, inviting Nellie Grant to go with them. On board the ship she met the young Englishman, who had been assidious in his attentions and, though almost every intimate friend had filed a protest against the marriage, the general and Mrs. Grant felt they could not hold out against Nellie's expressed wish to be allowed to marry the man of her choice.

The President and Mrs. Grant had a bitter trial in yielding to the importunities of Mr. Sartoris, and allowing their daughter and idol to marry and go to England to live without any hope of her ever returning to America. Their daughter's happiness, however, was paramount to all else with them, and, though they did not approve of her choice, when they found that she could not be persuaded out of it they allowed her to have everything as she desired.

Undoubtedly Nellie Grant's was the most elaborate wedding that ever took place in the White House. Social affairs in Washington were never brighter than in the spring of 1874. The city was full of officers who had won distinction in the army and navy during the Civil War. The Diplomatic Corps was composed of representative men. Many of them, as also numberless citizens, were rich and entertained constantly. President Grant could count wealthy friends by the score who were glad to do anything they could for him or his family. Nellie was so young and so much beloved by every one that, while they hated to think of her going to England, they were, in consequence, ready to lavish everything upon her. No bride was ever more beloved or received a greater number of magnificent presents than did Nellie Grant. The 21st of May, 1874 was a glorious spring day. The soft air was laden with the perfume of the magnolias and catalpas of the parks. Everything was full of life and happiness. The executive mansion had been elaborately decorated. The crowd was not as great as at an evening reception, as only the most distinguished and special friends of the President and Mrs. Grant were invited. Many members of the cabinet, justices of the Supreme Court, senators, representatives, and distinguished officers of the army and navy were there. Sir Edward and Lady Thornton were there as friends and sponsors for the bridegroom. A dais had been placed between the windows of the east side, above which hung a floral bell with long smilax ropes attached. At eleven o'clock Doctor

Tiffany of the Metropolitan Methodist Episcopal Church, entered and took his position on the dais. The Marine Band played the wedding march and announced the approach of the bridal party. All eyes were turned to the entrance from the corridor. The bridegroom, Mr. Sartoris, and Lieutenant-Colonel Fred D. Grant approached, followed by Miss Edith Fish and Miss Frelinghuysen, Miss Sherman and Miss Porter, Miss Drexel and Miss Dent. Next came Mrs. Grant, attended on either side by her two sons, Ulysses and Jesse. The President and the bride brought up the rear, the bridesmaids separating so as to form a circle, the President and bride stepping on the platform where the bridegroom advanced to meet the bride. Miss Edith Fish stood on the other side as maid of honor, Mrs. Grant and her sons standing immediately behind them. Doctor Tiffany, a man of imposing appearance, who had a fine voice, pronounced impressively the ceremony according to the ritual of the Methodist Church, Mrs. Grant's tearful eyes betraying the deep emotions of her mother's heart in giving up her daughter. A superb breakfast was served in the State dining-room; the customary boxes of bride's cake were distributed, after which the guests made their adieus, and the bride and groom prepared for their departure for New York to sail on the *Baltic* for England. The story of the life of Mrs. Sartoris, the death of her husband, her return to her native land, and her recent marriage to Mr. Jones of Chicago—a man of high standing and character—is well known. Of her three children, her son and one daughter reside in France; the other daughter lives in the United States.

Congress adjourned in June, and we returned to our home in Chicago.[8] We had been away from southern Illinois for four years, and many of our interests there required General Logan's attention. He spent several weeks looking after our affairs and meeting old friends, and came home much rested from the fatigues of the long and trying session of Congress. We had the pleasure of enjoying our home for a longer time during the summer of 1874 than we were privileged to do afterward.

In October 1874, we were summoned to attend the wedding of Lieutenant-Colonel Fred D. Grant, eldest son of General

Grant, to the lovely Miss Ida-Marie Honoré. The Honorés had a beautiful house in the centre of South Park in Chicago, which was surrounded with grand old trees and was in every sense a charming summer home. It was ideal in its interior appointments. Mrs. Potter Palmer having previously lived in the house, it was filled with statuary and other articles of virtu, among them Miss Hosmer's *Puck*, *The Veiled Cupid*, or *Secret 7*, *Love*, by Rossetti, and a replica of Randolph Rogers's exquisite statue of *Nydia, the Blind Girl of Pompeii.* The ceremony was performed by Reverend Mr. Errett, of the Christian Church, Mr. and Mrs. Honoré being members of that church. Miss Honoré was attended by Miss Levy, Miss Rucker, Miss Houston, and Miss Hall, while Lieutenant-Colonel Grant was attended by his brother Ulysses. The bride and groom left that afternoon for their bridal tour, Colonel Grant carrying away from Chicago one of its most attractive young women.

CHAPTER 11

End of the Grant Era

General Sherman's daughter Minnie was married October 1, 1874. Thus three important weddings had taken place in the families of General Grant and General Sherman—those of Nellie and Fred in Grant's family, and Minnie in Sherman's family.

When we arrived in Washington early in December we found that Colonel Fred and Mrs. Grant were ensconced in the White House and were to spend the winter with the President and Mrs. Grant, Colonel Fred being on duty in Washington. The presence of the fascinating Mrs. Grant, Jr., in the White House and the promise that Nellie would soon return for a visit to her native land, were a guarantee that Mrs. Grant's receptions would be very brilliant during the season. In fact, the society season began December 1, and promised to be unusually gay.

King David Kalakaua and his suite arrived December 12. Much ado was made over the fact that a real king was to visit Washington. As I remember it, Congress made an appropriation of twenty-five thousand dollars for the entertainment of His Majesty during his stay. Secretary Fish, Secretary Belknap, and Secretary Robeson joined the committee to welcome the King on his arrival. He was escorted to his apartments which had been prepared for him in the Arlington Hotel. Unfortunately, on account of a severe cold which he had contracted, the King was unable to carry out part of the programme which had been arranged for him, but was able to attend the theatre to hear Clara Louise Kellogg in *Mignon.* He displayed his gallantry by showering flowers on the prima donna. In appearance, the King was a fine specimen of a man. He was very tall, broad-shouldered, with a dark-olive complexion and very black hair and eyes. He looked more of a king than he was, and the devotees of titles went wild over this dusky sovereign. President Grant accorded him a brilliant reception and a state dinner. The Japanese minister and his lovely wife, Madame Yoshida, were among the guests who were invited to do honor to the King. A more magnificent costume was never worn in the White House than that of Madame Yoshida's. The material was of the rarest and most lustrous kind, and the gown had been made in the fashion of a full Japanese court dress. Mr. Yoshida, of course, appeared in the regulation court dress of his native country. King Kalakaua and his suite appeared in full dress evening suits, except two of his generals, who wore the uniform of the Hawaiian Guards. General Logan and I attended both functions, and of the many occasions of this character at which I have been present at the White House none have been more attractive in the matter of appointments. Congress, and official and civilian Washington entitled to invitations to such affairs, were there in full force, the ladies rivalling each other in the splendor of their costumes. Very few who participated in the attentions to King Kalakaua anticipated what the future held for Hawaii, or that the King and the royal family were doomed to close their imperial careers in a few brief years.

There was an unusual number of famous people in Washington that year. Many of the houses, especially on K Street, were occupied by persons who had made their impress on the history of their country. Alas! the majority of them have passed away, and their places have not been filled by persons who are their equals in extending hospitality and cordial greetings. There was much excitement over the approaching centennial exposition in Philadelphia. Every one was busy with some feature which was to be used to add to the attractiveness of the celebration of our glorious victories one hundred years before. Among the entertainments which were given to raise money was a centennial tea in the rotunda of the Capitol on December 16, 1875, in which every person at all prominent in society took a very active part. There were thirteen tables to represent the thirteen original States, and it was gratifying to see the taste and the strict adherence to the custom and style of refreshments of Colonial days. The ladies who presided over these tables were attired in gowns of the days of seventy-six, many of the dresses belonging to the wardrobes of their illustrious ancestors. The tables of North and South Carolina were especially attractive, the ladies who presided being typical of their native State. The beautiful flowers and delicious fruits which characterized these States were in abundance, while Maryland and many of the other States had innumerable revolutionary relics displayed. The rotunda was decorated as never before. Boxes of tea in imitation of the Boston Tea Party were in evidence. Tea was served in cups marked George and Martha Washington. These were sold at one dollar apiece, and I have the pleasure of still retaining the one which I purchased. Liberty bells which had been rung in those historic days were on exhibition. On the committee of arrangements were prominent army and navy officers and officials of the Government. Senator Hawley of Connecticut and Secretary Robeson made eloquent addresses, and the Marine Band discoursed patriotic music during the afternoon and evening.

At the opening of the exposition General Logan attended with the congressional committee, who were handsomely entertained by the commission at Horticultural Hall. In August I took our two children and their governess, Miss Parke, to Philadelphia where we spent two weeks in seeing everything of interest at the exposition and enjoyed every moment. At the time I had not visited Europe, as I have done many times since, and therefore there were to me very many novelties and interesting exhibits. I had not previously appreciated the advancement of my own country and was delighted to find so many evidences that the wheel of progress had been busy developing our resources and bringing to our land the fruits of a higher civilization. The Centennial Exposition was a good thing for our country. If it did nothing else, it was the initiative in the opening of the way for its successors.

During the winter General Sherman's memoirs appeared and brought forth much adverse comment from various quarters, on account of the fact that they reflected strongly his natural prejudices and, it was frankly said, unjust criticism of distinguished officers under him in the service. He was especially severe on General Logan and General Frank P. Blair, two volunteer officers, whom he characterized as "political generals," notwithstanding the fact that they had arisen to the rank of major-general by their military skill in handling troops—many times in independent command—and their gallantry on the field of battle. While he had to comment favorably upon their action in battle and their soldierly conduct, he could not give them the praise they deserved because of the fact that they were not graduates of the military academy at West Point. If I remember correctly, Frank Blair died without Sherman ever having corrected his unfair estimate of Blair's military career.

In the case of General Logan it was different. There was an additional reason for Sherman's criticism of General Logan—on account of the fact that General Logan was the author of the bill for the reduction of the army after the close of the war, and had greatly offended Sherman by recommending a cut in his salary. Although Sherman wrote a very bitter letter to Congress denouncing the bill, the majority of Congress considered that its provisions were just, and General Sherman was unable to prevent its passage. This, in addition to the fact that General Sherman had recommended General Howard to supersede General Logan in command of the Army of the Tennessee, after General Logan had won the great battle at Atlanta, and after Sherman had assured Logan that he should retain the command, intensified the antagonistic feeling existing between General Sherman and General Logan. General Logan, however, was conscientious in the preparation of the bill and had not taken occasion to be revenged on account of General Sherman's unkind treatment of him. General Logan was entirely vindicated by the army and was restored to the command of the Army of the Tennessee. He had no malice toward Sherman about the matter, because he felt that it all came from the prejudice existing against a man not a graduate of West Point. General Logan knew he had never lost a battle or in any way failed in the execution of orders issued to him during the war, more than which could not be said of graduates of West Point. He never at any time felt that the latter had much the advantage over faithful, conscientious, brave volunteer officers, whose patriotism guided them in their services to the country. General Logan believed if a man were desperately in earnest in his desire to serve his country, he would not be long in mastering military tactics and in fitting himself for any emergency which might arise. There is no doubt at all that General Logan's military genius was inborn. General Grant was lavish in his praise of him as a soldier and commander, and would undoubtedly have retained him as commander of the Army of the Tennessee had he (Grant) been in command of the Western Army at the time. It was a source of gratification that the scene at the Corkhill Banquet, described in the earlier pages of this autobiography, was enacted, and that there was a reconciliation between General Logan and General Sherman before they passed to that land from which no one returns.

The New Year's reception of January 1, 1875, was in many respects more brilliant than any previous one. The New Year's reception at the White House was then, as now, the signal for the beginning of the round of social events for the winter. Dinners, luncheons, receptions—official and otherwise—were the rule. In January Mr. and Mrs. Sartoris returned and took up their abode in the White House, greatly to the delight of Mrs. Grant, who now had her daughter and Mrs. Fred Grant to assist in the discharge of her social duties. Her Saturday afternoons were especially attractive and, she often told me afterward, were really the most enjoyable social functions that were held in the executive mansion. Persons came in so informally and received such a cordial welcome that they were at once made to feel it a privilege to pay their respects to the occupants of the White House. People wandered about through the red room, blue room, green room, east room, and the beautiful conservatories then at the west end of the corridor, and the state dining-room. Mrs. Grant seemed very happy when she had Nellie standing beside her. Nellie had not contracted any European airs, but stood beside her mother the same unpretentious, lovely, girlish woman whom everybody was delighted to welcome back to Washington. Perhaps it is a matter of prejudice, but it seems as if the representative ladies in Washington in those days were far more attractive than the majority we meet now. I have sometimes thought that the frequent intercourse with Europe and the contracting of the habits of cocktail-drinking and cigarette-smoking have affected the cordiality and simplicity of the manners of American women. I can remember when the suggestion was made that the ladies of the White House and the wives of members of the cabinet and other officials should not shake hands with their callers because it was supposed to be a matter of too much fatigue. I confess that the custom which causes a hostess to stand erect with a bouquet in her right hand and a fan or something in her left, which prevents her from extending a more cordial greeting than a stiff bow to her callers, is not calculated to put people at their ease or make them feel that their calls are appreciated. There never was any reason why Americans should ape the airs and stiffness of any European court. We welcome to our shores people from all lands and extend to them the privileges of life, liberty, and the pursuit of happiness: and why we should erect a barrier against those of our kind whom we recognize as fitting persons to be invited across our thresholds is an incomprehensible question, which has not been satisfactorily answered. Cordiality and hospitality are supposed to be the chief characteristics of Americans, and I regret to see any departure from the customs and manners which have ever been the charm of our people. Of all women in the world, American women should be considered the most sincere and attractive as hostesses.

Every year it seems that attractive features of society

grow fewer and fewer. Horatio King, John J. Nicolay, and Mrs. Dahlgren formerly had regular evenings in their homes, when musical programmes were rendered, impromptu papers read, and lectures delivered by able persons, among them General Garfield, General Logan, Librarian Spofford, Senator Ingalls, Jean Davenport Lander, and a daughter of Mrs. Scott Siddons, then a resident of Washington. Readings and recitations from Shakespeare and other classics were given, much to the enjoyment of the persons fortunate enough to be invited to these literary gatherings. The Schiller Bund gave delightful entertainments, when lectures were given, and the programme usually closed with amateur theatricals. Miss Edith Fish and Miss Nannie Jeffreys figured prominently in these plays. Miss Jeffreys won an enviable reputation as an amateur actress in her part in *Meg's Diversion.*

When we came to Washington, early in December, General Logan was just recovering from a very serious attack of illness. He had been a victim of inflammatory rheumatism contracted at Fort Donelson and, after a political campaign, frequently was confined to his bed for weeks. The opening day of Congress the galleries of both houses were packed. Sir Edward and Lady Thornton and Hon. William M. Evarts were in the diplomatic gallery, as were also Mrs. Grant and Mrs. Fish. The people of the whole country were very much interested in the proceedings in Congress, as it was known that the matter of the reconstruction of the Southern States was still at white heat, and it was supposed that the Louisiana question would furnish food for many an exciting controversy in the Senate.

Mr. Pinchback had been elected United States senator from Louisiana, and was bitterly opposed because of the fact that it was said he had colored blood in his veins. Every day some member of the House or Senate was heard in denunciation of the privileges and protection extended to the colored men in the South. There were outbreaks of Indians in the West, and a serious controversy arose over the Black Hills Reservation, as gold had been discovered there, and the Indians sternly opposed the influx of gold-seekers into their domain.

There were constant charges and countercharges of corruption and defalcations of officials, the Whiskey Ring figuring conspicuously at this time. Charges of membership in the Whiskey Ring were made against persons in official positions under the very roof of the White House. Grant himself did not escape the insinuations on the part of these marplots that he, if not a member of the ring, was cognizant of the connection of those intimately associated with him; and his accusers went so far in their persecution as to make it necessary for General Babcock to demand an investigation of his conduct. He was, of course, exonerated, but the authors of these charges had accomplished their purpose of throwing discredit upon the administration.[1] Men in the Republican party who advocated the election of Mr. Blaine, and other prominent men, took an active part in the warfare upon the integrity of the appointees of General Grant. The political campaign of 1876 may be said to have begun in 1875, since long before the holding of the convention for the election of delegates to the national convention to be held at Cincinnati, the champions of candidates had exhausted much of their ammunition in trying to kill off the rivals of men whose cause they advocated. Men opposed to Mr. Blaine retaliated by making grave charges as to his connection with various questionable schemes. Blaine's reading of the Mulligan letters on the floor of the House of Representatives is perhaps the most remarkable incident of a personal explanation that has ever occurred in Congress. Subsequently Nast's caricature, appearing originally in a New York paper, showing Mr. Blaine as the "Tatooed Man," was without exception the most cruel persecution ever inflicted upon a public man.[2]

There were innumerable resignations of men holding high positions by appointment. Some resigned from disgust and some to avoid the humiliation of investigations. Senators whose term expired March 4, 1877, were much concerned, as candidates for the members of the legislature would be elected on the ticket that would be nominated in 1876. Hence they had not only to be on the lookout in the interest of the candidates for the Presidency and Vice-Presidency but had to watch every movement, politically, in their home States, to be sure that their party was successful.

The national convention was held in Cincinnati in June 1876, and it was thought that Blaine, notwithstanding the intense abuse heaped upon him, had a majority. The convention was very largely attended by legions of Republicans who were not delegates, but who had gone there for the purpose of advocating or opposing Blaine's election. General Granville M. Dodge recently explained how Blaine's defeat was really brought about. He was a Blaine delegate in the convention and strongly advocated the election of Hon. James F. Wilson of Iowa, as permanent chairman. Mr. Wilson was one of the ablest and most experienced statesmen of the nation. Don Cameron wanted McPherson of Pennsylvania, then clerk of the House of Representatives and compiler of the "Political Hand Book of the Republican Party." Dodge worked very hard for Wilson and thought his election was agreed upon. He retired to get a few hours' sleep and rest, during which time the opponents of Wilson succeeded in electing McPherson as permanent chairman. This was the beginning of the blunders that led to Blaine's Waterloo. McPherson, as Dodge had suspected, was unequal to the position. He was too unsuspecting for the wily politicians who were inimical to Blaine, and at a critical moment entertained a motion to adjourn, which was followed by boisterous commotion and confusion, intensified by the trick of turning off the gas and enshrouding the hall in total darkness. Caucusing was the rule during the hours between the fatal adjournment and the meeting of the convention the following morning. No sleep was allowed to jeopardize the schemes of the anti-Blaine delegates, which culminated in nominating Rutherford B. Hayes of Ohio, for President, and William A. Wheeler of New York, for Vice-President. Mr. Hayes was the weakest man, save one, ever elected to the Presidency.[3] His associate on the ticket, Mr. Wheeler, was really a nonentity.

It would not have been possible to have nominated two more non-committal, conservative men. They were the very antipodes of the candidates prominent before the convention met. They were the usual types of compromise candidates, and brought no strength to the ticket. As a matter of fact, no one anxious for the success of the party wanted either of them.

The whole campaign of 1876 was characterized by the most virulent abuse of the candidates, active persons of both parties striving with each other in making charges of fraud, irregularities, and malfeasance on the part of officials and members of their respective parties. Nominees on the tickets for the various offices from President down were anxious as to the results. In addition, reformers were busy advocating all kinds of isms and theories. The hapless farmers, the inevitable prey of political demagogues, came in for unusual attentions. They were persuaded that they were the victims of merciless injustice; that their only hope for relief was through the election of reformers to the house and senate of the legislatures of the States most interested in agriculture. Illinois, the great "Prairie State," was completely overrun by "Grangers," who were posing as the farmers' special friends. They declared, if they were put in power they would readjust the management of the railroads and secure a change in the freight schedules, so that the products of the farm could be set down at the great market points for half the rate then in existence. They would, in fact, procure high prices for every commodity the agriculturist had to sell. A majority of the Republican county conventions had instructed their nominees for the house and senate of the Illinois legislature for General Logan for re-election to the United States Senate, which event was dependent upon the election of these instructed candidates. Hence the campaign had scarcely begun when importunities came from every quarter urging General Logan to visit almost every county in the State to speak in behalf of the election of the candidates instructed for him. Congress was in session for some time after the adjournment of the Republican national convention.

Loyal and far-seeing Republicans realized the full force of the mistake the national convention had made, but there was no alternative but to make the best of it, and if possible elect Hayes and Wheeler. Strangely enough, it was during this campaign that the Democratic party, while boasting of Jeffersonian simplicity, began to intimate that Mr. Tilden's "barrels of money would enable them to win a Democratic victory all over the United States." They claimed that the solid South, supplemented by the influence of money, would put their party in power—nationally and locally. When the election returns were in the people were amazed to find that their predictions had come so near being true. The election of President and Vice-President was in controversy and had to be finally settled by the famous Electoral Commission, under a special act to provide for the settlement of the important question as to who had been elected President and Vice-President in 1876.[4] Republican majorities had fallen off everywhere. In Illinois the political complexion of the legislature was in doubt, depending largely upon the party—Republican or Democratic—with which the "Prohibitionists," "Grangers," "Reformers," and "Independents" would co-operate.

It would be difficult to imagine with what disgust General Logan confronted the situation in the legislature when he found that old farmers, who were supposed to be the soul of honor and integrity, and had been for years enthusiastic supporters of himself, had been changed by some surreptitious influence. While they claimed to be undecided as to whom they would support for the Senate, nothing could induce them to commit themselves to General Logan. Upon investigation later it was found that these men had received from three to five thousand dollars each, with which to lift the mortgages off their farms, from their Granger friends, who had been using the money of ambitious aspirants to the Senate. So trustful was General Logan that it was some time before he could really credit the indubitable evidence that was laid before him of the dishonesty and duplicity of these old friends. The designing political jugglers had skilfully bought up just enough of the senators and members of the house to prevent General Logan from having a majority in either. The legislature had not long been in session when it was found that a part of the scheme was to defeat General Logan by the election of Hon. David Davis as Associate Justice of the United States Supreme Court to prevent him from being chosen on the Electoral Commission. Somebody's barrel accomplished the purpose of defeating General Logan for re-election and put David Davis in the Senate in his place. Mr. Davis regretted this as seriously as any one else, and did not hesitate to maintain that both he and General Logan had been sacrificed to the stupendous scheme of political demagogues. For weeks the election of the United States senator from Illinois was in doubt. The action of the legislature was so uncertain because of the instability and lack of integrity on the part of members of both houses. This may be said to have been the beginning of the political demoralization of the great State of Illinois, and was, perhaps, the first instance of the flagrant use of money to influence the action of the legislature in the election of a United States senator. I was with General Logan at Springfield, and shall not forget to my dying day the deep humiliation and suffering which he experienced as day after day he discovered fresh evidences of the duplicity of men whom he had trusted in war and in peace. He felt that he had served his State honorably and acceptably from the day he took the oath of office as a member of the Illinois legislature in 1856, through all the trying years of the war, to that hour. Believing as he did that the people approved of everything he had done, and desired to reward him by a re-election to the United States Senate, he could not bear to think that their will was being thwarted by the use of money, a force which it was impossible for him to combat.[5]

I hope it will not be considered indelicate to say that these reverses came at the most unfortunate time in our whole lives. General Logan devoted every hour of his life and time to the discharge of his public duties, and therefore was obliged to neglect opportunities for money-making. It will be remembered that the salary of a United States senator was at that time only five thousand dollars a year. We had lived very prudently in inhospitable boarding-houses, and in many ways practised self-denial and economy. But the unavoidable demands that have always been made upon public men, for political and other purposes, including requests by individuals to whom public men consider themselves under obligations, for the indorsement of their notes for financial responsibilities—nine times out of ten the indorser having to pay these notes—all these things made accumulation almost impossible for a United States senator. General Logan, like many others, had encroached upon the savings of years to meet these various demands, and was at a loss to know just what he should do at the expiration of his term, March 4, 1877.

Prior to that time the Electoral Commission had declared Hayes and Wheeler elected President and Vice-President, and every one supposed that General Logan would be offered some position within the gift of the President. He received no such consideration, notwithstanding the fact that some of his friends had gone to the President and explained to him General Logan's necessities. We were both too proud to make any sign.[6] I begged him to let me go down to southern Illinois and dispose of some lands which we had owned for years. With great reluctance he agreed to let me try to see what I could do. When I arrived in Carbondale I was received with so many manifestations of genuine friendship and interest in our welfare that I felt no hesitancy in going to the substantial men who I thought wanted the property and could afford to buy the land which we had to sell. Memory will forever retain the tenderness with which these dear old men responded to my request that they buy this land and relieve our embarrassment. They gave me exactly what I asked for the property and said that they were ready to carry for an indefinite length of time any notes which General Logan had given, and would give him cash for his land beside. I could only express my gratitude by tears which they hastened to wipe away, and to say: "Be cheerful and happy. Your discomfiture is only a brief affair. Two years hence we will send him back to the Senate or die in the attempt."

POSTLUDE

1877–1923

THE SOUTHERN ILLINOIS friends were right. In only two years Mr. Logan was back in the senate. But the early months of this period were troubled. Mrs. Logan, resentful of the Hayes administration's seeming unwillingness to take care of her husband with an appointive job at first urged him to forsake politics. The General had not forgotten how to practice law and soon he was earning more than a senatorial salary.[1]

Private life had its advantages: it was good to forego being errand boy for a host of constituents. In November of 1887 "Dolly" became the wife of William F. Tucker of Chicago. The Logans left the young couple in the Chicago house and returned to "Mrs. Rhine's boarding house" at 812 Twelfth St. N.W., in Washington, a prestigious place of its kind, and were soon enjoying the kind of Washington social life to which they had become accustomed.

Mrs. Logan became fond of the President's wife, Lucy Webb Hayes—she who first banished alcohol from the White House—although she continued to feel distain for the president himself, a notably weak president in her eyes. She was able to write that she and her husband "had a very happy winter, in that we were able to read aloud to each other, accomplishing more in that direction during this winter than we had been able to do for many years. We read a great many interesting books, and went to many lectures, dramatic performances, and social affairs. We had more time to enjoy our friends than we had ever had in Washington."

Meanwhile, Mr. Logan's friends had been busy in Illinois securing written pledges for the senatorial vacancy which would be filled in January, 1879. Both Logans went to Springfield to preside over a notably smooth political activity. It was all most different from 1877, "the Reformers had had their day and been retired to private life." Although there was a bevy of candidates in both political parties the Logan Republicans were firmly in command and the vote on January 17 was Logan 80, General Oglesby—the retiring governor—26.

The Logans returned happily to Washington "under very different auspices from those of 1877," to resume the good life at their boarding house. They found most of their old friends still in congress and some interesting new faces. Mrs. Logan was especially impressed by Blanche Kelso Bruce, the Negro senator from Mississippi, "a very agreeable man [who] conducted himself with the utmost propriety, winning the regard of his colleagues without distinction of party." [2] In the atmosphere of what might now be called the post-Reconstruction Era, she found kind words for a number of Democrats and ex-Confederates, especially L. Q. C. Lamar, the "other" senator from Mississippi, who was later to become a justice of the Supreme Court.

Senator David Davis who had displaced Logan in 1877 had assisted in the recent election. He and Logan now became highly congenial, but Mrs. Logan, who ascribed his leaving the Supreme Court for the senate to presidential ambitions, was willing to concede that this 350 pound statesman was big in body, brain and heart but she found him "absolutely unfitted" to be a senator.

Enough Republican politicians were dissatisfied with President Hayes to lead to a bumper crop of potential candidates as the election year 1880 approached. These included, in addition to several others, Grant, Blaine, Washburne, John Sherman, and Garfield. Mrs. Logan, much impressed with the role statesmen's wives play, reviews the wives in her *Reminiscences.* After generously agreeing that any of them would have been "acceptable" in the White House, she contributed some observations. Mrs. Blaine was a tall, large woman "of rare intelligence" who "was, unfortunately very pronounced in her opinions." Treated unjustly by newspapermen, she was "generally misunderstood." Mrs. Washburne was gentle, lovable and cheery, but had a "very imperious, irritable husband." Mrs Sherman was kind and considerate, "but was so modest and retiring that she was never properly appreciated." Mrs. Garfield, "one of the most womanly of women" would have served with credit in the White House had her husband not been assassinated.

General Logan's share in the super-heated political atmosphere of that year was to receive the brunt of a personal attack—one which had repercussions. Congressman William H. Lowe of Alabama, on the floor of the house, "revived the infamous slander" that during the crisis of 1861 Logan had tried to raise an Illinois regiment for the Confederacy. This was an old canard which had long ago been proved false. It was concerned with the recruitment efforts of Thorndike Brooks, formerly of Baltimore, whose activity in southern Illinois had resulted in a badly-under-strength "company," from Marion and vicinity, which he led south. Logan was extremely annoyed. He "posted" Lowe as a "poltroon and a coward." Lowe's response was to challenge Logan to a duel, much to the distress of Mrs. Logan.

The General contemptuously refused, and announced that if Lowe "did not retract the scandalous lies," and "should ever cross his track, he would break his neck." Shortly thereafter the two men were passengers on a Fortress Monroe steamer, but a confrontation was averted by Mrs. Logan. A few days later an alarmed Alabama colleague briefed Lowe "and told him what he knew of the General's skill as a shot," that "General Logan had a pair of the finest duelling pistols in the country . . . that he used to practice . . . shooting at a cap-box on the head of a colored boy who thought it was a great thing to have General Logan shoot the box off his head." This frightened Lowe into the desired apology. For his part, Logan read a collection of affidavits into the senate record which he hoped would end this accusation forever. An approving press printed so many comments on the affair that Mrs. Logan filled four books with clippings.

The summer of 1879 was momentous to the Logans because of the arrival home of General Grant from his world tour. The great political questions were: would Grant accept the third-term nomination his faction wanted for him, and, could the nomination be secured.

Mrs. Logan was in her glory in helping to refurbish the Grant house at Galena—unoccupied for many years—for a Welcome Home celebration. When the great day arrived the Logans and the Elihu Washburnes were permitted to spend the night as house guests of the Grants, and to sit up very late while the taciturn Grant held them spell-bound with his unexpected loquacity.

Inspired by this contact and by the unusually warm welcome the ex-president received at a veterans convention in Chicago, Logan exerted himself to organize the Republicans of Illinois to support the nomination of his now willing idol.

With the gathering of the 1880 convention at Chicago it was soon obvious that a Grant nomination would not come easily. The Blaine delegates were numerous and determined. James A. Garfield was active in promoting John Sherman's candidacy, although in Mrs. Logan's view he was chiefly advertising and promoting himself.

When it was apparent that neither Blaine nor Grant could win, the search began for a compromise candidate. "Overtures were made daily to General Logan," his wife wrote, "urging him to allow his name to be substituted for Grant's, and there is no doubt but that when it was discovered that Grant could not be nominated because of the third-term cry, General Logan could have carried the nomination. He scorned the suggestion and could not see it in any other light than that it would be treachery to Grant. He preferred to go down with Grant rather than even seemingly to betray him."

The convention was in no mood to draft a resistant Logan. The deadlock was broken with the nomination of James A. Garfield and Chester A. Arthur.[3] Logan stifled his distaste for

Garfield, campaigning throughout much of the country for him. Then, after victory, he waited nervously to see if Garfield's cabinet choices would further widen the party split.

In the preceding winter General Logan had put himself in the public eye by making an all-out effort to frustrate attempts being made to rehabilitate one of the regular army generals of the Civil War. This was the Fitz-John Porter case. In it he may have satisfied the sense of justice of many of the veterans among his supporters, but his attitude was that of a self-appointed avenging angel. During the second Bull Run battle General Porter and his 5th Army Corps were a short march from the battlefield, with orders to provide support to the sore-beset General John Pope, under whose command Porter was. These orders he ignored, and for this offense he was tried by court martial. The initial decision of the court was that he was guilty as charged and should be shot. This sentence seemed excessive to President Lincoln, who directed the court to ponder the matter further. He signed the second report "which deprived General Porter of his rank in the army and its pay and emoluments."

Porter felt humiliated and ill-used. He and his many friends inside and outside the army worked many years to attempt his reinstatement so that he could then honorably retire. Finally a board of review recommended this. Logan had no personal animus against Porter, but he believed Lincoln had been just and perhaps overly-lenient, and in January of 1880 he began devoting almost every evening to studying the voluminous records in the case, working until two or three o'clock in the morning. Mrs. Logan was his faithful helper in this task.

Finally, on March 2, in his capacity as chairman of the military committee, he began his four-day speech before the senate—a speech which covered 891 pages of manuscript, equal to fifty pages of the *Congressional Record.* As Mrs. Logan put it: "The ten days devoted to the preparation and delivery of his argument . . . was the greatest drain on his nervous system and the most onerous work of his life. After his speech it was said that it had been clearly demonstrated that Porter should have been shot." [4] If this herculean performance is an indication of the senator's priorities among the problems confronting the nation it is not surprising that there were Republicans who did not consider him their best presidential possibility.[5]

Both Logans were proud of a piece of constructive legislation which the General offered in 1882. It had long been one of his publicly stated views that the ignorance of the southern masses had made it easy for "false" leaders to take them into secession and the Civil War. Since they continued ignorant, in his opinion, he now offered an early version of federal aid to education.

He proposed that the revenue from the excise tax on liquor should be distributed among the states, according to population, to support "such instruction as is provided in the curriculum of the public schools . . . , and also the establishment and maintenance of normal schools, teachers institutes, and instruction in the industrial and mechanical arts." To be eligible to receive this money a state or territory had to require school attendance of all children between age seven and age twelve and had to provide all necessary buildings. Logan thought of this measure as a prod to the laggard states. He proudly claimed that Illinois spent annually 1 per-cent of its assessed valuation on education, while Georgia spent only one-tenth of 1 per-cent and North Carolina one-quarter of 1 per-cent. The bill never cleared the committee on Education and Labor because of Good people. In Mrs. Logan's opinion they thought it would give "respectability" to the liquor industry.[6]

Notwithstanding her factional disapproval of both President Hayes and President Garfield, Mrs. Logan enjoyed life during their administrations. She was pleased when Mrs. Hayes sought her assistance in White House entertainments. She was pleased that the White House was full of Garfield children, and pleased that the billiard table was "restored" to the mansion, both for the children's use and to make it possible for the president "to take much needed exercise." General Logan had demonstrated that he was a good loser and had campaigned vigorously for Garfield, who rewarded this loyalty by consulting him frequently and by placing his nominee, Robert Todd Lincoln, in the cabinet as Secretary of War.

When Garfield was shot by Charles Guiteau, a disappointed

office seeker, and later died of the wound, the Logans were shocked and dismayed. They appear to have considered the shooting an anarchist plot and General Logan "wondered if the anarchist organization had on their list other men in authority." [7] President Arthur, a widower, turned out to be Mrs. Logan's beau ideal as a President. One of his first acts was to order a large scale refurbishing and redecoration of the White House, a work "personally" directed by him. "He displayed such exquisite taste in the changes he made that no one could believe but that some woman's taste and dainty fingers had given the delicate touches which lent to the staid old mansion such a homelike air." Furthermore, the numerous parties he gave were always distinguished by the "rarest and most delicious refreshments" and the excellent performance of professional musicians. No longer need White House guests "listen to the mediocre repertoire of local amateurs."

Arthur had charisma. In addition, he was making an unexpectedly good record during his fragment of a term. But he was a political accident whose only office prior to the vice-presidency had been the collectorship of the port of New York, and many important Republicans were soon being "talked of" as candidates for the presidency. As Mrs. Logan listed them, they were: "Logan, Robert Lincoln, President Arthur, James G. Blaine, ex-Senator Conkling, General Grant, and Governor Foster of Ohio."

In January, 1884, Logan was hearing from friends on this subject. In March General Grant gave an interview urging his nomination. Assured of his own state's support as a favorite son, General Logan adopted a modest position of wanting "the office to seek the man," and was anxious not to appear self-seeking. He wrote Mrs. Logan that "Blaine's friends are at work but his boom will play out because it scares so many men who say he cannot be elected." General Logan had opposed a Blaine nomination in earlier conventions because he thought the man was tainted with personal corruption: he still thought so.[8]

Logan was believed to command the support of Methodists and Negroes but his chief support was supposed to come from "the veterans." When the convention met in Chicago in early June the men put in nomination were Blaine, Arthur, George F.

Edmunds, Logan, John Sherman, Joseph R. Hawley and William Tecumseh Sherman.[9] On the first ballot Blaine was the front-runner with President Arthur a substantial second; Edmunds was third, with Logan close behind. Logan lost a few votes on each of the first three ballots, and then before the third ballot was completed he gave up, sending telegrams to his delegates asking them to vote for Blaine. Blaine was promptly nominated. The nomination of Logan for vice president quickly followed, and was by acclamation. Some of the incredulous Arthur men suspected a deal, but this is denied by George F. Dawson, Logan's intimate and biographer. According to Dawson, Logan refused to answer questions, stating merely that he did not want the vice presidency, but would accept, out of a sense of duty, if nominated.

A sense of mystery hovers over all this. The mystery is deepened by the fact that Mrs. Logan, in her *Reminiscences,* leaves the convention all but unmentioned, and by the absence from the Logan Papers of any correspondence of significance.[10]

The presidential campaign of 1884 was the first lost by the Republicans since 1856. There were many Americans in their thirties who could not remember a Democrat in the White House. Because there was no significant difference between the Republican and Democratic platforms the contest turned into a shrewish exchange of personal depreciation. Logan was right in his belief that a Blaine candidacy would bring on serious questioning of the candidate's public morality. The Republicans attacked the private morality of the Democratic candidate, Governor Grover Cleveland of New York. He had earlier acknowledged being the father of an illegitimate child. The Republicans began their campaign with a great post-convention "reception" for Blaine at Washington. Mrs. Logan recalled that: "General Logan was very much disgusted because the speakers at the reception . . . began to explain and apologize for Mr. Blaine's record, in reply to charges that had been made against him by the opposition." She added that "no charges were made against General Logan for his record was an open letter and he invited a search-light investigation of his whole life."

Logan was faced with a dilemma. He believed that attempts

to "defend" Blaine's record were folly; there were no platform issues; he "would not stoop to the personalities so wantonly and fatally indulged in during that campaign." Yet he believed in an aggressive campaign. His solution was once again to "wave the bloody shirt," to pillory the opposing nominees as the representatives of a party made up of Confederates and Copperheads, in the hope that the passions of the Civil War era could still be fanned into a victory at the polls. With Mrs. Logan at his side he stumped many states from Maine to Nebraska, performing very well this now time-worn routine.[11]

In early October a national committeeman from New York advised the General that the election hinged on New York state, and especially on the Irish and German voters, with two-thirds of the Irish then leaning Republican and the Germans standing 50–50. This may have been in Logan's mind when he tried to veto the national committee's plan to finish the campaign with a Blaine dinner in New York city. He thought a "dinner" would automatically exclude too many supporters, and according to Mrs. Logan he anticipated "someone's indiscreet utterances." His worst fears were fulfilled. The Reverend Dr. S. D. Burchard made his famous remark branding the Democrats as the party of "Rum, Romanism and Rebellion," which a weary and unlistening Blaine failed to repudiate. New York was lost by a narrow margin, and with it the election.[12]

Logan had to console himself with a sense of having been right. On election morning he rebuked Mrs. Logan for trying to cheer him up by saying: "My dear, do not delude yourself. It is all over, and we are defeated." He may have been consoled by letters saying that if he had been at the top of the ticket the results would have been otherwise, and urging him to look forward to 1888.[13]

In the long retrospect permitted by her *Reminiscenses* Mrs. Logan, always the loyal wife, offered her opinion: "There is no gainsaying the fact that General Logan was the choice of the people for the Presidency in 1884, but Mr. Blaine had behind him the moneyed men, who saw in Mr. Blaine a more pliant character for their schemes than in General Logan, who steadily opposed all kinds of subsidies for railroads, steamships, and other gigantic enterprises based upon Government aid for their furtherance. He was known as an anti-monopolist and the enemy of wildcat schemes. He was therefore, not a favorite with the class of men who all too frequently dictate nominations in spite of the expressed will of the people."

Defeated for the vice presidency, General Logan quickly found himself involved in the fight of his political life for reelection to the senate. All the ticket splitting that had gone on in the election had produced an Illinois legislature of uncertain political affiliation, with the "independents" holding the balance of power. Daily votes for the senatorship for weeks on end failed to produce a majority for any of the several candidates, furthermore, as Mrs. Logan put it: "Old and tried Republican friends, it was found, had been completely demoralized by the use of money in the redemption of their farms and other financial inducements to vote for an independent or Democrat." The agonizing deadlock attracted the attention of the whole country.

On April 12, 1885, a Democratic legislator died. An ingenious plan for getting out the Republican vote in his district led to the election of a Republican as his successor, and that man's vote for senator meant that after "a struggle of four months and nineteen days" General Logan was elected for another six year term.[14]

Returning to Washington, the Logans resumed residence at 3 Iowa Circle N.W., a large brick house they had rented after the vice presidential nomination, when they believed they needed a place large enough to entertain in and to have houseguests. Mrs. Logan so enjoyed this non-boarding-house existence that she persuaded her husband to let her look for a house they could buy and could occupy at least during the six years of the new term. While the General busied himself chiefly in preparing his book *The Great Conspiracy,* Mrs. Logan, looking long and hard, discovered the "Stone mansion" on Columbia Heights, which then belonged to Senator John Sherman. Bought and occupied late in 1885, it was the scene of the predominantly happy last year of General Logan's life. John Jr. was at home. The General was able to have his army son-in-law, Major Tucker, transferred to Washington, with the result that the Logans had son, daughter, and grandchildren gathered close at hand.

This happy atmosphere was made even happier by the many indications that a considerable number of Republicans were anxious to support the General for the presidency in 1888. A trip to San Francisco brought forth tumultuous, clamorous enthusiam to the surprise and delight of the Logans.

Unfortunately, the General's health was failing. The vice presidential and senatorial campaigns had exhausted him. Since early manhood he had been troubled from time to time by "rheumatism," but had been much improved by a stay at Hot Springs, Arkansas, in 1883. A prolonged cold and increased rheumatic pain in 1886 prompted Mrs. Logan to do what she could to get him to return there, but he insisted on postponing such a trip "until the Christmas holidays."

On December 15 he suffered such severe rheumatic pain while at work in the Capitol that he had himself driven home and put to bed. His doctors soon had him sitting up in a chair for an hour each day, but on the morning of December 22 "a paroxysm of excruciating pain seized him in the arms and about the heart." His alarmed physicians called in a consultant; his mind began to wander, and at three o'clock on Sunday, December 26, he died.

The old soldier lay in state in the Capitol Rotunda for two days. The casket was deposited temporarily in the mausoleum of Rock Creek cemetery, then removed to a granite mortuary chapel in the Soldier's Home cemetery erected by Mrs. Logan.

Loyal and companionable wife that she was, Mrs. Logan believed that her husband would not want his death to delay the forthcoming marriage of their son. Consequently, she put aside her mourning to appear at the wedding of John A. Logan, Jr., and Edith Andrews on March 22, 1887. The bride's father, a respected and substantial resident of Youngstown, Ohio, had no son "and at once adopted John A. Logan, Jr., as his own." In deference to Mr. Andrews' wishes the young Logans lived at Youngstown.

In the autumn of 1887 Mrs. Logan was rescued from her loneliness by being asked to chaperon Florence and Harriet Pullman, the daughters of Mr. and Mrs. George Pullman, on an extended European trip. She enjoyed the Pullman girls, enjoyed her first ocean crossing and found Europe fascinating.

With the Logan prestige and the Pullman money, with the charming girls and influential friends, she found most doors open. She and her charges were among the privileged people admitted to the throne room at Berlin to hear William II make his coronation address as the new emperor. Other interesting events and social contacts made the five months in Berlin meaningful. With similar excitements during somewhat briefer visits in Austria-Hungary, Italy, Switzerland, France, and England it is not surprising that a woman of Mrs. Logan's inquiring mind and zest for life should have acquired an appreciation of foreign travel which was to make trips abroad a fixed feature of her life for years to come. London, where Robert Lincoln was the American envoy, was a special joy. There she met Queen Victoria, "the most remarkable woman of the time" and was surprised at her "simplicity of dress" and at how "large" she was.

Before leaving Washington Mrs. Logan had entered into an agreement to become the editor of a new women's magazine ("founded on my name"), to which she would contribute while in Europe while a deputy, her friend Mary Safford, performed the editorial duties. This was a fortunate circumstance since it not only provided congenial occupation for a woman accustomed to work and work hard but carried "a good salary" and provided a berth as an assistant editor for Mary Logan Tucker, her daughter "Dolly."

Home Magazine flourished for six years under the Logan editorship, reaching a circulation of 300,000—a large one for that time. The magazine was an extension of its editor's personality and interests. The first issue carried a favorable statement on Woman's Suffrage, a cause that Mrs. Logan and her husband had both been supporting for some time. There were frequent little articles on public men, both here and abroad, and an occasional one on public affairs, such as "President Making in the United States." From time to time there would be an article on some accomplished woman, contemporary or historical. There were short short stories and short poems, always by authors whose names are unknown today. Innumerable issues contained short installments of a German romantic novel, *Mortal Foes*—author unnamed—translated by Mary Safford, who continued as an assistant editor.[15]

Mrs. Logan was obviously out to improve and to broaden the minds of her readers, but she did not entirely neglect the traditional materials of a women's magazine. Each issue contained one page of "fashions," two dresses and a few accessories being the sole content. The short "Recipe" section would be devoted to such simple things as salt-rising bread, soda biscuits, and how to make a boiled cake icing. The "Little Folks Column" was given over to a Bible story each issue. There would be practical little accounts of "How to Figure Interest" and "How to Get Rid of Crow's Feet."

Physically the magazine was not attractive, reflecting the low production budget that went with a modest subscription price of fifty cents a year. In the early years each issue consisted of fourteen pages, but this had been increased to twenty seven by 1891. It was printed on newsprint, with fairly good illustrations in black and white. The advertiscments were neither large nor numerous—probably a portent of the magazine's demise. It is perhaps worthy of note that they did not include the many remedies for "female trouble" which were characteristic of the press of the time.[16]

In 1891 Mrs. Logan solaced herself for the loss of her editorial job with a trip to England and France. Her abundant energies found a new outlet in 1893 when she was appointed to the Board of Lady Managers of the Chicago World's Fair. This task completed, she had the privilege of turning down President Harrison's request that she accept the important but politically ticklish job of Commissioner of Pensions.

The Spanish American War brought her tragedy. John A. Logan, Jr., the apple of her eye and the image of his father, joined the army only to be killed during his first day of action in the Philippines. Mrs. Logan's greatest personal contribution to the war was a magazine article on the sorry plight of the sick veterans of the Cuban campaign who were being held in quarantine at Montauk Point, Long Island.

Whatever else she might be busy with she was continually

concerned that General Logan's military service should be properly appreciated and properly commemorated. She had a continuing interest in the planning and placing of the two great equestrian statues of him; the one by Augustus Saint-Gaudens in Grant Park, facing Michigan Avenue in Chicago, and the one by Franklin Simmons which was made in Rome and which stands in the center of Logan Circle in Washington.

Having tasted the pleasures of writing for publication Mrs. Logan was pleased when William Randolph Hearst in 1902 employed her as a writer for his newspaper syndicate, a connection which went on until 1910.

Her name appeared as author or editor on the title pages of several books. She seems to have been proudest of *The Part Taken by Women in American History* which she wrote in 1910–11 with the assistance of her daughter, a 907 page volume. Although Mrs. Logan's thoughts on women appear in the introduction to some of the various sections, this book is primarily a biographical dictionary, both contemporary and historical, in which sketches of 928 women appear. It is as remarkable for the women it omits as for those it includes but is a treasure trove of material on nineteenth- and early twentieth-century women, many of them rather obscure.[17]

Earlier, in 1901, she had brought out *Thirty Years in Washington, or Life and Scenes in Our National Capital,* a 752 page work, profusely illustrated. It is not autobiographical, except incidentally, but is a miscellany of articles of a chatty character on everything that a proper lady of the time might like to know about. There are kindly remarks about the McKinley-Roosevelt administration, descriptions of the public buildings and what goes on in them; how the government operates; how the secret service catches counterfeiters, and so on. The reader is taken on a tour of the White House and treated to gossipy anecdotes on its former inhabitants, especially the wives of presidents. Much of this material she had used earlier in a compendium called *Our National Government.*

Her final literary achievement was the *Reminiscences of a Soldier's Wife,* the earlier part of which appeared as ten installments in *Cosmopolitan Magazine* in 1913. Her greatest honor was the presidency of the American Red Cross. Although her latter years were devoted chiefly to her grandchildren and great grandchildren she was a staunch relief worker and a fervent patriot during World War I, a conflict in which John A. Logan III served as a combat officer in the A.E.F. At eighty-one she was vigorous enough so that friends did not think it ludicrous to try to get her a seat in President Harding's cabinet.

In the early winter of 1923 she summoned her energies for a final fight: to prevent the removal of the Logan statue in Chicago from the spot Saint-Gaudens had selected for it. On Lincoln's birthday she was sick with a cold, but against her doctor's orders she insisted on attending the open-air Lincoln ceremonies. The cold turned into influenza, and the influenza into pneumonia. On the next patriotic occasion, Washington's birthday, being in her eighty-fifth year, and after thirty-eight years of widowhood, she died. She was layed to rest beside the husband of whom she was so proud.[18]

NOTES

Prelude, 1838–1859

1. Unless otherwise noted, the data and quotations in the Prelude come from Mrs. John A. Logan, *Reminiscences of a Soldier's Wife: An Autobiography* (New York, 1913), Chaps. 1 through 3.

2. Readers who would like to look further into the history and folklore of southern Illinois are referred to John W. Allen, *Legends and Lore of Southern Illinois* (Carbondale, 1963), *passim.*

3. Captain Cunningham had served in the Black Hawk War as an Illinois militiaman. He served as county clerk of Williamson County as well as sheriff and in 1845 was a member of the state legislature. Later he had an appointment as a United States Marshal in the Southern Department of Illinois.—*National Cyclopedia of American Biography,* IV, 299. *See also,* George Francis Dawson, *Life and Services of Gen. John A. Logan as Soldier and Statesman* (Chicago and New York, 1887), p. 537.

4. John Alexander Logan was born Feb. 9, 1826, on a 160 acre farm which lay within the limits of the present city of Murphysboro, Illinois. He was the son of Dr. John Logan, a Scotch-Irish medical practitioner, and Elizabeth Jenkins Logan. His first schooling was at Brownsville, Illinois, at the age of seven. In 1842 when he was sixteen, he and his brother Tom went as boarding students to Shiloh Academy, in Randolph County, where they spent three years studying spelling, grammar, and arithmetic and began Latin. In 1845 they were brought home to continue studies with a tutor who had been employed by Dr. Logan to teach all his children, who numbered eleven. On May 9, 1847, John enlisted in what became Company H. of the 1st Illinois Volunteers. He served as adjutant for that portion of the regiment which held Santa Fe, the remainder being stationed at El Paso. The regiment arrived home in September, 1848. Logan learned some law by working in the office of his mother's brother, but

diverged to serve as county clerk of Jackson County after his election in 1849. He graduated from the law department of the University of Louisville in 1851 and was elected to the lower house of the Illinois legislature in 1852. After taking his seat in January 1853, he became a member of the Judiciary Committee and the Banks and Corporations Committee. In 1852, aged 26, he was elected prosecutor of the Third Judicial Circuit.—James Pickett Jones, *"Black Jack": John A. Logan and Southern Illinois in the Civil War Era,* Florida State University Studies, No. 51 (Tallahassee, 1967), pp. 1–15; Allen, *Legends and Lore,* pp. 28–29; John Howard Brown, ed., *Lamb's Biographical Dictionary of the United States* (Boston, 1903), p. 108; *Dictionary of American Biography,* VI, 363–64.

5. Mary showed notable reluctance until late in the courtship, at first neglecting to answer her suitor's letters. Logan proposed shortly after her graduation and was annoyed by her inability to give him an answer. From the first he was insistent on a prompt marriage, not later than the end of August. During this period she was receiving sentimental letters from an unidentified "Harry," who wrote from Lebanon, Illinois in the summer, and in the fall from West Point, where he was a cadet. In his last letter—November 4, 1855—he remarks that he has not heard from her in a long time and that he was gratified to receive "the papers" and to realize "you was [*sic*] not indifferent to me and that you had not entirely forgotten me."—Various letters, John A. Logan to Mary Cunningham, and Mary to John, especially J. A. L. to M. C., Feb. 14, 1855, and Aug. 15 and 20, 1855; M. C. to J. A. L., Aug. 11, 1855; "Harry" to Mary Cunningham, Letter, Nov. 4, 1855, John A. Logan Family Papers, Library of Congress.

6. For example, Mary Logan to John A. Logan, Letters, March 4, March 8, April 26, May 2, 1858, Logan Papers.

7. Logan's quick leap to prominence in the legislature was based on the hard line he took toward Negro migration. The state constitution of 1848 forbad Negro migration into Illinois but left details to the legislature. That body neglected to legislate in the matter and Logan's election campaign in 1853 featured promises to force the issue. It is ironic that this man who was later to become a prominent political friend of the Negro and a Republican, should have put through the notorious Logan Act in his first term. The act provided a stiff fine for anyone introducing a Negro into the state. Furthermore, any Negro who entered was to be fined and ejected. If he could not pay, which was likely, he was to work out the fine and court costs. The act passed the house 45 to 23 with all delegations south of Springfield solidly supporting it. Six days later it passed the senate with a four vote margin. It made enemies for its sponsor in northern Illinois, where antislavery men had been trying to get

legislation to improve the dubious status of the five to six thousand Negroes in the state. It made him a hero in southern Illinois.—Jones, *"Black Jack,"* pp. 17–20.

8. In 1858 Logan spoke from the same platform with Douglas at Chester, Cairo, Benton, and Centralia.—*Ibid.*, pp. 37–38.

9. Logan went off to Washington to begin his congressional career alone. It was thought that Dolly was too young for the hardships of travel. Mrs. Logan, as might be expected, was thoroughly discontented with the separation. She solaced herself by envisioning her absent husband as performing protean deeds for "the preservation of our Glorious Union." Just before Christmas she indicated her impression of the seriousness of possible secession as follows: "my own notion is that were the Union dissolved, the Constitution of the United States would be powerless, and that *each* State would be a republic of itself and would only be governed by its own laws without any regard to the Constitution and the consequence would be an incessant Civil War." She then begs her husband to give her his thoughts on this subject.—M. L. to J. A. L., Letter, Dec. 23, 1859, Logan Papers.

1–The Eve of Secession

1. Logan's first election to Congress was a notable triumph. He received 15,878 votes while David L. Phillips, the Republican, and W. K. Parish, the "Lecompton" (i.e., Administration) Democrat, received 2976 and 200 respectively. The move from Benton to Marion was politically motivated. Logan had learned of a "conspiracy" in the legislature to delete Franklin County (Benton) from the Ninth Congressional District in order to gerrymander him out of his seat.—James Pickett Jones, *"Black Jack": John A. Logan and Southern Illinois in the Civil War Era*, Florida State University Studies, No. 51 (Tallahassee, 1967), pp. 40, 76.

2. Harriet Lane was the young and widely admired niece of President Buchanan. She served as White House hostess throughout the administration of her bachelor uncle.—*National Cyclopedia of American Biography*, V., 9.

3. The Crittenden Compromise never came to a definitive vote. It involved the following points: (1) There was to be no slavery in territories north of the 36–30 line, but slavery was to be protected south of it. (2) Future states might come into the Union with or without slavery as they pleased. (3) Congress was to restrain from abolishing slavery in territory which was surrounded by slave states. (4) Where intimidation prevented the recapture of a slave the United States was to fully compensate the owner, recovering costs from the county. (5) There was to be full enforcement of the Fugitive Slave Act and Congress was to urge the repeal of State

"Personal Liberty Laws." All of this was to be made into a constitutional amendment "and no further amendment was to be made which would authorize Congress to touch slavery in any of the States."—J. G. Randall and David Donald, *The Civil War and Reconstruction*, 2d ed. (Boston, 1961), pp. 150–51.

4. The dates in 1860–61 on which the States seceded were as follows: South Carolina, Dec. 20; Mississippi, Jan. 9; Florida, Jan. 10; Alabama, Jan. 11; Georgia, Jan. 19; Louisiana, Jan. 26; Texas, Feb. 1; Virginia, April 17; Arkansas, May 6; Tennessee, May 7, and North Carolina, May 20.—*Ibid.*, pp. 136–41, 180–89.

5. William M. Gwin (not Gwyn) was a Tennesseean who served as senator from California from its admission until 1861. Notably pro-Southern before the War, he left the country after a brief imprisonment in 1861, spending the war years in Mexico and France. When he returned after peace came he was held in prison for eight months by the Federal government. He had no further political career.—*Dictionary of American Biography*, VIII, 64–65.

6. The battle of Ball's Bluff was fought Oct. 21, 1961.—Randall and David, *Civil War and Reconstruction*, p. 281.

7. Southern Illinois was overwhelmingly anti-Republican. In 1858 some counties voted 50 to 1 for Democrats; in 1860 only four counties were carried by Lincoln—St. Clair, Madison, Bond, and Edwards, counties where there was a strong German vote. But the region was overwhelmingly pro-Douglas, and its adherence to the Union, initially due to Douglas' prompt and firm stand during the Fort Sumter crisis, was solidified in the late summer by Congressman Logan's appeals. The strength of anti-secession feeling is attested by the fact that throughout the war volunteering was always over-quota and it was never necessary to impose the draft.—Edward Conrad Smith, *The Borderland in the Civil War* (New York, 1927), pp. 45, 68, 138, 182, 184.

8. The Ohio and Mississippi Railroad, connecting Cincinnati and St. Louis, later was merged with the Baltimore and Ohio. It was sometimes thought of as the northern boundary of Southern Illinois.

9. On May 24, 1861, having given his family only one hour's notice, Hybert B. Cunningham ("Bub"), Mary's beloved younger brother, left with a small group of young men to join the Confederate Army. When his enlistment expired he presented himself at Logan's headquarters and was accepted as a volunteer aide. General Logan asked Governor Richard Yates for a captain's commission for him, which was granted. He continued to serve on Logan's staff to the end of the war. In writing her husband the news of Bub's departure, Mrs. Logan, in her frustration, made some remarks which were not compatible with the stout Union views she would soon have to profess: "God alone knows what will come [for] we have lived to see the day

when men dare not call themselves free men or exercise the rights of free speech and since we are thus near a despotism . . . the Administration and his advisers have already their work of invasion; their arrogance and power have hurried them on. . . . The day will soon be here when every man must take sides in this conflict and never before were their [*sic*] two extremes so objectionable for one cannot honestly and honorable [*sic*] or justly endorse the course of the President."—Mary Logan to John A. Logan, Letter, May 25, 1861, and John A. Logan to Gov. Richard Yates, Letter, July 16, 1864, Logan Family Papers, Library of Congress. See also, Jones, "*Black Jack*," pp. 83–84.

10. Since General Logan was to be spoken of as a Judas and an arch opportunist by many Democrats in the postwar years it is important to review the agony of indecision which he went through for many months of 1861. On January 1 he wrote a seventeen-page letter to I. N. Haynie (of Cairo) in which he said the secession crisis was "a joint conspiracy of abolitionists and Ultra Southerners, *both* of whom want the Union broken up." He believed that separation would "lead to strife," that the question of free navigation of the Mississippi would arise, and must be insisted upon by the North "at any cost." The moderates of both sections must turn on the extremists and throw them out. "Let every state have unquestioned the institutions it wants." He wanted to reassure and appease the South so that its extremists would not prevail. On February 5 he addressed the House, pleading for Union, but without the use of force. He worked hard to further the Crittenden Compromise and on July 5 he wrote his wife that all of the Kentucky congressmen and a majority of the Missourians were for the Union; that nearly all the soldiers at Washington were Democrats. On July 6 and 16 he wrote Mary that he was not well, but on July 20 he told her he had fought for four hours, musket in hand against the Confederates at Blackburn's Ford, a skirmish which preceded Bull Run by three days. On July 25 he wrote that he wanted to "Join the Army," but would come home and consult her first—a promise he did not keep, for on August 11 Yates offered him the colonelcy of a regiment and demanded an immediate answer. Actually, June 18 was probably the day Logan crossed the Rubicon of publicly avowing willingness to support coercion of the South. On that day he addressed Grant's 21st Illinois Volunteers, urging the men to reenlist. In July and early August rumours that he was planning to raise a regiment were so rife among his constituents that Mrs. Logan repeatedly asked him what she was to say to inquirers, and added that his supporters did not believe the rumours. —J. A. L. to I. N. Haynie, Letter, Jan. 1, 1861; J. A. L. to M. L., Letters, July 5, July 6, July 16, July 20, July 21; M. L. to J. A. L., Letters, July 22, July 25; Richard Yates to J. A. L., Letter, August 11,

1861, Logan Family Papers, Library of Congress. *See also*, Jones, *"Black Jack,"* pp. 67–73, 88–89; 96–99.

2—Espousing the Union Cause

1. Mrs. Logan spent a considerable part of the time with her husband during the period the 31st Illinois was in camp at Cairo. Her principle reason, as stated at the time, sheds a poignant light on the "Brothers War." In a letter written in late September or early October, 1861, she says: "the unnatural and piercing feelings our families feel about your being in the Service makes it awful to be with them while you live; and when I think of many things you said and affirmations you made last spring in your speeches against the war I can trace the foundation of their feelings. They will never feel right the fact of your having to join with Republicans under Lincoln's administration to fight the South when they (the South I mean) have made no invasions, and will ever keep alive that bitterness which they will not hide."—M. L. to J. A. L., Letter, Logan Family Papers, Library of Congress. Of the whole Logan family only the younger brother, James, approved John's course. His brother Tom loudly proclaimed pro-Southern feeling; his brother-in-law, Dr. Israel Blanchard, attacked him. "His mother's hostility was most difficult to bear." She "upbraided" him.—Jones, *"Black Jack": John A. Logan and Southern Illinois in the Civil War Era,* Florida State University Studies, No. 51 (Tallahassee, 1967), p. 101.

2. Cairo was the southern terminus of the Illinois Central Railroad at that time. Passengers and freight were there either transferred to boats or were ferried twenty miles south to Columbus, Kentucky (soon to be occupied and fortified by the Confederates) where they could regain railroad connections to New Orleans. For a dismal picture of the Cairo of 1861 as seen by a distinguished English novelist, *see* Anthony Trollope, *North America* (Philadelphia, 1862), II, 11.

3. The troops at Cairo had the usual high sick rates from "childrens diseases" which were characteristic of all troop rendezvous points in 1861, but complicated by much incidence of the malarial fevers. The want of adequate drugs and medical supplies was notorious in the west in 1862. This was remedied by the creation of an enormous medical supply depot at Louisville in 1862 in charge of the assistant surgeon general of the army.—George Worthington Adams, *Doctors in Blue: The Medical History of the Union Army in the Civil War* (New York, 1952), pp. 15, 16, 20.

4. This was the usual reaction to amputations. It is true that early in the war most of the "surgeons" were inexperienced and inept, but they learned fast and as time went on amputations were performed by teams of "specialists." A review of the statistics, long

after the war, is convincing that the amputees stood a better chance of survival than the men who were treated by "conservative" methods. This was because nearly all wounds were infected and because the principal missile of the war, the Minié ball, usually fragmented large segments of bone.—*Ibid.*, Chap. 6 *passim.*

3—*Armageddon—a Wife's Vigil*

1. Logan's promotion to brigadier general was requested by General Grant on March 14, 1862. He was returned to active duty on April 7, 1862. As the battle of Shiloh was fought April 6 and 7, he was just too late to participate.—George Francis Dawson, *Life and Services of Gen. John A. Logan as Soldier and Statesman* (Chicago and New York, 1887), p. 24.

2. This was not exactly as Mrs. Logan understood it. Grant, as commander of a military district, was the subordinate of Halleck, the department commander. Halleck decided to come to the scene of action partly because of the rumours mentioned but also due to the curious situation which developed because a traitorous telegrapher with Grant had neglected to deliver some of Halleck's messages to Grant and had neglected to send some of Grant's messages to Halleck, planting in Halleck's mind the idea that Grant must be insubordinate or out of his head.—Bruce Catton, *Grant Moves South* (Boston, Toronto, 1960), Chap. 5 *passim,* and pp. 186–288.

3. General Logan's initial response to the Emancipation Proclamation was that it was "foolish," would lengthen the war and would confuse the issue of what the war was about.—J. A. L. to M. L., Letter, December 12, 1862.

4. Logan's promotion to major general came after his electioneering in Illinois in November, 1863. He was given command of the Fifteenth Army Corps, which had been successively commanded by Grant, Sherman, and James B. McPherson.—Dawson, *Life and Services,* pp. 49–50. Logan was highly popular with his soldiers partly because of his dash and high spirits. The distinguished war correspondent Sylvester Cadwalader, observing him during the Vicksburg campaign, thought he had not yet grown up to the "conventional requirements" of a brigadier general. On one occasion "I saw him . . . with nothing on him in the way of clothing but his hat, shirt and boots, sitting at a table on which stood a bottle of whisky and a tin cup, and playing on the violin for a lot of darky roustabouts to dance. . . . Yet he was never accused of drunkeness—was not intoxicated from the beginning to the end of the war, so far as came to my knowledge."—Sylvester Cadwalader, *Three Years With Grant: As Recalled by War Correspondent Sylvester Cadwalader,* Edited and with an introduction and notes by Benjamin P. Thomas (New York, 1956), pp. 66–67.

5. The question of Southern Illinois' loyalty to the Union cause is a vexed one. Volunteers for the army presented themselves in sufficient numbers so that the draft was never invoked in the Ninth Congressional District, which included most of the region; but this may have been a reflection of the relatively poor economic possibilities there as compared with the rest of the state. After the Emancipation Proclamation turned the war into one of Liberation there were abnormally high desertion rates in some of the Southern Illinois regiments in the south. It was felt necessary to disarm one regiment in Mississippi because of "fraternization" and desertions. A regiment at Memphis was reduced to 35 men by desertions. There were disturbances in three of the counties adjoining Jackson County (Carbondale), but even greater disturbances occurred in Central Illinois. Logan's seat in Congress was filled by a Peace Democrat and the Peace Democrats in the State Legislature followed an obstructive policy; but with peace and the return home of the soldiers the region was anxious to elect Logan and other Republicans and remained Republican for a century.—Cf. Edward C. Smith, *The Borderland and the Civil War* (New York, 1927), pp. 333, 338–41; Wood Gray, *The Hidden Civil War: The Story of the Copperheads* (New York, 1942), p. 155; Ella Lonn, *Desertion During the Civil War* (New York, 1928), pp. 152–55, 204, 234; Arthur C. Cole, *The Era of the Civil War, Centennial History of Illinois,* III (Springfield, 1919), Chap. 13 *passim.*

4—"Politicking" in Illinois, 1864

1. Grenville Mellen Dodge, 1831–1916, was to have a notable postwar career as a railroad builder, serving as chief engineer of the Union Pacific 1866–70 and of the Texas Pacific 1871–81.—*Who Was Who in America* (Chicago, 1963), p. 329. Francis Preston Blair, Jr., 1821–75 was the brother of Montgomery Blair, Lincoln's Postmaster General. He had been the leading Unionist politician in St. Louis early in the war and came into the army as a brigadier general. In 1868 he was the Democratic candidate for vice president.—*Dictionary of American Biography,* I, 332–34. For excellent accounts of the Atlanta campaign *see* Bruce Catton, *Never Call Retreat, The Centennial History of the Civil War,* III, E. B. Long, Director of Research (Garden City, N. Y., 1965), and Jones, *"Black Jack": John A. Logan and Southern Illinois in the Civil War Era,* Florida State University Studies, No. 51 (Tallahassee, 1967), Chaps. 12 and 13.

2. General John B. Hood replaced General Joseph E. Johnston as the Confederate commander July 17, 1864.—Catton, *Never Call Retreat,* p. 329. William Joseph Hardee, 1815–73, an 1838 graduate of West Point, was the author of *Rifle and Light Infantry Tactics* (Philadelphia, 1855) which was the tactical "Bible" of both sides.—

Dictionary of American Biography (hereafter to be cited as *D.A.B.*), IV, 239–40.

3. General Oliver Otis Howard, 1830–1909, a Maine man who was a graduate of both Bowdoin College and West Point, was widely known as the "Christian General" because of his sincere devotion to evangelical religion and his sometimes prissy ways. Best known for his Directorship of the Freedmen's Bureau (1865–74), his character and his performance at the Bureau are somewhat unappreciatively examined in William S. McFeely, *Yankee Stepfather: General O. O. Howard and the Freedmen* (New Haven, 1968), *passim*. For Howard's attitude *see Ibid.*, pp. 10–13.

4. In denying Logan the command of the Army of the Tennessee, General Sherman must have been influenced by the strong hostility to Logan of General George H. Thomas, the commander of the Army of the Cumberland. The Thomas-Logan "feud" stemmed from a quarrel over Logan's claims to partial control over the Louisville and Nashville Railroad which lay wholly within the territorial limits of the Department of the Cumberland.—Lloyd Lewis, *Sherman: Fighting Prophet* (New York, 1932), p. 346. It may be noted that altho Sherman sometimes liked to tease Howard by using profanity, he admired him.—*Ibid.*, p. 349.

5. Sherman's decision to name Howard was not immediately arrived at, and was confusing to Logan and to others. On July 25 Sherman wrote Logan, addressing him as "Commanding, Army of the Tennessee," to counsel him on one of the powers of an Army commander, the power to send a general away from the Army. General Dodge wanted to get rid of one of his brigadiers. Sherman tells Logan this is within his rights as Army commander but urges "delicacy" in the use of this power.—Sherman to Logan, Letter, July 25, 1864, Logan Papers. Two days later, having decided on Howard, Sherman wrote Logan as follows: "I assure you in giving preference to Gen. Howard, I will not fail to give you early credit for having done so well. You have command of a good corps, a command that I would prefer to the more complicated one of a Department and if you will be patient it will come to you soon enough." This letter begins: "Take a good rest. I know you are worn out with mental and physical work."—Sherman to Logan, Letter, July 27, 1864, Logan Papers. On that same day General Joseph Hooker, commander of the Twentieth Corps and former commander of the Army of the Potomac, wrote Logan to express outrage that Howard had been preferred over Logan and to state that he is writing to request he be relieved.—Hooker, to Logan, Letter, July 27, 1864, Logan Papers. Logan's reactions as shown in his letters to Mrs. Logan, are interesting. On August 31 he wrote her at length, first describing the battle and his victory, then telling her about Howard getting the command.

He leaves Sherman unmentioned and says Howard was assigned "by the War Department." On August 6 he is rancorous about Sherman: "West Point must have all under Sherman who is an infernal *brute*. As soon as this campaign is over I think I shall come home, at least I will not serve longer under Sherman." In his letter of August 21, he shows his hurt when Mary has brought the matter up, by stating that the Army of the Tennessee wants him, and writing that he will "sometime be vindicated."—J. A. L. to M. L., Letters, July 31, August 6, August 21, 1864, Logan Papers. That this psychological wound continued to fester throughout his life is attested by Mrs. Logan's treatment of the matter in the text. William Eidson, a careful and thorough student of Logan's career, believes that the Army of the Tennessee would have remained Logan's except for the strong opposition of General Thomas, who threatened to resign as commander of the Army of the Cumberland.—William Eidson, "John A. Logan," Manuscript Biography, Vanderbilt University. Sherman himself, in explaining his desire for Howard to General Henry W. Halleck, gave unstinted praise to Logan's handling of the Army after McPherson's death, but states that the command of the large Military Department of the Tennessee was involved, not merely the field Army of that name.—Sherman to Halleck, August 16, 1864, Logan Papers. James P. Jones seems to think that Sherman's doubts of Logan's ability to maneuver three army corps was central in the decision. Jones, *"Black Jack,"* pp. 219–20.

6. Despite Logan's bitterness in having to give up the command of the Army of the Tennessee, perspective leads irresistibly to the conclusion that he served the Union cause much better by "politicking" in Illinois than he could have in leading that Army during its innocuous march with Sherman "from Atlanta to the sea." His brief dip into Illinois politics in 1863 had made it clear that he was unalterably opposed to stopping the war short of victory. But it had not indicated that he was prepared to give up his status as a "War Democrat" and become a Republican. It is not surprising then that the military celebrity he acquired in 1864 led a number of Democratic politicians to assail him with pleas that he enter active Democratic politics for the presidential campaign, possibly as the vice-presidential candidate, or even as the presidential candidate. Apparently he gave no answer to such enticements, and after McClellan was nominated the appeal was that Logan could serve the Union best by giving support to "Little Mac."—Francis G. Young to Logan, Letter, August 12, 1864; J. W. Sheehan to Logan, Letter, August 31, 1864; William Allen to Logan, Letter, September 29, 1864, all in Logan Papers. However, his old and valued friend and fellow Democrat, Isaac N. Haynie of Cairo, having heard that Logan was going to support McClellan, wrote him saying he did not understand how "any

man of my views can support him" and urged the general to make clear his stand.—Haynie to Logan, Letter, September 9, 1864, Logan Papers. *See also* Jones, "*Black Jack,*" Chap. 14 *passim,* and Eidson, "Logan," pp. 146–49. It was Congressman Washburne, the man who had been so instrumental in advancing his military career in 1861 and 1862, who persuaded the Administration to ask a leave for him and who wrote him persuasively that it was his duty to come home and carry Illinois for Lincoln.—Elihu B. Washburne to Logan, Letter, September 12, 1864, Logan Papers.

5—*New Horizons at War's End*

1. The United States Sanitary Commission had been organized and given a semi-official status in 1861. Something like the later Red Cross, it conceived itself as having the double role of advising the army on all matters concerning the health of the soldiers and providing comforts in the shape of hospital supplies and food delicacies. Local chapters were organized in most Northern communities to provide the supplies and food and to raise money. Adams, *Doctors in Blue: The Medical History of the Union Army in the Civil War* (New York, 1952), pp. 5–22, 47, 77, 82, 109, 150–52, 158, 165–68, 190. The standard book-length treatment is William Q. Maxwell, *Lincoln's Fifth Wheel* (New York), 1956.

2. Ulysses S. Grant, *Personal Memoirs of U. S. Grant* (New York, 1886), II, 379–84. Grant was aware of Logan's bitter disappointment at not receiving command of the Army of The Tennessee, and he implies the view that he thinks Logan should have had it. But he says he does not doubt that Sherman was acting for what he believed "would be to the good of the service."—*Ibid.*, pp. 352–54.

3. The burning of Columbia is one of the noisiest and most long-lived of the controversies to come out of the war. General Wade Hampton denied flatly that any cotton was burned on his orders. Much of the Confederate testimony is to be found in the *Congressional Record* (May 15, 1930), pp. 8981–9026. The latest scholarly treatment of the subject is that of Bruce Catton who agrees that Sherman did not *order* Columbia burned. He finds Sherman's explanation hard to believe, and adds: "but it is also necessary to realize that if the fire had not started so it would have been started in some other way, because, as the capital of the first state to secede, Columbia was certain to go up in flames as soon as these soldiers reached it."—Catton, *Never Call Retreat, The Centennial History of the Civil War,* III (Garden City, N. Y., 1965), pp. 434–35.

4. Consciously or unconsciously, Mrs. Logan gives the impression that the two great Union armies marched on the same day. The Army of the Potomac marched on May 23; Sherman's Westerners on May 24.

5. "They want to make me a Brigadier in the regular army but I think I shall quit the business and try peaceful avocations for a while: and see how I will be used by the country and that may determine me as to the army." He proudly states to Mary that his Corps "now has 23,000 men present for duty . . . and could march all over Texas if ordered to do so."—J. A. L. to M. L., Letter, April 27 (Raleigh, N. C.), Logan Papers.

6. Throughout 1865 Logan was excited by career possibilities. He had barely rejoined his troops when he was hoping for election to the vacant U. S. Senatorship. His friend Haynie believed he could have had it had he been on the ground in Springfield. Haynie explained to Mrs. Logan that Washburne and Ex-Governor Richard Yates were "about the only candidates" and it looked as though Yates would get the plum. To console her he added: "If virtue and sobriety secure *defeat*—and their opposites secure promotion how long will it take this world to become good?"—I. N. Haynie to M. L., Letter (Springfield), January 4, 1865, Logan Papers. He was referring to Yates' unfortunate slide into alcoholism, for which *see* Richard Yates and Catherine Yates Pickering, *Richard Yates: Civil War Governor* (Danville, Ill., 1966), pp. 267–78. *See also,* J. A. L. to M. L., Letter, January 20, 1865, Logan Papers.

From Savannah, Logan indicated his worries on his financial future, and on what career he should follow: I "may loose (*sic*) my energy to some extent then I feel I shall have to struggle all my life for a bare living but I can make one and will do so. . . . I would like somewhere that I could move in good society and properly place my family in the elevated scale of the world where ability and wealth could be properly estimated and appreciated."—J. A. L. to M. L., January 22, 1865. With victory his morale improved. From Chicago, in late summer, he wrote "the people seem glad to see me and unless I am very much fooled I will have but little trouble when the time comes in securing any position I may desire."—J. A. L. to M. L., September 4, 1865. During the fall Logan spent some time in the east repairing his fortunes. On November 3 a banker friend made him a $5000 profit on the stockmarket. He was so pleased that he decided to put all his money in the friend's hands and "try it again." —J. A. L. to M. L., November 4, 1865. Three days later his profits had mounted to $6100: "I shall close at that and think I have done well don't you think so?"—J. A. L. to M. L., November 7, 1865.

It was in November that the Johnson administration tried to capture him by offering appointment as minister to Mexico and indicating he could have the mission to Japan if he preferred it. Matters were pushed to the point that Secretary Seward actually sent him his commission as minister to Mexico, and demanded a prompt answer. Governor Oglesby wrote him that he was wise to turn down the Japanese appointment, but thought he ought to accept the Mexican opportunity. "If I were not Governor of Illinois I would take it at once." In his decision to turn down both diplomatic appointments, Logan was influenced by his older backer, Congressman Washburne, who advised against Mexico and who promised support for the senatorship and promised not to be a candidate himself.—J. A. L. to M. L., Letters, November 4, 1865; November 7, 1865; December 8, 1865; William E. Seward to Logan, November 16 and November 22, 1865; Logan to Seward, November 29, 1865; Richard J. Oglesby to Logan, November 28, 1865, Logan Papers.

7. Mrs. Logan's memory seems to be at fault here. Logan did not resign his seat until early in 1862. On January 4 he wrote her to explain that he could be both a member of congress and a colonel in the army but cannot be paid for both offices, "and therefore am not willing to do the duties of both. . . . I shall resign one or the other and I certainly cannot resign my army commission after getting the boys into it."—J. A. L. to M. L. (New York), January 3, 1862.

8. Sen. Ira Harris was elected to the senate from New York in 1861 to replace Wm. E. Seward. He left the senate in 1867.—*The National Cyclopedia of American Biography* (New York, 1899), II, 96. Sen. Willard Saulsbury (*not* Salisbury) was senator from Delaware, 1857–71. Perhaps Mrs. Logan considered him "eccentric" because he favored the restoration of civil rights to former Confederates. *D.A.B.*, XVI, 378.

9. The Washington scene could differ as seen by a victorious northern woman and a defeated southern man. Contrast Mrs. Logan's happy view with that of Confederate General Richard Taylor, upon his first postwar visit to the city. "The marshal tread of hundreds of volunteer generals, just disbanded, resounded in the streets. Gorged with loot, they spent it as lavishly as Morgan's buccaneers after the sack of Panama. Their women sat at meat or walked the highways, resplendent in jewels, spoil of Southern matrons. The camp-followers of the army were here in high carnival, and in character and numbers rivalled the attendants of Xerxes. Courtesans swarmed everywhere, about the inns, around the Capitol, in the antechambers of the White House, and were brokers for the transaction of all business."—Richard Taylor, *Destruction and Reconstruction: Personal Experiences of the Late War*, ed. Richard B. Harwell (New York, London, Toronto, 1955), p. 296.

10. The Logan's Carbondale house is a commodious but unpretentious two-story frame dwelling, now altered by structural change, on the northwest corner of Oak and Pine streets. The 1870 population of Carbondale was 3370 (of whom 383 were Negro). No figure is given in the 1860 census.—*Ninth Census*, June 1, 1870, I (Washington, 1872).

11. Veterans of earlier wars were not numerous enough to constitute a "problem." For an illuminating and interesting discussion of the Veteran Problem of the Civil War *see* Dixon Wecter, *When Johnny Comes Marching Home* (Cambridge, Mass., 1944), pp. 101–254.

12. In early June, 1865, the Johnson administration was actively seeking the support of popular generals. On June 7 a "Union" meeting, inspired by Democrats, was held at Cooper Union in New York City, with Grant, Logan, and Frank Blair present by invitation. Grant acknowledged an ovation merely by bowing. Logan made a speech in which he stated a "wait and see" policy regarding President Johnson, whose name had been loudly applauded. Logan suggested that Britain be asked to settle the Alabama claims, that Maximillian be asked to leave Mexico and that the validity of the national debt must not be questioned. The New York *Herald* quoted him as having said that the states had never been out of the Union.—Dawson, *Life and Services of Gen. John A. Logan as Soldier and Statesman* (Chicago and New York, 1887), p. 105; Eidson, "John A. Logan," Manuscript Biography, Vanderbilt University, p. 198. For Logan's immediate postwar political attitudes and activities see also Jones, *"Black Jack": John A. Logan and Southern Illinois in the Civil War Era*, Florida State University Studies, No. 51 (Tallahassee, 1967), Chap. 16 *passim.*

6—*Life Among the Reconstructionists*

1. Benjamin Franklin Stephenson, 1823–71, Illinois born, was surgeon of the 14th Illinois Volunteer Infantry, 1861–64.—*Who's Who in American History,* p. 504. Mrs. Dearing, the authority on the G.A.R., thinks the real founder was Governor Oglesby, assisted by Logan, who used Dr. Stephenson as their instrument.—Mary R. Dearing, *Veterans in Politics: the Story of the Grand Army of the Republic* (Baton Rouge, 1952), pp. 81–84. Logan had already participated in the founding of the Society of the Army of the Tennessee in the spring of 1865, while the war was still in progress.

2. This was a small proportion of the men eligible for membership. For a comment on the G.A.R. as an "adjunct" of the Republican party see Randall and David, *Civil War and Reconstruction,* 2d ed. (Boston, 1961), p. 588.

3. By the spring of 1866 Logan had arrived at the view that "Johnson seems determined to force the Copperheads into power again."—J. A. L. to M. L., Letter, April 29, 1866, Logan Papers. For a recent balanced view of Johnson's Reconstruction policies see Kenneth M. Stampp, *The Era of Reconstruction, 1865–1877* (New York, 1965), Chapter 3 *passim.* After posturing as a Radical at the

start of his administration, with remarks such as "Treason is a crime" and must not go unpunished, President Johnson settled down to an approximation of what Lincoln seems to have had in mind. As he saw it, the war had been one for Union and Freedom. The Thirteenth Amendment took care of the "freedom" part, as he viewed it: "union" was to be obtained by a program of pardon and amnesty to those ex-Confederates who would take the oath of allegiance and cooperate in forming state governments under new constitutions which abolished slavery and recognized the permanency and legitimacy of the government at Washington. Believing that reconstruction was an administrative prerogative, Johnson worked fast to push his plans as far as he could while Congress was not sitting. On May 29, 1865, he appointed a provisional governor for North Carolina who was to call a convention to make a new constitution, the makers to be elected by all who had received presidential pardons or been "amnestied." He then used the same proclamation for other states. Ultimately, on December 25, 1868, he made pardon and amnesty universal and restored civil rights to all who had been stripped of them. The passage by Southern legislatures of "black codes" to control the freedmen, coupled with massive race riots in New Orleans and Memphis, led radical Republicans in Congress to the conclusion that Johnson was trying to restore slavery under another name and resulted in the passage of the Civil Rights acts and the fourteenth and fifteenth Amendments. Congress was determined to take control of the reconstruction process, which it did by refusing to seat congressional delegations sent to Washington by Johnson's new state governments.

4. Since the division of the South into districts to be administered by generals was an important part of Congressional Reconstruction, the Radicals were anxious that the Secretary of War should be the kind of man with whom they could work. Stanton was such a man, and his retention was supposedly guaranteed by the passage of the Tenure of Office Act which stated that an officer whose appointment required senatorial confirmation could be removed only with senatorial agreement. To test the constitutionality of this act President Johnson suspended Stanton in August, 1867, and persuaded General Grant to accept interim appointment as Secretary of War, believing he had the general's promise to cooperate. Grant did not see it this way and stepped aside in favor of Stanton. This led Johnson into a violent letter of denunciation which drove Grant into the camp of the Radicals. On February 21, 1868, Johnson appointed Gen. Lorenzo Thomas as interim Secretary of War, notifying Stanton that he was removed. Stanton then stood siege in his office, supported by Logan's stout G.A.R. men. This imbroglio was the basis for the

radicals' decision to impeach the President, a course which had been under serious consideration for a long time. *See* Stampp, *Era of Reconstruction*, pp. 147–50 and 152 *n*.

5. Samuel Clarke Pomeroy, 1816–19. He had been one of the leaders of the New England settlers in "Bloody Kansas" from the beginning and was prominent in national Republican politics from 1856 on.—*Who's Who in American History*, p. 417. Benjamin Franklin Butler, 1818–93, was one of the most controversial characters of the era. Originally a Massachusetts Democrat, and a proponent of Breckenridge in 1860, he entered the Union Army as a Brigadier General in 1861 and following an extremely spotty career as a "political general" turned Radical Republican after the war and served in the House of Representatives 1867–75.—*Ibid.*, p. 180.

6. Charles Sumner, 1811–74, represented Massachusetts in the Senate from 1851 until his death. An elegant, highly educated man, he stood out throughout his long Senate career as an extreme anti-slavery man and Radical reconstructionist, devoted to what he considered the best interests of the freed Negroes and known for the harsh acerbity he showed his political opponents.—*Ibid.*, p. 515.

7. B. F. Stephenson, the "founder" of the G.A.R., wrote Logan a long letter in January, 1868, telling him that he was preferred over Grant by the G.A.R. members for the presidency and urging that the veterans should attempt to control the Republican convention.—B. F. Stephenson to L., Letter, Springfield, January 30, 1868, Logan Papers.

8. The English-built Confederate cruiser *Alabama* had had sensational success in sinking or capturing large numbers of United States merchant ships and in forcing still more into foreign registry because of greatly increased insurance rates. It was the contention of the United States Government that the British were in violation of international law in permitting the construction of the *Alabama* and consequently owed the United States and its citizens vast sums as indemnity. It was agreed that the matter should be judged by an arbitration commission consisting of representatives selected by the United States, Great Britain, Switzerland, Italy, and Brazil. After long deliberations this body on September 14, 1872, concluded that Britain should pay $15,500,000. The matter was of great interest and importance as a landmark in the settlement of this kind of international quarrel.—H. C. Lincoln, *Great Britain and the United States: a History of Anglo-American Relations 1783–1952* (New York, 1955), pp. 513–17.

9. Mrs. Logan's account of the origin of Memorial Day does not receive full credence in Carbondale, Ill., where John Allen, a highly respected local historian, has produced evidence that a similar cele-

bration, with General Logan present, had been held earlier. A number of other communities have advanced similar claims.

7—*Confidants to the First Family*

1. There are interesting similarities and dissimilarities between Logan and Benjamin F. Butler. Both were red-hot Democrats before the war; but Logan was a staunch Douglas man and Butler was the nominator of Jefferson Davis in 1860. Both entered the army in 1861; but Butler was a brigadier general and Logan a colonel. Both were objects of considerable newspaper attention during the war, with Butler getting more space than Logan. Both controlled the destinies of captured cities: Logan at Memphis and Vicksburg, Butler at New Orleans. The latter made himself so hated by the population he governed that he received the nickname "Beast Butler," chiefly because of his notorious order to treat insolent Confederate women "as women of the town," and partly because of good things he did such as the enforcement of such rigorous sanitary regulations that New Orleans became both clean and healthy for the first time in its history. Butler was the first to command a field Army, but won no laurels: Logan, in various ranks, won high distinction as a soldier on numerous major battlefields. After the war they both became prominent as Radical Republicans and played major roles in Congress, becoming, in the eyes of Democrats, the two Judases. Then Butler forsook his Republicanism to become the presidential nominee of the Greenback Party and the Anti-Monopoly Party, while Logan, tho he had flirtations with inflation in the form of Greenbackism, remained a Republican Stalwart, who immolated himself in a lifelong devotion to advancing the career of President Grant. In the course of war and politics Butler made a fortune: Logan died a relatively poor man.

2. Isaac P. Christiancy, 1812–90. His offense seems to have been that as an elderly man he married a young girl. An act which has roused the wrath of some women in later periods of our history.

8—*Memorable Years in the Senate*

1. Logan, at the behest of some of his friends, had given some thought to the governorship in 1868, but decided in favor of the Congressman-at-Large position.—*See* Letters of J. H. Haynie to Logan, February 14, 1868, James Fishback to Logan, February 23, 1868, and J. James Ren to Logan, February 3, 1868, all in Logan Papers. When the Yates senate term expired in 1870 Yates was unable to prevail against the pro-Logan forces for reelection. He himself thought this was due primarily to his reputation as an alcoholic. On January 6, 1870, he wrote Governor Palmer: "I feel very bad that by force of a bad habit, I am to see those timid creatures

who stood way back, saying I was playing hell with the party, taking the place which it has cost me a lifetime to reach. Yates and Pickering, *Richard Yates: Civil War Governor* (Danville, Ill., 1906), p. 263.

2. In 1870 Logan was antiprotectionist in tariff matters. On March 6 he wrote Horace White, the strong antiprotectionist editor of the *Chicago Tribune:* "I am gratified to know that you appreciate and understand the iniquity and folly of the existing tariff."—Logan to White, Logan Papers.

3. Late in 1865 and early in 1866 Logan spent considerable time away from home acting as attorney for northern cotton claimants against the Federal Government. This was remunerative, as was his incursion into the stock market. He had also invested in real estate. —Eidson, "John A. Logan," Manuscript Biography, Vanderbilt University, pp. 204–6. In a letter to Mrs. Logan in 1871 the Senator tells of selling a Chicago lot of 100 front feet (off a ten acre tract he had bought earlier in the year) for $20,000 and remarks that he has bought another speculative tract for $26,000.—J. A. L. to M. L., Letter, August 7, 1871.

4. This was Adelbert Ames, 1835–1933, the beau ideal of Carpetbaggers, who was representing Mississippi in the Senate and had been and was again to be governor of that state. Originally from Maine, his talents took him from 2nd lieutenant to major general in the Union Army during the four years of the war.—*D.A.B.*, XI, pp. 27–28, and *Biographical Directory of the American Congress, 1774–1961,* House Document 442, 85th Congress, 2d Session.

5. This was a contest as to who should be seated as senator from North Carolina. Its significance is that Abbott was a carpetbagger from Boston and Ransom was a Confederate veteran.

6. William Sprague, former Governor of Rhode Island. Mrs. Sprague divorced him after a public quarrel and lived in straitened circumstances until her death in 1899.—*Who's Who in American History,* p. 499.

9—*1872: A Time of Troubles*

1. The unflinching devotion of General and Mrs. Logan to Grant is both inspiring and pathetic. Grant had recommended Logan for his first star and his second star; Grant had thought he deserved to command the Army of The Tennessee when Sherman designated Howard; Grant had sent Logan to relieve Thomas if Thomas was not in action at Nashville when he arrived. A review of the Logan correpondence indicates that neither the general nor his wife was so naïve as to believe that all was right with the Grant Administration, but to both of them Grant was a great and good man betrayed by

some of his underlings, and he could do no wrong. Logan's wholehearted devotion to the Third Term cause in 1880 was at the expense of his own political advancement.

2. The purpose of this spectacular Japanese embassy was to renegotiate the treaties that had been more or less forced on Japan by the Pierce Administration. After twenty years of confusion they had decided on a policy of all-out modernization which involved the selection of many foreign "experts" and new treaties with the United States and a number of other nations.—Payson J. Treat, *Japan and the United States, 1853–1921* (Stanford, 1928), Chap. 6 *passim.*

3. The death of Mrs. Greeley on October 30, 1872, followed by his defeat for the presidency in the next week, brought Mr. Greeley to a severe mental breakdown and to his prompt death on November 29.—*Who's Who in American History*, p. 216.

4. Analysis by elimination would indicate that Mrs. Logan is aiming her scorn at Mrs. William Howard Taft.

5. Horace White, a friend and correspondent of General Logan, represented the *Chicago Tribune.*

10—Chicago and Washington, 1873

1. In 1874 General Logan paid $40,000 to acquire a one-seventh interest in the Dives Mine at Silver Plume, Colorado. He raised the money by selling some of his Chicago real estate.—Eidson, "John A. Logan," Manuscript Biography, Vanderbilt University, p. 294.

2. In 1865 Levi Z. Leiter joined with Marshal Field to buy the Potter Palmer Store, later known as Marshal Field and Co. In 1881 he sold his interest and devoted his attention chiefly to real estate. He was known as a cultivated man of bookish and artistic interests. He was the father of the future Marchioness Curzon of Keddleston and Vicereine of India. *D.A.B.*, VI, 157.

3. George M. Pullman, 1833–97, married Harriet Sanger in 1867 who was to become a lifelong and intimate friend of Mrs. Logan. He was the inventor of the Pullman car and the founder of the Pullman Palace Car Co. which became the largest railroad car manufacturer in the world.—*Who's Who in American History*, p. 427.

4. In a corrupt time and region Louisiana was outstanding in its corruption, with all parties sharing in the looting. In 1872 the Warmoth Republicans (anti-Grant) joined with the Democrats to support John McEnery for governor. The pro-Grant Republicans supported William P. Kellogg. Both sides claimed victory at the polls. The State returning board said that the McEnery group had won both the executive and legislative branches. The Kellogg group organized their own board, and using "pseudo returns" elected Kellogg and a Republican-majority legislature. Grant recognized the Kellogg fac-

tion, would not listen to the McEnery adherents, and used U. S. troops to keep Kellogg in power.—Randall and David, *Civil War and Reconstruction,* 2d ed. (Boston, 1961), pp. 624, 691–93.

5. The Freedmen's Bureau was the Federal Government's first experience with large-scale Welfare. Established by Congress on March 3, 1865, as a bureau of the War Department, it was to feed the starving in the South, irrespective of race, and was to perform various functions toward the freed slaves during an initial two-year period. It established the latter upon public lands to a limited degree, supervised labor contracts, protected them against unfair state legislation and established schools for them. One of Johnson's early presidential acts was to appoint General Oliver Otis Howard, then commanding general of the Army of the Tennessee as its head administrator. A bill to renew the bureau more or less permanently was vetoed by Johnson on the ground that since the Federal Courts were now open and functioning the bureau was unnecessary. Cordially disliked by Southern whites, it became the darling of the Radical Republicans who believed it essential if the Freedmen were not to be "re-enslaved."—*Ibid.,* pp. 576–78. The authoritative monograph, George R. Bentley, *A History of the Freedmen's Bureau* (Philadelphia, 1955) holds that on balance it did a useful job under difficult circumstances. The most recent work, William S. McFeeley, *Yankee Stepfather: General O. O. Howard and the Freedmen* (New Haven and London, 1968) takes the position that it was derelict in its duty in protecting black men's rights, especially in not establishing more of them as peasant proprietors on confiscated land.

6. Allan Nevins, the greatest authority on the Civil War period, states that "the next generation" criticized Cameron "more harshly than he deserved." Cameron ". . . was honest and did his best. But he was a misfit . . . clumsy, forgetful, unsystematic . . . his executive feebleness soon made him a sore clog upon the administration."—Allan Nevins, *The War for the Union,* I, *The Improvised War 1861–1862* (New York, 1959), 408–15.

7. The handling of the Belknap resignation was one of the most maladroit acts of this unfortunately maladroit president. Belknap, to please his first wife, had made appointments as Indian Agents to persons who "kicked back" annual sums of money to Mrs. Belknap and other favorites, one of whom was Orville Grant, the president's brother. When Belknap learned that a House committee was about to recommend his impeachment he rushed to Grant with a resignation which he believed would prevent the impeachment. Grant, who was to claim ignorance of the whole matter, despite ample ventilation in the New York press, accepted the resignation immediately.—Allan Nevins, *Hamilton Fish: The Inner History of the Grant Administration* (New York, 1936), pp. 804–10.

8. Logan, faced with increasing Greenback (inflation) sentiment in rural Illinois, and increasing Granger influence, had reason to need a fence-mending trip home. He had been deeply disappointed when Grant had vetoed the currency expansion bill, so much so that in April his wife had written him to keep his temper in the senate and to say "cooly that you are convinced the people desire more currency the President's veto to the contrary not withstanding."—M. L. to J. A. L., undated letter (but undoubtedly April), Logan Papers. Logan thought the Greenbacks outstanding should be increased to $800 million. "He believed that his struggle against all the bankers and importers in the country equalled any fight in which he had ever engaged."—Eidson, "Logan," p. 276.

11—End of the Grant Era

1. Despite considerable evidence against Babcock he was acquitted, chiefly because Grant's deposition "exonerating" him was so very positive that conviction would seem to make the President guilty either "of complicity or incredible blindness."—Nevins, *Hamilton Fish: The Inner History of the Grant Administration* (New York, 1936), pp. 800–803.

2. The "Mulligan Letters" spoiled Blaine's chances for the presidential nomination in 1876. They were letters written by Blaine which indicated he had accepted financial favors from the Little Rock and Fort Smith Railroad while he was Speaker of the House and while federal aid for the railroad was before the House. They were produced by James Mulligan of Boston who appeared before a House investigating committee.—*Ibid.*, 826 ff.

3. Mrs. Logan's judgment of President Hayes is colored by both factional partizanship and personal pique. Hayes had been elected to "clean up the mess" of the Grant administration, and so was disliked by Grant "Stalwarts" like the Logans. Furthermore he ignored Logan's requests for a lame-duck appointive position when Logan lost the senatorial election in Illinois, for which see below, note 6.

4. The disputed election of 1876 has remained disputed ever since that time. The electoral votes disputed were one from Oregon on a technicality, and all those from Louisiana, South Carolina, and Florida, according to which set of returns, offered by rival returning boards, were accepted. The Electoral Commission, voting strictly on party lines, awarded all the votes to Hayes, with a majority of one on each disputed question. The most recent, and highly qualified historical expert's opinion is: "The consensus of recent historical scholarship is that Hayes was probably entitled to the electoral votes of South Carolina and Louisiana, that Tilden was entitled to the four votes of Florida, and that Tilden was therefore elected by a vote of 188 to 181.—C. Vann Woodward, *Reunion and Reaction* (Boston, 1951), p.

19. No one questioned the fact that Tilden had won a substantial majority of the popular vote. It may be mentioned that Logan and Blaine both had strong support for the Presidential nomination in the Illinois Republican convention of 1876, the delegation finally being instructed to vote for Blaine.—Ernest Ludlow Bogart and Charles Manfred Thompson, *The Industrial State 1870–1893, The Centennial History of Illinois,* IV (Springfield, 1920), pp. 111–12.

5. Historians were later to ascribe Logan's loss of his senate seat to other causes. Dissatisfied farmers and other debtors were riding high in Illinois politics in the mid-seventies, both within the major parties and as an independent force. The Grangers held the balance of power in the legislature elected in 1876. Logan controlled the Republican Caucus and John M. Palmer the Democratic, but neither could win without Granger support. When the Republicans dropped Logan in favor of Judge Charles B. Lawrence the Democrats substituted Justice David Davis of the U. S. Supreme Court and won with him. This election took place on January 25, 1877, the day the bill creating the Electoral Commission to decide the disputed Presidency passed Congress. According to the batting order provided for the five Supreme Court justices who were to serve on this commission, Davis would have been the fifteenth member of the commission. His election to the senate thus removed him from having what was thought of as the deciding vote in the choice between Hayes and Tilden and brought about the election of Hayes since the justice put into the fifteenth commission seat was a thoroughgoing partisan Republican.— *Ibid.,* Chaps. 4 and 5, *passim,* and pp. 121–22. *See also* Stampp, *The Era of Reconstruction, 1865–1877* (New York, 1965), Chap. 7 *passim.*

6. General and Mrs. Logan were deeply disappointed at losing the senatorship and were bitter about what happened next. Logan had confidently, perhaps fatuously, trusted that President Hayes would take care of him with a major appointment to a cabinet seat or a diplomatic mission. Early in February he wrote his wife: "I like St. Petersburg, St. James', Paris or Brussels, and I am sure you would. Spain would suit nicely, too." When inauguration day came with nothing definite in sight, Mrs. Logan wrote her husband a letter full of disgust with Hayes and his Administration. She saw trouble ahead with a cabinet containing Democrats and other strange people but not her husband. On March 8 the General responded: "Now you know all by the papers. You see that Hayes has sold us all out and the base ingratitude shown . . . to those that elected him has disgusted all . . . here. I just got your letter saying 'let us go to France.' I would be glad to do it but my treatment has been such by this outfit that I cannot honorably accept anything at his hands." Three days later he added: "I am not saying anything but if ever any man has

been treated badly by those who should have been my friends I have been. My present feeling is to never again have anything to do with political life."—J. A. L. to M. L., Letter, February 9, 1877; M. L. to J. A. L., Letter, March 4, 1877; J. A. L. to M. L., Letters, March 8 and March 11, 1877, Logan Papers.

Postlude, 1877–1923

1. Unless otherwise noted the source of all data and quotations in the Postlude is Mrs. John A. Logan, *Reminiscences of a Soldier's Wife: An Autobiography* (New York, 1913), Chaps. 14 through 16.

2. Senator Bruce was reputed to be the richest American Negro of his time.—*Who's Who in American History: Historical Volume, 1607–1896*, (Chicago, 1963), p. 81.

3. The Illinois situation was complicated. Until the end of April Elihu B. Washburne, longtime backer of both Grant and Logan, was cooperating to win the Illinois delegation for Grant. He then joined with Blaine men to try to purge the state's delegation of Grant delegates.—Washburne to Logan, Letters, April 10 and 30, 1880; Logan to J. D. Cameron, Telegram, May 10, 1880, Logan Family Papers, Library of Congress. *See also*, William Eidson, "John A. Logan," Manuscript Biography, Vanderbilt University, pp. 307–8.

4. Contrary to the impression given by Mrs. Logan, the bill to restore Porter to the army passed. Bruce Catton considers that the original court martial had been, at least in part, a political warning to "malcontents" gathered around McClellan.—Bruce Catton, *Never Call Retreat, The Centennial History of the Civil War*, III (Garden city, N. Y. 1965), 68, 69, 96.

5. This is the personal opinion of the editor. Such an idea would be inconceivable to Mrs. Logan.

6. George Francis Dawson, *Life and Services of Gen. John A. Logan as Soldier and Statesman* (Chicago and New York, 1887), pp. 110, 298–306.

7. Here either Mrs. Logan's memory is seriously at fault or she is quoting her husband's immediate reaction before he knew the name of the assassin. Charles Julius Guiteau was a longtime Republican politician, and of the "Stalwart" wing of the party, who was nettled by Garfield's civil service reform tendencies and who was disappointed in his ambitions for a consular appointment. He stated at his trial that he was a "Stalwart" who wanted Arthur to have the presidency.—*Dictionary of American Biography*, IV, 149; *Who's Who in American History*, p. 223.

8. J. A. L. to M. L., Letter, March 22, 1884, Logan Papers. Friends of the General were telling him that he was strong vis-a-vis Blaine west of the Mississippi, except in Iowa, and strong in Illinois except for the support of Blaine by the *Chicago Tribune*.—Oliver C.

Sabin to J. A. L., Letter, Jan. 15, 1884, and "Mc" [unidentified] to J. A. L., Letter, April 24, 1884, Logan Papers. George Franklin Edmunds, 1828–1919, senator from Vermont was a distinguished lawyer and a man of integrity. He was the candidate of the liberal-reform element of the party. The desertion of the ticket by many of his followers—"Mugwumps"—was a major reason for the defeat of Blaine and Logan.—*D.A.B.*, III, 24–27.

9. Joseph Roswell Hawley, 1826–1905, had reached the rank of major general in the Union army and was senator from Connecticut. A strong protectionist and "sound-money" man, he had been chairman of the Resolutions committee at the 1876 Republican convention.—*D.A.B.*, IV 421–22.

10. The Logan Papers contain only one communication from Blaine to Logan during the months of the campaign—a short, inconsequential note—and no copy of anything from Logan to Blaine, leading to the suspicion that some items may have been removed before the papers were deposited in the Library of Congress. Mrs. Logan's view of Blaine reflects her fierce loyalty to her husband. Blaine's distinguished biographer presents him as the more "virtuous" of the two, and says that Blaine was willing to have Logan as his running mate to get the votes of veterans. "If politics made these uncongenial candidates bedfellows," he wrote, "preference kept each of them on the extreme edge of his side of the bed."—David Saville Muzzey, *James G. Blaine: A Political Idol of Other Days* (New York, 1934), pp. 72, 307. Dawson's account of the convention and campaign may be accepted as Logan's own, since they were in such close contact.—Dawson, *John A. Logan,* 309 ff. If Logan was involved in any "deal" to acquire the vice-presidential nomination he kept it a secret from his family. His daughter was surprized and incredulous that he would accept the nomination.—Mary Logan Tucker to "Papa and Mama," Letter, June 7, 1884, Logan Papers. Although Logan had the "favorite-son" support of Illinois there was strong support for Blaine in the state convention. See Ernest Ludlow Bogart and Charles Manfred Thompson, *The Industrial State 1870–1893, The Centennial History of Illinois,* IV (Springfield, 1920), pp. 145–46. See also, Edward Stanwood, *A History of the Presidency From 1788 to 1897* new ed. rev. Charles Knowles Bolton (Boston and New York, 1928), p. 427. It may be worthy of note that Blaine offered discreet support to Logan for the presidency *pro tem* of the senate upon the death of Vice President Hendricks in late November of 1885. He was unanimously elected to that office but declined.—James G. Blaine to J. A. L., Letter, Nov. 29, 1885, Logan Papers. *See also* Dawson, *Logan,* p. 402.

11. Thomas J. Pressly, *Americans Interpret Their Civil War* (New York, 1962), pp. 70–73.

12. George F. Dawson to J. A. L., Letter, Oct. 8, 1884, Logan Papers. The idea that Dr. Blanchard's "Rum, Romanism and Rebellion" lost the election is based on the fact that a change of 600 votes in New York would have elected Blaine and Logan.—*D.A.B.*, III, 325–26.

13. N. E. Dawson and P. Donnan to J. A. L., Letters, June 30 and July 18, 1885; M. H. McCord to J. A. L., Nov. 15, 1884, Logan Papers.

14. For a detailed account of this unusually complex and interesting election see Bogart and Thompson, *The Industrial State*, pp. 149–58.

15. Mrs. John A. Logan, *The Part Taken by Women in American History* (Wilmington, Del., 1912), p. 12; *National Cyclopedia of American Biography*, p. 301.

16. This description of the contents and appearance of *Home Magazine* is based on an examination of the files. Mrs. Logan has nothing to say on these subjects in the *Reminiscences*. She also does not mention that in October, 1898, her name appeared as one of three editors on the masthead of a new magazine, *The American Sentinel: a Patriotic Illustrated Monthly*, whose mottoes were "The Youth of Today are the Patriots of Tomorrow" and "Teach Patriotism in the Public Schools." This was a slick-paper, well-illustrated periodical. The October number (Vol. I, No. 1) included Mrs. Logan's article on the Rough Riders at Montauk Point, an inspirational article on the United States by Edward Everett Hale, a poem on the Goddess of Liberty by Ella Wheeler Wilcox and a number of similar items. Pasted on the inside cover of the Library of Congress copy is a letter from Mrs. Logan to the Librarian in which she explains that she has withdrawn her name upon learning that the publishers lacked the capital to publish a magazine, and "as I was unwilling that they should use my name to obtain subscriptions which they would never fill."

17. It is not surprising that Victoria Woodhull, Tenney C. Claflin, Madam Jumel, Mrs. Surrat, and Frances Wright do not appear, for Mrs. Logan believed in propriety. But one wonders at the omission of Jane Addams.

18. The sources for Mrs. Logan's life after she had written the *Reminiscences* are various obituary news stories, as follow: The *Chicago Daily Tribune*, Feb. 23, 1923; The *New York Times*, Feb. 23, 1923; The *Illinois State Register* (Springfield), Feb. 22, 1923; The *Illinois State Journal* (Springfield), Feb. 23, 1923; The *Marion Semi-Weekly Leader* (Marion, Ill.), Feb. 27, 1923; The *Carbondale Free Press* (Carbondale, Ill.), Feb. 22, 1923.

Index